An Endangered Species

Jerry Daly, MSC

To Dan Eiffe

You might find bits
of book interesting

An Endangered Species

The Life of a Priest

Jerry Daly

the columba press

First published in 2016 by

the columba press

55A Spruce Avenue,
Stillorgan Industrial Park,
Blackrock, Co. Dublin

Cover design by Helene Pertl | Columba Press

Origination by The Columba Press
Printed by SprintPrint, Dublin

ISBN 978 1 78218 294 8

Acknowledgements

Without the affirmation and professional help from my nephew Danny Daly this book would not have happened. Also practical help from my nephew Dónal Daly. I am also grateful to Christine Stroyan for transcribing my scribble into a Word document.

Contents

Preface

At the end of 2014, the Archbishop of Tuam, Dr Michael Neary, warned that 'on the very edge of Europe, we are hearing the last vestiges of Christendom in their death rattle'. He went on to say that the church in Ireland found itself at a rather bewildering crossroads. The outright hostility from sections of the media and the political establishment had curiously abated and he gave the reason for this: 'A great struggle, social, political, intellectual and profoundly cultural has been fought, and we have lost.'

I believe that this is the first time that a member of the Irish hierarchy has spoken so openly and honestly about the reality of the crisis facing the Catholic Church in Ireland. What a contrast this is to a statement by the Archbishop of Dublin, Diarmuid Martin: 'For the moment, what we have to do is find worthy candidates who are able to live as celibate priests as in the tradition in the Latin rite. I believe that there are candidates but we are not reaching them.' In spite of the work of a vocation director, the archdiocese got one vocation entering Maynooth in 2014.

Fr Brendan Hoban, in his timely book *Who Will Break Bread for Us?*, gives proof that the issue of priest vocations is now embarrassingly quantifiable: at the moment there are about 4,000 priests in Ireland. The vast majority of them are over fifty years old; many of them are over seventy years old. If we can only read the signs of the times, in twenty-five years there will be less than 200 active priests for the whole country. Some would say that this is an optimistic scenario.

Fr Hoban speaks about the sticking-plaster solutions proposed, such as ordaining male deacons, or importing priests from Africa, and clustering parishes. These measures will have no impact on the problem. He goes on to propose some solutions of his own. To ordain mature men who feel they have a vocation and to invite the many priests who have left to get married to return to active ministry. Even if the church were to agree, they would be only temporary solutions. These men would only have about twenty years of active service. I am also doubtful if many of these priests would return to active ministry in the present climate of the church.

Fr Hoban speaks about the loss of vocations being quantifiable. What he fails to mention is that the great fall in Mass attendance is equally quantifiable. It is now down to 40% nationally. In a few parishes in Dublin, it is down to 2%. In one of these parishes, some parents want their children to make their first holy communion. For a few months, the parents are asked to attend Mass with the children once a month. They have to be texted on the preceding Friday as a reminder. I say the 10 a.m. Sunday Mass in the neighbouring parish. The vast majority are over fifty years – many are over seventy years. It is very like the age profile of the clergy. In twenty-five years' time, there will only be tiny congregations in very large churches; there won't be that many eager to have bread broken for them. This rapid decrease of younger people attending Mass will very soon have financial implications on maintaining the present parish structures.

I passionately believe that only radical solutions will help. The leaders of the church cannot stand idly by. They must be proactive. The Holy Spirit will lead us down roads that many will find difficult to accept. The proposed Diocesan Synod in Limerick in 2016 may be a first step on this road.

I am not a scripture scholar or a theologian, but I would like to digress for a moment. From the very cradle of the church, there were the Petrine and Pauline principles. The first calls the church to be true to its origins and the truth of the gospels, to teach and apply these truths through its magisterium and to maintain the bonds of communion across the world and across the centuries.

The Pauline principle (named after St Paul) sends the church ever outwards, fulfilling its missionary mandate, to every time and culture, meeting people where they are and trying to enculturate in new times and new situations and, especially, listening and discerning the movements of the spirit of God by attention and carefully reading the 'signs of the times'. These tensions run right through the history of the church from New Testament times.

Whichever principle predominates, the abuse of power and authority is a very human problem. In Jesus' own lifetime, the disciples quarrelled with one another about who might have the greater authority. Jesus felt it necessary to severely rebuke them. In His kingdom, the greatest must become the least of all, servant of all – He Himself came to serve, not to be served.

When the Emperor Constantine converted to Christianity, everything changed. From a persecuted minority religion with no churches or wealth, Christianity became the religion of choice for the powerful. The property and possessions that belonged to a new empire were at stake. As Mark Vernon, in his book *The Big Questions: God*, wrote: 'By donning the old imperial purple, popes showed that heaven was a place on earth, and they were in charge.' There was a new model of the church – the model of a pyramid: all power and authority is from the top down. This model is with us to this day. The exercise of priesthood took on a new role. It was no longer a ministry of presiding at the breaking of bread. They were told that they were a tribe set apart; they were not like other Christians. They could cure souls; they were more virtuous than others.

Bertrand Russell, discussing the failures of religion, said: 'Any average selection of mankind, set apart and told that it excels the rest in virtue, must tend to sink below the average.' Some eight centuries after Constantine, the clergy were told celibacy was not an option, but a rule of life for them. This set them apart from the rest of Christendom evermore. The Petrine principle became dominant. Some priests joined monasteries and became monks. When St Patrick came to Ireland in AD 432, it was a monastic model of clergy he brought with him – hence the great outreach to missionary activity that enriched parts of Europe for centuries. The Roman Empire became the great vehicle for the spread of Christianity. On the downside of this, the church took on all the trappings of power.

All of this is just a brief summary of the roots of all that has gone wrong in the use of power and authority. Pope Francis is very aware of the tension between the Petrine and Pauline principles. He wants to keep the tension creative rather than destructive; thus his insistence at the recent synod in Rome that everyone should be free to speak and be listened to. The dialogue must be ongoing, charitable and mutually respectful. But the same Pope Francis had no qualms in lambasting the severe abuse of power and prestige in the Vatican Curia.

So why do I have to write a book? I have been a missionary priest in the Missionaries of the Sacred Heart for fifty-eight years. I have worked in South Africa, Indonesia and done extensive parish work in England. Because of the dramatic decline in priestly and religious vocations in the First World, we are becoming an endangered species. I believe my story as a priest during all these changes has some value. I am totally convinced that Christ will be with the church till the end of time. It cannot fail; the Spirit that raised Jesus from the dead will lead us into new ways to live the kingdom values that Jesus lived and preached.

I believe that it is possible to look at new ways of being a priest. Some of these I have mentioned at the end of the book. I believe that moving from the model of a pyramid to that of a circle will one day become a reality in the church. I agree with the Archbishop of Tuam, Dr Neary, who said: 'If we are to manage this enormous transition to a smaller but more dynamically evangelical Church, we will need people. Not primarily money or structures, however important they may be.'

As a priest, working with different peoples and different cultures, I have always been impressed with the goodness of most people, and I have tried to give some concrete examples of this here. One of my strongest convictions is the importance of the role of women in the church. I feel so sad that the church has never practically appreciated their value. I wish that some scripture scholar or theologian could come up with some argument or proof that they can never preside at the eucharist. Then, and only then, it might make some sense to me why we cannot discuss the possibility.

I thank God that one of the gifts He has given me is a sense of humour – to see the funny side of many human situations. I hope this has come through in my story.

Part I

This book is not an autobiography. They are two a penny – buy one, get one free! *An Endangered Species* is not primarily about my life, but a glimpse of a hundred thousand other missionary priests, Brothers and Sisters. As we approach the one hundredth anniversary of the founding of the Irish State, I want this book to be a reflection of the thousands of unsung heroes who left everything to go to Africa, Asia and South America, to bring not just the good news of the gospel, but also liberation from disease and the gift of education. Many of them died prematurely from tropical diseases. I want this book to reflect the tsunami of changes that have taken place in the church, society and technology (especially IT), and how all of this has impinged on my life as a missionary and parish priest in the UK. Just to give one example, when I went to South Africa in 1958, it took ten days on a liner from Southampton. Three years later when I went to Indonesia, it took nine weeks. We went on a cargo ship that took a few passengers from Milton Haven in Wales. It took three weeks to Jakarta. It took three weeks to get the necessary paperwork there, and another three weeks on a local cargo ship to the Moluccas Islands. The only connection with the outside world there was a small transistor radio. Post from home took two to five months to arrive!

I have recently returned from a pilgrimage to Lourdes. I discovered that for the town of Lourdes there are only two priests, who also cover twenty-two local villages, each with its own beautiful church. They get Mass a few times a year. In my lifetime as a priest, we have become an endangered species. I have a niece who is teaching RE in secondary school and who is so disillusioned with the unchanging attitude of the church. She said a few years ago she could engage the children in a discussion on some aspect of church teaching; now things have changed so radically and they have not the slightest interest in church teaching. It has become irrelevant – few of them attend Sunday Mass. We have lost two, if not three, generations of young people.

I was encouraged to write this book because I saw some light at the end of the tunnel of fear that stopped even cardinals speaking out. Cardinal Martini, Archbishop of Milan, waited until after he died to have an interview published in which he suggested that the church had been left behind for 200 years. What are we afraid of? The church must recognise its mistakes and must follow a path of radical change, starting with the pope and bishops. Our culture has aged, our religious houses are empty, the bureaucracy of the church accumulates, our rituals and clothes are pompous. Debate and discussion are vital. Cardinal Hume left a similar posthumous message; why were they afraid to speak out while they were alive?

But the greatest beacon of hope has been Pope Francis – what a radical statement he made when he said: 'We cannot insist only on issues related to abortion, gay marriage and the use of contraceptives. We have to find a new balance; otherwise even the moral edifice of the church is likely to fall like a house of cards, losing the freshness and fragrance of the Gospel. The church sometimes has locked itself up in small-minded rules.'

I would like to reflect on the compulsory link between priesthood and celibacy. It is estimated that 6,000 priests have left to get married in the USA and Europe in the last forty years. There are some wonderful married men who would like to be ordained priests. Nuns and Brothers are an even more endangered species than priests. I aim to cast a long look on the massive contribution they have made to Irish society and elsewhere.

I have been very involved in my ministry, especially in the UK, in Marriage Encounter and the preparation of engaged couples for marriage. My experience in this has been very rewarding and hopefully of some interest. I am also a political animal. My experiences in South Africa in the late 1950s and later in the 1980s and 1990s, and the evils of apartheid, will be highlighted in some of my stories, along with my admiration for Nelson Mandela. Also, I will describe working in a very English parish of St Albans during Bloody Sunday and its aftermath, my admiration for most of the Irish who found new life in England, and my admiration for my English parishioners. But I am aware of the crimes against humanity that involved British rule in Ireland before, during and after the Famine.

I hope that there will be a lighter side to my story. My late vocation as a golfer and my fanatical support of Manchester United should interest some readers.

When I reached the golden age of eighty, I came to our retirement home in Western Road, Cork. It was strange coming back to life in Ireland after so many years. I do Sunday Mass in the old church in Ballincollig, as well as a couple of weekday Masses. I tell my friends that I am slowly giving up golf, as I now only play three times a week. Now I must briefly return to my roots and start my story.

1932 was the 1,500th anniversary of the coming of St Patrick to Ireland. In the middle of that year, on 3 July, I was born – the ninth of ten children – to Daniel Daly and Margaret Mary Cronin. It was also the year and month of the Eucharistic Congress in Dublin which drew massive crowds to Dublin, and during which John Count McCormack made the famous rendition of 'Panis Angelicus'.

My father was one of two boys and four girls who grew up on a small farm facing beautiful Dunmanus Bay on the Sheep's Head Peninsula. Two of the girls, Nora and Margaret, went and made nursing careers in New York; neither of them married. The other two married local farmers, both named O'Donovan. My father Daniel, being the suitable height of 6 feet, joined the Royal Irish Constabulary and was posted to Ennistymon in County

Clare. My brother James, who stayed at home to run the farm but was more interested in horses and drink, decided to run away to Australia and was never heard of again. Daniel's parents asked him to give up his police job to come home to run the farm. He built a new farmhouse, unusually large for its time, with five bedrooms. He fell in love with a very beautiful girl called Margaret Mary Cronin. He was in his thirties; she was only eighteen. They got married on the eleventh day of the eleventh month of 1911.

In the first six years they had four children: Nora, Joe, Anna Marie and James. I never knew Anna Marie as she died at the age of ten. In hindsight, it is certain that she was a coeliac, a disease which was only discovered after World War II; several of my nieces and nephews have coeliac disease. Anna Maria was misdiagnosed with appendicitis and went for an operation in Cork, from which she never recovered. Her death broke my mother's heart.

They went on to have six more children, but there were some big gaps between them. Danny went to join the Irish army at eighteen, and Michael, who was the tall, dark, handsome one, went to England to work during the war and later joined the Palestine Police. Francis, also known as Frank, was six years older than me. Martina was two and a half years older. My younger sister Mary was five years younger than me. There was a gap of twenty-five years between Mary and Nora. Joe was nineteen when I was born and he was my godfather. I looked on Frank, Martina and Mary as siblings; the rest were too adult to look to as siblings. I became very close to Mary.

The period before and after I was born was painfully difficult economically. In 1916 there was the Easter Rising, so brutally put down. There was the struggle for independence through guerrilla warfare, whose hero was Michael Collins. There was the meeting of Irish leaders with the clever, Machiavellian Churchill, where partition was agreed on as only a temporary solution. This was followed by the Civil War, during which Collins was assassinated. After the truce, Whitehall imposed economic sanctions on Éire; this was called the 'economic war'.

England refused to buy farm produce – cattle and sheep – from Éire. My older brother James took on the responsibilities of an adult farmer with my father. He was ploughing at the age of fourteen. We had all the basic home-grown foods. The wheat was ground to make beautiful soda bread; Nora made the best I have ever eaten. Oats were sent away to be made into oatmeal, which we had with lots of milk before we went to bed. James was expert at growing all the vegetables. A pig was occasionally killed and pickled in lots of salt. My mother was incredibly industrious. She was asked to pioneer a poultry farm by the new Department of Agriculture. She had several hundred pure-bred hens. The local farmers' wives came to buy the eggs, which they hatched to improve the laying productivity of their hens. She also reared a flock of turkeys, which were sold before Christmas.

One of my earliest memories is of Joe, my godfather. I don't know how my parents were able to afford it, but he spent a couple of years in Rockwell College. Apparently, he won prizes at sprinting. My father had a bull to which local farmers brought their cows to be serviced. One day the bull got loose just as Joe happened to come into the field. From a safe vantage point, I can remember the bull chasing Joe. As the bull was gaining on him, he sailed over a fence, at the same time throwing the hat which he always wore back over his head. This seemed to distract the bull, which gave Joe the chance to get away. I thought the spectacle was hilarious – I was so young and foolish, I had no idea of the mortal danger Joe was in.

At the age of four and a half, my mother walked me the 1.5 miles to Kilcrohane School. The two teachers, Mr and Mrs Hurley, were elderly, having reared ten children of their own. Mrs Hurley said to my mother that this was the last of the Daly family, not knowing she was pregnant with my sister Mary.

Reflecting on teaching in rural Ireland at that time, it wasn't great. The two classrooms were very basic. They relied for heating in the winter on donations of peat from the parents. The fireplace was behind the teacher, who benefited most from it. The schoolbooks were basic. Mr Hurley was keen on maths and I got my love of maths from him. In hindsight, what I got most of all from them was a deep sense of faith. Three of their sons became missionary priests and one of their daughters a nun.

Our recreation involved games of running. I used to love to run barefoot. My closest friends were Connie Murphy, who at the age of nineteen emigrated to the Rocky Mountains, where he later inherited a ranch from an uncle. He also bought other ranches, and from a 30-acre farm in Ireland he now owns a 30,000-acre ranch. There was Patrick Donovan, who married and reared a family of six. All of the sons are now married and live locally. The fourth member of the gang was Johnny Donovan, who also became a farmer.

There was a short catechism which was used to prepare us for holy communion, and a long catechism for confirmation. The teachers spent a fair number of classes on these as a diocesan priest came annually to inspect us. I remember one of these occasions, when he asked a question about scripture. He asked who said 'all I have is yours'. No one raised a hand. Eventually I blurted out 'the prodigal father'. Both teacher and priest found this amusing, as I should have said the father of the prodigal son.

My first holy communion was a very important day in my life. Shortly afterwards I became an altar server. This I enjoyed very much. In the old Latin Mass, we had to learn the Latin responses as well as quite a number of ways of moving from one end of the altar to the other. Our soutane was purple with a white surplice. I remember the Forty Hours Adoration, which was a momentous occasion for me. I think the seeds of a vocation were starting to grow. During Lent, we did a very hasty Stations of the Cross (maybe two minutes) during our lunch break. My aunt, Mrs Fitzpatrick, was married to the local publican – Martina and I brought sandwiches and she made cocoa for our lunch.

* * *

I suppose lots of children have phobias unknown to their parents. Mine was unusual: a beggar man who used to visit once or twice a year. The poor man had had one of his legs amputated below the knee. He went around on crutches. I had a peculiar fear of him, especially my first year when I came home from school alone – every turn of the road I was afraid I might meet him.

On 3 August 1937, Martina and I were told to go out of the house to play and not to dare come in until we were told. I remember so well my aunt Elsie Fitz shouting to us about midday that we had a baby sister. My mum's tenth child was delivered like all the rest of us. I presume there was a midwife there too. I remember later that year being jealous of the attention Mary got, especially from Nora. But later Mary became the best friend I ever had – more about that later on.

As we grew older, there were lots of chores we had to do when we came from school. We had to go out to find where the cows were and bring them home for milking. We spent hours minding them in a field, preventing them from going near other crops. In those days, there was no rural electricity and no tap water. Some rainwater was stored in concrete tanks, but cooking water had to be fetched from a well quite a way away.

In rural Ireland, there was an ample provision of primary schools. There were six small schools in my parish. Children had to walk to school. But if it were not for the Sisters and Brothers we would have almost no secondary schools. There was very little secondary education provided by the State controlled from Whitehall – educated peasants could cause trouble for the Empire! For rural children it was a matter of leaving school at the age of thirteen or fourteen. They would work on the farm for a while. Then most would emigrate to the UK or USA, or elsewhere. A few would stay at home and become tradesmen, and very often the oldest boy would inherit the farm. There were only a few families in my school who could afford to send their children away to boarding school. As I drifted to the top class, I wondered occasionally what I might do.

It happened at that time that the teacher's eldest boy Diarmuid was ordained a priest and when he said Mass in the morning, Mrs Hurley used to ask me to serve him. The seeds of becoming a priest were beginning to grow in my mind. But I wasn't going to tell anybody about that just yet.

Around that time, an older girl joined our school. Her name was Noreen Donovan. I liked her very much; I even stole apples from the master's orchard and gave them to her. After a year, she won a scholarship to go to Dublin to study for the Civil Service, and the childhood romance came to an abrupt end. But we have always kept in touch. She married a wonderful husband, Des Brennan, and set up home in Clontarf, Dublin. When I came from Mission later on, I used to visit them and have said Mass in their house. One of her daughters, Morah, married Gerry Ryan of radio fame, who died tragically.

Back to Kilcrohane School. When I was fourteen, I was quite convinced I wanted to become a priest. Now I would have to tell someone. One day I plucked up the courage to tell Mrs Hurley. I am not sure if she was surprised or not. She must have discussed it with her son Fr Diarmuid, because the next day she called me aside and told me about the Missionaries of the Sacred Heart in Cork, who had a small boarding school for boys who would like to be priests. The fee they charged was very reasonable. My next hurdle was the most difficult one. How was I going to tell my mother I wanted to become a priest – would she laugh at me? But she was great. She said the most wonderful thing to me: 'Don't ever worry if one day you change your mind. You do what you think is the right thing.' Mrs Hurley wrote to the MSC College, and they wrote back to me and invited me to come for an interview and a small exam.

To wind the clock back a few years, in September 1939 adults were all excited about the outbreak of war. I was too young to grasp the significance of it and thought it some sort of row between strangers. But it had a very significant side effect for the young Irish economy. Now England was anxious to buy all our farm produce – they even bought our rabbits. The latter was a great window of opportunity for my brother Frank and I to avail of a new source of pocket money. We became very skilled at snaring rabbits. We did not give our new riches over to the family income, which meant that our rabbit operation was done in secret. It wasn't always easy to find the necessary time to set snares and kill the poor rabbits if still alive – they had to be gutted and hung up in some safe place before selling them. We got three or four shillings for a rabbit – untold riches for us.

Another thing that benefited our family was that James and Joe joined the local coastguards, which paid them a weekly wage. James still had lots of time to work on the farm. My aunt Helena was old and asked my father to work her farm. Frank was very busy working with James. Farming was a back-breaking business then, with horses and machinery and very long hours.

As the war went on it was very exciting to see some British destroyers come down Dunmanus Bay as far as Ahakista. They wanted the locals to go out in their small boats with items such as vegetables, chickens and eggs – for which they got an inflated price. Frank and I could not think of any way of getting our rabbits to them!

As I grew older, I did more and more chores on the farm, but I never did any milking of cows. That was playtime for many of us. We invented our own type of hurling, with a stick with a knob on it and a tennis ball.

The war brought great opportunities as many young men and women of twenty said goodbye to Ireland and moved across the channel to find work. Many of the girls became nurses. Some men joined the British army and navy. Two of my cousins joined the navy; one died in a Japanese concentration camp in what is now Indonesia.

* * *

In April 1947, my mother and I went to Sacred Heart College for interview. I was accepted as a new boarder in September. We got a list of clothes to bring – one item was a black suit and tie. I was due to join the men in black!

I left home on 3 September and got a lift to Bantry, where I stayed in the Bantry Bay Hotel – Mrs Nellie O'Callaghan was a cousin of mine. I met two other boys in black going back to Sacred Heart College for their third year. They were Jim Dudley from Dursey Island and Dan O'Neill from Castletownbere.

How travel has changed! They came by ferry boat from Castletownbere to Bantry – CIE buses only went as far as Glengarriff. As it happened, there was a bus strike on. The next day, we took the train from Bantry, which took nearly two and a half hours! As there were no buses we had to take our own cases and walk all the way to Western Road – two days travelling to get to Cork!

On reflection, going to boarding school was traumatic. It was however a necessary evil, as there was no other alternative if one wanted to become a priest. The thirty-six students slept in a large dormitory. The first night, I went sleep-crawling. I woke up under a bed and had no idea how to return to my own bed. I woke up a few students, which seemed a great cause for laughter and fun. There were none of the modern facilities like showers or hot water. The two bathtubs were on the ground floor, to be used very rarely. All of this wasn't too great a problem as we came from farmhouses or places with similar deprivations.

We discovered there were all sorts of restrictive rules and regulations. The great freedom we had enjoyed whilst growing up was curtailed. I soon discovered that the priest in charge of students, whom we shall call by his nickname Hardy, was a brutal tyrant who required little or no excuse to beat and sometimes to kick and batter us. In hindsight, I think he was a sadist. He was fanatical about speaking Irish and there were continual reminders of the evil of all things British, especially their games of soccer and rugby.

Across the road was the Mardyke Sports Ground, where his 'foreign' games were played; even looking in that direction could get you a beating. We had our own little playing pitch, on which – because of overuse – there was not a blade of grass. Hardy joined us playing matches of hurling and football. On one occasion, in my efforts to kick the ball over the bar, I kicked it into the River Lee, which was only 25 yards away. I immediately got this awful kick from this grown Kerry man up the backside. A couple of the team were instantly dispatched with pole and wire basket to run down to the bridge near the Bon Secours

Hospital and await the advent of said football. All of this took some time. I felt so guilty for spoiling the match. (I also felt the effects of that football boot for a few days.)

There was a study, where we spent most of the day. This became the classroom for first years during morning and early afternoon. Three classes moved across the corridor with a flimsy partition. The top year met in the priests' library / community room.

What were the teaching staff like? Fr Jim Murphy had a BA before joining the MSCs. He was a very good English teacher, giving us a love of Shakespeare and poetry, and like the rest of the priests apart from Hardy, he was a gentleman. The remainder of the staff had no teacher training or qualifications and were, in hindsight, rather poor. The one exception was Fr Michael Carrick, who was an excellent maths teacher.

Apart from classes, recreation and time in the oratory, we spent our time in the study. We each had our own desk. One of the students was prefect and was supposed to keep law and order. Hardy also made quick visits, and woe to the boy whom he deemed to be talking. I will always remember one such late-evening visit when he found Jim Mannix asleep on the desk with his head on his hands. He hit him such a blow on the back that I can still hear the moans and groans from poor innocent Jim. On Sundays, we were allowed to read books, which were collected in the evening.

We had a dining room, which we shared with the fathers. There were three tables of students sitting opposite the fathers. The food was very poor: bread and tea every morning and evening, with a little bit of butter. At lunch we had potatoes, vegetables and nearly always stewed meat, which was more bones and gristle than meat. The prefect at each table tried to divide this out as fairly as he could. The dessert was usually tapioca, which even our hunger did not make appetising – it always looked like sticky frogspawn. We could also see what the fathers were having, which made us more hungry. We had our turns at serving them from the hatch. When my turn came, I became adept at stealing a rasher, holding it in the palm of my hand while serving and then making a visit to my place and leaving it on my plate. This was reckless behaviour.

We were allowed to get parcels from home. Because we were not allowed to have any money, we gave them the message that butter was most acceptable, where they would hide a half crown. We always shared the butter and other goodies with our friends at the table. How did we spend the money? At least once a week all the students would have to go for a long walk. We had a plan: some would stay at the end of the group and walk slowly, delaying the priest in charge at the back. Those with money would walk fast, giving them time to go into a shop to buy the most welcome bar of chocolate or sweets. I think most of the priests knew what we were up to but turned a blind eye.

There was another window of opportunity. I don't know why, but I was appointed sacristan for the Sacred Heart Church, which wasn't the parish church but was the most popular for Sunday and weekday Masses. Being sacristan gave me access to the altar boys, who were quite willing to be messengers in buying things for us. This was also risky behaviour, but breaking rules and taking risks brought its own excitement. They once bought me a box of cigarettes; the first one I smoked in the sacristy toilet. I don't think it tasted that good, but it was the ultimate act of rebellion.

Going home at Christmas for the first time was heaven itself. Being back with siblings and parents and those who returned for Christmas brought a feeling of intense joy. I never told the family about the beatings of Hardy; they would not have believed me. As a young boy, my father never once laid a hand on me, although I had one narrow escape (I pulled Martina's hair – she liked to make me angry – and he did get the cane, but I made myself scarce and returned later when all was calm).

But the holidays came to an end, and it was more difficult going back the second time. The second term was short and then it was holiday time again. Going back after Easter, I clearly remember saying goodbye to my father. I never saw him alive again. Two weeks later, John O'Mahony was in Cork for business and got a message to collect me and bring me home.

My father had died on a trip to Bantry by pony and trap. Mary, who was only ten years old, was with him when he collapsed from a massive heart attack on the street. He was much older than my mother; he was seventy-one years old. They did not tell me the full truth, but said that my father was very ill. But somehow I feared it was worse. Most of the family were still in Bantry, but when I went into my home Frank was crying his eyes out. I knew my father was dead.

It was my first encounter with death. Sudden death leaves everyone numb. Later on as a priest, I was most sensitive to families who were grieving, doing everything in my power to help them. Very often, what was needed most was someone to listen to their story of pain and grief. My mother said she never got over the first pain she got when told of Dad's death. She was now head of the family on her own. But she was the most resilient of women.

A few days later I returned to Sacred Heart College. I don't remember any of the priests expressing any word of sympathy or kindness to me. In later life as a priest, I realised how important it was that there be some counselling, especially for children who suddenly lose a parent. In that spartan boarding school, there was none.

I must now relate something that I never told my family till this day. My brother Michael, who emigrated to work in Rugby during the war and joined the Palestine British Police for the short term before the foundation of Israel, was on his way home by boat when my father died. When he arrived in Cork he came up to Sacred Heart College to see me. He had a short time before catching the train to Bantry. We met in the visiting parlour. It was so painful to tell him that our father had died ten days before. He wanted to know all the details. Time was running out, so he asked me to walk back to the station with him. I went up to Hardy's room to get permission. His death notice in the paper said he was an ex-Royal Irish Constabulary man – in Hardy's sick mind this was another word for a collaborator with the hated English. The answer he gave me was in Irish. He said to clear out of his sight, no permission. I had to go back to Michael with tears and sadness to say I did not get permission. I have never fully gotten over this inhumanity. I have often said in my homilies, for evil to prosper all that is necessary is that good people do nothing. The priests in the college were good men; they knew what Hardy did to us. Mere cowardice prevented them from intervening.

During daylight hours, all our recreation was playing hurling or football, with matches on half-days. Some afternoons we had interested spectators looking in over the high wall. They were teenage girls on their way home from school, surveying the talent on the pitch. We never spoke to them, but were very aware of their interested presence. One of our students had flaming red hair and seemed to be the object of their desires. He was Jerry Looney, since dead. He somehow got to know the name of one of the girls; she was the sister of two of the altar servers. One Wednesday half-day we were confined to the study because of rain. Jerry decided to write a love letter to Peggy. As he was deeply engrossed in wording this message of love, he was unaware that Hardy had come into the study. Hardy looked over his shoulder and read the romantic letter. A terrible hiding followed, with threats of expulsion. As always happens, boys will be boys and can be cruel to each other. There was a rock candy called Peggy's leg and we sometimes asked poor Jerry if he fancied Peggy's leg. Like his hair, he had a flaming temper and you made sure to keep some distance away.

A couple of weeks after my father's death, I was told that I was skipping from first class to second class. Liam Callaghan went from second to third. It was not an easy thing to do. Although I was excellent at maths, I was not that good at languages. No one made an effort to help me catch up with the year's lessons that I had skipped. I don't know how I managed, but my exam result was 'Pass' at the end of the year.

I was now in the same class as Tim Gleason and Dennis McCarthy – or Donncha MacCarthaigh, as he prefers to be called – and we became close friends. How strange that we are all three in the retirement home now. We were later ordained together with Narciso Tiro in Moyne Park.

A scarcity of bread for our morning and evening meals was a regular occurrence. I don't know how it came about, but on one occasion we organised a sit-down strike! It was customary that when the fathers got up from table, we all got up to say the prayer. This evening, we all remained seated. We could feel the consternation. There was a shout from the Superior to stand up. A slow response followed. We were asked later what it was all about, and we mentioned our grievance about bread. Later that evening, I was called up to Fr Scriven in the Superior's room. It appeared that the fathers had had a meeting and they wanted to find the ringleader. They picked on Liam Callaghan and me. He told me that I might be expelled. I started to cry and tried to deny that I was a ringleader. I was told to go back to the study and they would think about it. I did not hear any more about it. The bread situation improved.

Toward the end of August 1950, I got a letter from the Sacred Heart College telling me there would be a delay in starting the new school year. They had purchased a large house and farm in Carraig na Bhfear (Carrignavar) which would be used for the top two classes. It would take a few weeks to refurbish it as a school. We got there at the start of October. It was the most pleasant surprise. We were back on a farm in the countryside again. The food was far better there, and there was much more freedom.

The house was ill-prepared to be a school, but we managed to live in dormitories without any central heating that winter. In the mornings the coverlet was wet with condensation. Unfortunately, Hardy came as one of the staff, and although he was no longer officially in charge, he found ample opportunity to continue his reign of terror. He was teaching Irish and history through Irish. In class, he was like a bomb primed to explode.

For me, there was one wonderful newcomer to the staff: Fr Morgan Curran, our Latin teacher. Because of my skipping class I would never have passed the matriculation exam in Latin without him. I did all my Latin in one year.

There was a great window of opportunity, we were free to roam around the 200-acre farm and its lovely wooded valley. It was home to many rabbits, and the UK was still anxious to buy rabbits from Ireland. Tim Gleason, Dennis McCarthy and I discovered there was money out there in them there rabbit burrows. Johnny, the farmworker, brought snares for us. We found time and opportunity to set them. Every morning, in the little time we had before class, we ran around there. Most mornings produced at least one rabbit. If it wasn't already dead, we killed it and hung it up on a tree. When we had a few, we gutted them and gave them to Johnny to sell them. It was a covert operation trying to outwit Hardy, but the pocket money made it worthwhile.

We were studying hard for our final exam, but we also had time for hurling and football, played on real fields. June came and we sat for the exam in the Great Hall of UCC. I remember one hot afternoon when the lady invigilator fell asleep. We did not take advantage – the consequences were too great.

It was back to my family in Kilcrohane for a last summer school holiday. Always at the back of my mind was the fear that I may not have passed Latin. I enjoyed helping on the farm. I was a big lad, now almost 6 feet tall. I remember having one difference of opinion with my mother. There was a local dance in the tiny hall in Kilcrohane on Saturday night. I asked her if she had ironed my favourite white shirt. She said, 'What do you want it for?' I told her that I was going to the dance. Her response was that since I was going on to be a priest, why should I want to go dancing with those young girls? She did now know that there was one I was keen on, Mary Hurley. (She later tried her vocation as a nun for a few years.) She did iron my shirt and I did dance with Mary Hurley, but in my mind I was determined to follow through my desire to be a priest. I would have to forego any close relationship with girls.

One day, the postman delivered a conical parcel, inside which was my certificate for passing my matriculation exam. A few years later this exam was replaced with the Leaving Certificate. I wrote to Cork asking them to accept me as a candidate to Myross Wood House near Leap in West Cork. It was in the most beautiful setting, with a wood in the background and sea at the front. The Missionaries of the Sacred Heart had purchased it in the early 1940s from the former landlord, who was called Townsend. Lots of refurbishing took place to make it into a novitiate and house of philosophy. I had a long list of things to bring with me, including a black suit, black raincoat and black hat.

On 20 August 1951, a good neighbour drove my mother, Martina and me to Myross Wood. The long journey to the priesthood had taken a new and serious phase. There was a one-month introductory course, where we were with the novices who were completing their novitiate year. They were due to make the temporary vows of poverty, chastity and obedience before starting their philosophy course in the other part of the house. Our intake was seven: five from our school in Carrignavar (Dennis McCarthy, Tim Gleeson, Sean O'Mahoney, Martin Murtagh and myself) and Hugh Slattery and Eugene Clarkson. We had to call each other 'Brother'. The person in charge of novitiates was called 'Novice Master'.

So, I was not just going to become a priest, but first and foremost a religious priest, with vows in contrast to the priests working in the local parishes, who were called secular priests. The novitiate was a spiritual year devoted to the formation and growth of the students' personal life. It would involve lots of time for prayer, meditation, spiritual reading, reflection and getting to know the spirit and charism of the society. There would be a forty-day retreat during Lent, with complete silence except for a few breaks.

* * *

Who are the Missionaries of the Sacred Heart? They were founded by a French parish priest, Fr Jules Chevalier, working in the small town of Issoudun in the year 1854. He was deeply moved by the apathy of religious practice and also by the evils that afflicted the people of his time as he contemplated the Heart of Christ in which is revealed the compassionate love of the Father. He discovered there the remedy for the ills of his time.

In the words of the founder, 'Jesus was happy to pour out the tenderness of His Heart on little ones and on the poor, on those who suffer and on sinners, on all the miseries of humanity.' The spirit of our Society is one of love and kindness, humility and simplicity; it is, above all, one of love for justice and concern for all, especially the poor. Because Mary is intimately united to the mystery of her Son's heart, we pray to her under the title of Our Lady of the Sacred Heart.

Jules Chevalier gradually formed a community of like-minded priests and got approval for a new congregation. Some time later, the Holy See asked him to send some of the new missionaries to Papua New Guinea and the South Sea Islands. In the late 1930s some of our Irish priests became missionaries in New Guinea. Two were murdered by the Japanese and the rest taken into concentrations camps. They survived.

Some time was spent on reflecting on the vows we were about to make. We were tested in little ways. Our main manual work was doing the washing-up after lunch and evening meals for the whole community in the house. We were fortunate to have as our cooks the Daughters of Our Lady of the Sacred Heart. It took some time to do all that washing-up. If we broke any of the ware we would have to go to the Novice Master's room to confess. On one such occasion, he rather sarcastically said, 'Brother, break a few more.' You just had to bite your tongue! We were living on one side of the building with our own oratory. We were not allowed to have any communication with the students who were studying philosophy on the other side of the building. Our recreation was going for walks to nearby villages with our black clothes and hats. We played a little football and hurling, but with seven it was futile having matches.

What did the novitiate year do for me? On reflection, it was probably the most important year in my life. The Novice Master dictated some material every evening for meditation before Mass. This was very helpful. But what changed me most of all was the free time I spent in the oratory, in silence and quiet communication with the Heart of Jesus. The wilfulness to break rules was gone. There were so many aspirations rising in my heart – many of them unreal. At last I was slowly becoming a suitable candidate for the religious life and priesthood.

I must mention one other priest. Fr Morgan Curran was Assistant Novice Master and also taught scripture in the philosophy classes. He was the one who was my Latin teacher in Carrignavar. He was one of the most holy priests I have known. He was a living icon of the love of Jesus for us, truly meek and humble of heart.

One of the novices was feeling the pressure. During the forty days retreat, I was out walking after the evening meal near the wood when I heard his voice imitating Michael O'Hehir broadcasting the All-Ireland between Cork and Louth. The silence was too much for him, so he wanted to let off some steam. Sean left a few years later and became a detective in Dublin.

We were interviewed by Fr Scriven, who was the Provincial and who had threatened to expel me because he thought I was ringleader in the sit-down strike. The seven of us were accepted to make our first temporary vows for three years on 21 September 1952. My mother, Martina and Nora came to the ceremony. It was a joyful day of celebration. We moved to the other side of the house to start the philosophy course.

A word about seminaries for secular and religious priests. The secular priest had Maynooth and a few smaller ones in Ireland. Each and every religious and missionary order had its own house of study. Basically, they did two years of philosophy-related subjects and four years of theology. Rarely had they enough competent staff. They were all bound by the model of seminary dictated by Rome, which was the same for the whole world. I have strong feelings about this, which I will deal with later. The philosophy was called scholasticism, based on Thomas Aquinas, who lived in the twelfth century. He based his philosophy on Aristotle, who lived 2,000 years ago. To make matters worse, some of the textbooks were in Latin and the lecturers tried painfully to speak Latin, a dead language for 1,800 years.

There was none of the thinking of modern philosophers and there were no modern books available. We did two years of this, and, apart from the rules of logic, it had very little relevance for our future lives as priests.

During our holidays, we were never allowed to go home. They were spent either helping on the farm or playing football, hurling or tennis. Fortunately, we had a boat and were allowed to use it occasionally. When the tide was in, many took advantage of swimming.

We had one hairy experience with the boat. Eight of us set off for a picnic on an island which was out of the mouth of Glandore Harbour and to the right. Getting there was easy as the sea was calm. As the wind got up after many hours on Rabbit Island we decided to get home quickly. Fortunately we had Jim Dudley, born on Dursey Island, who had some experience. I had a little bit. The wind got stronger and stronger. Keeping the bow of the boat facing the ever-increasing waves was more and more demanding. We got past Adam Island, which was the scene of the greatest fishing-boat disaster in recent times – five people losing their lives there in 2012. Somehow we managed to get back to calmer waters and home. It was a recipe for disaster but thankfully no one was hurt.

As well as classes and long study time, we were also expected to do other chores. There was a hen farm to produce eggs for the large community. There, three of us were responsible for boiling potatoes, mixing them with mash and feeding the hens every day; collecting the eggs; as well as securing them in at night. This was a seven-day-a-week chore. I was also infirmarian, which meant taking meals to whoever was sick in bed – also demanding.

I inherited a problem with varicose veins from my mother. I had to go to the Bon Secours Hospital in Cork to have them stripped in both legs. How medical times have changed! I had to remain in bed for seven days with legs bandaged like a mummy. Nowadays you would be out of hospital in one or two days. Mr Kearney was the surgeon. He marched around the hospital with Matron trying to keep up – the sheet was pulled down and the top of the bandage opened. He then caught the end of the sticking plaster over the wound in the crotch and tore it off, with lots and lots of hair attached. This act of cruelty went on every day. I was glad to get back to Myross Wood.

At the end of every term there was an exam. A good memory helped. You had your notes and textbook and you had to regurgitate these at exam time. Most got fairly good marks. On reflection, what a pity we did not have modern books available, do essays or explore new thinking; maybe time for rational debate with freedom to express oneself. We had Fr Morgan Curran for some scripture classes. Scripture scholars might find them too pious, but they were helpful. Fr Coen did a basic course on astronomy, which was fascinating.

The long hours of study could be very boring. One afternoon I tried to bring some light relief. Maybe I was prone to do some practical jokes. This one backfired. Fr Warren was the Superior. He told me that the evening meal would be one hour early for some reason and to tell the bellman to ring the bell one hour early. I did not tell the bellman. When the time came I got up from my seat and made some awful groans and gestures and staggered towards the door and into the corridor where I rang the bell. They would all think I had gone mad and had some sort of breakdown. Eugene Clarkson ran to give me comfort, but before I could stop them Tim Cahalane and Michael Maher ran to Fr Warren's room. I soon recovered and returned to my seat before Fr Warren came down. He was not amused. In many little ways he made life more difficult for me while I remained in Myross Wood. You might say good enough for you!

There is one other incident that I regret. We had some robust games of football; during one of these matches Martin Murtagh kept fouling me. I gave him several warnings, and after one more bad foul I hit him with my fist. I got him under the eye and there was lots of blood. The match was stopped and he had to go and report to Fr Warren. Thankfully, he was economical with the truth and told him I got him with an accidental elbow. He had to be taken to Skibbereen to get it stitched. It was the last time I ever hit a person with my fist.

Every day we wore the MSC habit of soutane, cord and Roman collar. When we went out we wore a black suit with Roman collar and hat; in winter, a black overcoat. People were often amused to see these young boys with Roman collars. We were baby priests!

All our letters were left unclosed and went through the Director of Students. So did incoming mail, which he had the right to open before giving it to us. There was one landline phone outside the supervisor's door. The first time I used it, it was a call from my family to tell me that my elderly aunt had died. Can the youth of today, with all their sophisticated mobiles, believe I was twenty-one before I used a phone? The revolution IT has brought about!

We had no access to newspapers and the only time we could listen to the radio was the occasional GAA match. We were cut off from the big bad outside world. How strange: we were being prepared to minister to this bad world either at home or abroad and we were denied any current information about it!

* * *

The two years went by fast and it was time to leave and go to our Theology House in Moyne Park, Tuam, Co. Galway. We were allowed one night at home before heading to Galway. It was three years since we had seen the inside of our family home.

Moyne Park was a stately home and farm which the Missionaries of the Sacred Heart had purchased in the early 1940s. There was the main house and an outside house was adapted for about twenty students. We all had our own room for the first time; small, with no running water. The toilets and wash areas were less than basic, with no hot water. There was a large coke furnace which had to be lit and stoked by students on a rota basis during winter. This was going to be our home for four years. Fr Dominic Duffy was Superior and Director of Students. I always admired him. He had done postgraduate studies in theology in Maynooth. He would be our professor of dogmatic theology. In 1984 he volunteered to go to mission in

South Africa. He travelled with John Finn, who was just ordained, and I, who was returning to South Africa for a second time.

There was a very elderly priest, Fr Pat Long, teaching moral theology and Fr Tommy McGeogh was teaching canon law.

Sixty years have gone by since then. Reflecting back on those four years of theology, I must admit that in spite of all the efforts of these good priests, it was not the best preparation for ministry at home or abroad. It was not their fault – they were prisoners of their time.

Dogma was set in marble or stone. There could be no growth or change in truths that were formulated by very clever men, some of whom lived over a thousand years before. Any new insights were unwelcome. The writings of modern theologians were treated with suspicion and even disdain. So we had our textbooks and we took notes in class. We tried to remember and regurgitate them for our exams. Just to take one example, I was interested in evolution. We all take for granted now that evolution took place over millions of years. Yet when I was a student in Moyne Park you were supposed to take the biblical creation story literally, just like they do in some of the southern states of the USA. I got access to a new book on mitigated evolution by a person called Messenger. Once a year each student had to give a talk on whatever subject he chose. All the staff would be present. I tried to give all the obvious scientific reasons why we must accept the fact that evolution took place over millions of years and that at a later stage God intervened to create man. The general feeling of the audience was that it's just all theories – you have no proof.

I believe Jesus came to tell some of the secrets of God. He would try to tell us that God is a mystery and through every generation the Holy Spirit, through prophets and learned men, would reveal a little bit more of this inexhaustible mystery. Revelation is ongoing and never-ending. The ocean of God's truth is bottomless. With my little bucket I can take something from it. Thomas Aquinas with his gigantic bucket was able to take so much more.

That any theologian could claim that he has told us all that we can know about God in his learned books is a delusion. If we are told it is all set in stone or marble till the end of time it is an insult to our intelligence and freedom. At the end of my book I will return to this again.

For more moral theology we had Fr Pat Long, whom I liked. For some reason, he had the nickname of Toni. The older students kept telling us he always repeats his exams, of which they had quite a few. Toni must have got wind of this. He set a completely new exam and a few were found wanting and failed. There was a bit of an uproar about this and Toni was asked to retire.

As we were a very young congregation in Ireland, it was difficult to get suitable and competent staff. They asked Fr J.J. Cleary to go to Moyne Park to teach moral theology. He had not opened a theology book for twenty-five years. We just followed the textbook. When it came to the term that we were to do the whole question of the Sixth Commandment and human sexuality, he said we should just do it through Latin. It was a complete waste of time. Three years after my ordination, when returning from South Africa for a short holiday before going to Indonesia, we came up the east coast of Africa. While the ship was going through the Suez Canal we went for a short visit to Cairo. Some touts were trying to sell me condoms and I didn't have a clue what they were! The idea that the smallest offence against the Sixth Commandment was a mortal sin seems so absurd now. Teaching on the whole area of human sexuality was so negative that instead of it being one of God's great gifts to us, it was looked on as a necessary evil. I would like to reflect on this when talking on marriage.

Thankfully, Fr Tom McGeogh switched to moral theology, while the newcomer from Rome Fr J.J. O'Brien took over canon law.

We all had a bicycle and during holidays could go to Knock or Salthill in Galway and explore parts of Connemara, provided we got back for night. We helped with the harvest and the picking of potatoes, which no one liked.

We were fully grown men and had a good football and hurling team. We played St Jarlath's senior team as well as the Tuam Stars during the winter. The famous duo of Purcell and Stockwell were playing for them. When they beat Cork in the 1956 All-Ireland Final, Stockwell and some of the team brought the old Sam Maguire cup to Moyne to let us see it. I felt sad that it wasn't in west Cork. We were very impressed that they thought of us.

At the beginning of the year there was voting for people to take on certain responsibilities for the year. In Myross and again in Moyne Park I was chosen to put on some plays during the year. This took up a lot of time: getting a suitable play, picking the different characters and the time-consuming task of getting them to learn their lines off by heart. There was a problem in so far that men had to do the ladies' parts – some flatly refused. Those who did left something to be desired. But there was a great sense of fulfilment and fun on the night, although no Oscars were given out. It helped us to build confidence to appear before a congregation to preach and say Mass.

Fr Shanahan was in charge of our preparing and delivering of homilies. This was helpful.

Because money was scarce, the order got special indult to ordain students who were over twenty-four years during their fourth year of theology. This was so they could get a stipend for saying daily Mass. Tim Gleason, Dennis McCarthy, Narciso Tiro and I were to be ordained in the autumn of 1957. Mass was still in Latin. Fr J. J. O'Brien was to supervise us as we practised the many rubrics and got familiar with the Latin prayers. As we were all teetotallers, even tasting wine was necessary.

* * *

The day for ordination was fixed: 13 October 1957, which fell on a Sunday. Bishop Donal Lamont, a Carmelite missionary bishop home from Southern Rhodesia, was asked to do the ordination. It was his first ordination. We were allowed to bring parents, siblings and in-laws. It was a long journey from Bantry to

Athenry, where they stayed overnight. The local curate, Fr Lucey, came with them. To give an idea of how times have changed, while in the hotel in Athenry he got a few to sing. He had a new toy – a tape recorder. He played the songs back and they were dumbfounded.

It is so difficult to speak of my ordination day that I have laid my pen on the desk for half an hour. How can I describe the emotion of my ordination? It was almost eleven years since I first whispered to my mother that I wanted to be a priest. But not once during the ups and downs of those eleven years did I doubt my vocation to be a priest. In spite of my unworthiness, the Sacred Heart of Jesus had called me to be an instrument to spread His love. The four of us lay prostrate before the bishop, dressed in our white albs. It was a gesture of our total reliance on God to keep lifting us up every day. The *'Veni Creator'* rang out. Would that God's spirit would for ever more fall on us like the dew falls.

There was the firm laying on of hands by the bishop and priests, and the words of ordination. The part that moved me the most was the anointing of the palms of our hands with chrism and then folding them and tying them with white cloth. Those hands would lift up the bread containing the invincible risen Christ and the chalice of His blood. They would make the sign of the cross over repentant sinners and try to set them free. They would touch the forehead of the sick and dying, giving them reassurance of God's mercy and love. They would reach out to those who needed comfort in their pain and sorrow.

There was the symbolic handing of the chalice, as well as the clothing with the stole and chasuble.

We were ready to celebrate the Mass with the bishop. One moment I remember so well was after communion when I closed my eyes for a few moments as we knelt down. Not aware that we were due to move to the altar, I got the sharp end of Tim Gleeson's elbow. What a down-to-earth fellow my long-term friend is.

There was the meeting of our beloved families, an oasis of love and joy, and maybe a little bit of pride. We shared a lovely breakfast served by the students. Then there were the first blessings. Fr J.J. O'Brien took a lovely photo of me blessing the most wonderful mother in the world and the rest of my siblings.

There was a long journey back to west Cork through the narrow roads of Galway, then Limerick and onwards to Cork. There was another long day ahead tomorrow. Our Lady Star of the Sea Church in Kilcrohane, where I was baptised and had so often served Mass, would be the host of my first Mass. All the local people were in the full church. Each got an individual blessing after Mass – it was quite tiring. I remember a few old women went to kiss my hands, and their faith made me feel so humble.

We had a lovely breakfast for family and close friends. Now there was time to relax and take photos. Certain bottles of spirit were also passed around. We got two weeks' holidays before returning to Moyne Park to finish our fourth year of theology. It was a time to visit friends and neighbours. My brother Michael, who returned from New York for the ordination, purchased a second-hand Ford Prefect. I had no driving lessons; I just got into it one day and started to drive away slowly. There were very few cars on the roads to Kilcrohane. I had learned to drive – there was no driving test back then.

My brother Joe had also returned from New York, having been there since being made redundant from the coastguard in Sheep's Head Point. He had saved some money and decided to buy a pub in Cullen, near Millstreet. He was now forty-three years old. Someone made a match for him with Peggy Sheahan from Rathmore. She was in her thirties and fancied this Yank with the red hair. All this was taking place only a couple of months before my ordination. They decided to get married – and who better to do the ceremony than Joe's godson, just ordained! We had a lovely family marriage ceremony in St Patrick's Church, Cork. The next year, before I went to Africa, I baptised their first boy Dónal when, as the custom was then, the baby was only a few days old.

Back in Moyne Park, it was still pre-Vatican II. There was no concelebrated Mass. In the side altar, we all did our individual daily Mass. There were final exams to prepare for, including one oral exam where the professor came to us for mock confession. He had all sorts of complicated and unreal sins which we had to sort out.

* * *

Coming from a large family, it would be normal to have one or two family tragedies. I have had many more, including suicides, which I will deal with later.

My brother James inherited the farm. He married Mary Donovan and at the time of my ordination they had two children, Ita and Donie. There was a third one on the way. In early 1958 Mary went to a small hospital in Skibbereen to have the baby delivered. The attending doctor was keen on the local pub – maybe he went to play darts? The baby was dead in the womb a day before they discovered it. They rushed her to Cork, where it was impossible to save her life. James had gone by train to Cork only to be told bluntly, 'Your wife is dead.' He walked the streets of Cork not knowing what to do.

I got a phone message with the bad news and went home immediately. It was my first of many experiences in trying to deal with tragic death and grieving relatives. My mum and Mary's parents and brother were inconsolable. Then there were the two tiny children Ita and Donie. Who would look after them? There was the preparation for my first funeral Mass. What could I say in my homily that might make any sense to bring comfort and healing?

A day before my ordination Bill Barrow, a student, in a moment of reckless generosity gave me a silver rosary – all the beads were solid silver – which I have to this day. He had got it as a present from the USA. Clutching at straws in helping the parents of Mary, Stephen and Anne, I gave them the rosary, asking them to say the Sorrowful Mysteries of the Rosary. Holding this rosary for a few days seemed to bring a tiny bit of comfort.

After the sad funeral, the big question was asked: who would rear Ita and Donie? My mother, who had reared ten of us, said she would. My sister Mary had completed her secondary education in Kildare Convent as a day pupil, staying in Newbridge with my brother Danny. She was now in her first year of training as a student nurse at the North Infirmary Hospital, Cork. She got six months' leave from the understanding nun, and so started the rearing of Ita and Donie.

Back in Moyne Park, the three remaining students of the fourth year were ordained: Hugh Slattery, Eugene Clarkson and Martin Murtagh. We were all asked to state which ministry was our first and second choice. I think most put down mission as first choice. Only two of us were asked to go – the rest went to the University of Cork to be trained as much-needed teachers in the Sacred Heart schools of Cork and Carrignavar.

We got a well-deserved break of a couple of months. I remember being recruited on to the local parish team with the ambitious name of the 'Western Stars'. It would be my last opportunity to play Gaelic football. I was their centre half-back. Being known as a priest, the opponents treated me more gently than they might have otherwise.

Part II

In early September 1958 there was what they called a Missionary Departure Ceremony at Sacred Heart Church, where we got our Missionary Cross. Having got our injections, and proof that we didn't have TB, Fr Jerry Buckley, who was twenty-five years old and ordained with us, Hugh Slattery and I would depart from Cork on the Innisfallen ferry to Wales and by train to Southampton where we would get the liner for South Africa. James, Michael and Joe came to see me off on the boat. There will always be sad memories of sailing down Cork Harbour and away from the land I loved, going into the unknown. Three years later I did the same thing on my way to Indonesia. I might get sentimental if I write about kissing my mother goodbye.

It was exciting climbing onto one of the Union Castle liners bound for Cape Town. There were no commercial airlines then. Most affluent white South Africans, especially those of British descent, took a once-in-a-lifetime holiday to the UK and Europe. They all travelled by liner to and fro. The food and facilities on board were something we were not accustomed to. There were formal seating arrangements for lunch and dinner. How the ladies vied with each other in dressing up for dinner! The great honour they aspired to was an invitation to dinner at the captain's table. I am not sure what entitled them to this honour – there were whispers and maybe stories of jealousy! We were all allocated a table to sit at during the voyage. There were about nine missionary priests and two young nuns on board. Most of the priests were at one table. The two young beautiful nuns, who were going to Southern Rhodesia, and I – as well as a very elderly gentleman – were at another table. I don't know if the other priests were a tiny bit jealous, but one of them – a very elderly Benedictine priest – used to take the nuns to a secluded area every night to say the rosary (and maybe give them spiritual advice about the dangers of spending so much time with a nice young Irish priest!).

We joined in the deck games: the quoit throwing, a sort of tennis, and swimming in the large pool. There were concerts and cinema and dances. The South African Catholics among the travellers quickly made themselves known to us and tried to reassure us of all the good things about living and working in South Africa. Some of them served our individual Masses in the morning.

I am perhaps one of the world's worst sailors – I get seasick so easily. Having sailed away from the UK we soon came into the Bay of Biscay and a raging storm. For two days I stayed in my bunk without food. Things soon got calm as we sailed southward and I finally got my sea legs.

There was a special ceremony crossing the imaginary line of the equator as the young ones were happy to be thrown into the swimming pool under the eyes of King Neptune. We stopped at the beautiful island of Madeira for five hours. It was the first time I saw banana plantations. Twenty-seven years later, a very famous footballer – who played with Manchester United and Real Madrid – was born on this island: Cristiano Ronaldo. Kids dived into the ocean for coins thrown by passengers and we went onshore. As Hugh Slattery and I were gazing at the vista from outside the cathedral a man sidled up to Hugh, saying the word 'women'. For a few seconds Hugh was puzzled – and then it dawned on him that the man was a pimp. Hugh later became a bishop in South Africa, and I have often reminded him of this occasion in Madeira where he rather than I was approached by a pimp!

The next stop was Cape Town. I doubt if there is any more beautiful place in the world, with Table Mountain and the meeting of the Atlantic and Indian Oceans, its vineyards and beaches. We berthed after dawn under very blue skies and immediately the decks were swarming with black men eager to help passengers with their luggage. We had arrived in Africa. After all this time my mind is a blur about all the sensations of stepping on African soil for the first time. Fr Liam Long, working in Cape Town, took us on a tour of the city before bringing us back to the ship. We were to go on for one more day's journey to Port Elizabeth, where we disembarked.

Fr Tim O'Neill met us as we got off the boat. Fr Jerry Buckley went to a parish in Port Elizabeth while Hugh and I were driven the 100 miles to King William's Town. Travelling along the road, I was intrigued by the huge mounts of earth, most of them conical shaped, in the nearby veld. Tim told us they were anthills. I didn't believe him, but it was true.

* * *

Our order was founded in 1854 in France. It was over half a century later that Fr Michael Tierney, who joined the MSC in Australia and came to the UK to start the parish in St Albans, came to found the order in Ireland, through the Sacred Heart College in Western Road, Cork. He got his vocation in Ireland. However, students had to go to Belgium and Holland for their seminary training until the outbreak of World War II, when they had to establish their own in Myross Wood and Moyne Park. The first foreign missionaries went to the South Sea Islands and New Guinea in 1936. As a missionary congregation in Ireland, we were a small outfit among the great missionary congregations there. From the 1950s onwards we started to get an average of seven vocations annually. This was to increase. Our newly created province decided we needed our own mission field. The Benedictine Order had a vast territory in the North Transvaal and were willing to give us half of it. In 1950, the first three arrived, followed later by Fr Bill Cadogan, a veteran from New Guinea and former concentration camps. He would be the leader. This became our most successful mission as time went on.

The second mission field was to be Eastern Cape, with King William's Town as its centre. For a variety of reasons it did not work out well and those working there went to the mission territory in North Transvaal, where John Durkin became the first bishop. There were two major problems with starting a mission field in South Africa: it was, on the one hand, an industrial nation with vast resources, yet these resources were all entirely controlled by a few million white people. For nearly a hundred years the Catholic Church in South Africa mostly catered for its white Catholic population. The congregation of Sisters and Brothers were asked to provide schools for the whites only. There were exceptions to this, but not many. Many of the priests were secular and were not trained or interested in missionary outreach to the vast black population. The great Oblate Order tried to reverse this trend. But the greatest problem of all was the curse of apartheid. More about that when I return to South Africa in the 1980s.

In the summer of 1958 some congregation in Rome came up with a strange idea: religious priests would have to do a fifth year of theology. Hugh and I had arrived at King William's Town and were told that, to somehow fulfil this new law, we would be stationed in the parish of Fort Beaufort with Fr Owen Sullivan, where some of the MSCs would do some classes with us. It never materialised, as the priests felt unable or unwilling to do it. But the six months there were not a waste of time. We did a little Afrikaans language study, read books about Africa, got used to the climate, played some tennis with white parishioners, and passed our driving tests. It was a welcome rest after eleven years of studying.

After a few months I was asked to go to the university, but thankfully Fr Jerry O'Mahony went instead of me. It was decided that I would join the Mission in North Transvaal, 800 miles away. My chauffeur was Fr Jimmy White. He had gone to UCC and got a teaching degree. He was a very good footballer and played corner back for Cork under the name J. O'Brien. Priests were not allowed to play football at that level. He went to King William's Town to do some teaching. The day before we left he had been to a wedding. Returning home after the celebrations he bashed the end of the exhaust of the Volkswagon Beetle. The noise it made was horrendous as we drove up the east coast of South Africa at a ferocious speed. We stopped overnight in Ermelo in Natal with a Franciscan community.

We continued on our journey northwards and entered the south gate of the Kruger National Park. There were only dirt roads then, and there was no speed limit. With the thunderous noise of the car we frightened all the wildlife away. It was late when we arrived at Duivelskloof Catholic Presbytery, where Fr Bertie Murphy would be our host.

There were many small but important outreaches to the vast African population, notably by the great Oblate Order, who were responsible for the Dioceses of Johannesburg, Durban and Bloemfontain. The Benedictine Order, in spite of trying to combine monastic and missionary lives, had made some valiant efforts. The most important was at Doornspruit, where they invited Sisters and Brothers of charity to open boarding schools for black boys and girls.

This was my first appointment. It was hoped that Fr Andreas would teach me the African language while I would be chaplain to both of these schools. It was hard going, but I had some little success.

Also in residence was the first abbot and bishop of the area, who was retired and suffered from Alzheimer's. He was one of the holiest and most humble people I have ever met. We had a lovely relationship and one of my cherished duties was to look after him. All of our rooms had outside doors and mine was adjacent to his. At about 5 a.m. every morning I used to hear his door rattling. I had the key. He said it was time for community office prayers. I had to gently persuade him to get back to bed, where I treated him like a child, putting his long white beard over the blanket.

During the day, when he went into the toilet, sometimes he was unable to remember how to open the lock. I used to get in the window – I was rather slim then. He would say to me, 'Were you always here?' My answer was always, 'I just dropped in.'

Occasionally he had lucid moments. He told me that he and the Sisters of Charity physically built the church. They stopped to say the different hours of the Office Prayer. He sat on a seat outside the clinic saying some words to the African women in their language. His little luxury was a pinch of snuff.

MSC personnel were still scarce and Fr Bertie Murphy could not return for some time due to ill health. I was asked to go to Duivelskloof as the priest in charge of a small parish. The name of the small village is interesting. When the Afrikaaners went on the Great Trek into the hinterland they founded the Orange Free State, then moved northward to the vast territory they were to call the Transvaal. After many years of tribulation and with loss of life – first their oxen died from the tsetse fly and they themselves suffered from malaria – they had to cross the ridge of a mountain with the ox wagons. As they descended into the valley their wagons stuck in the many rifts and gorges; they cursed their luck when they came to this valley and called it Duivelskloof, which meant Devil's Valley. They moved on. Little did they think that this Devil's Valley would one day become a paradise of fruit farms. It is well to remember that these early settlers took all of the arable land in South Africa as their God-given right and left the rest to the vast African population. Emigrant fruit farmers from Italy and Germany came to this valley to purchase land and start growing fruit trees. With newly discovered machinery they were able to build dams and set up sophisticated irrigation systems. There were vast acres of orange trees, fragrant and beautiful when in blossom and sumptuous when the fruit was ready for picking. The climate was near-perfect, with not a hint of frost. There were thousands of acres of outdoor tomatoes. Full lorries left for the markets of Jo'burg every evening. There were banana farms and pawpaw fruit. I got to love avocado and mangoes. There was also a tea plantation sponsored by the government.

There were many Italian families and other Catholics from different parts of Europe among them. There was a lovely presbytery and church. Another cultural shock for me were the shacks where the black people lived with no proper sanitation.

They were the servants of the white people. They did have a primitive school, which was a help. The church was built in such a way that the main part was facing the altar, and built onto the side was a small section for the few African Catholics. Because of the new laws of apartheid it was illegal for them to be under the same roof, even for worship.

In one area where there were quite a few Catholic farmers we were able to start a small outreach to their workers. With the help of a voluntary black catechist, we were preparing children for their first communion.

The white families were anxious that I would visit them regularly and sometimes for meals. On Saturday afternoon I played tennis with them in the tennis club. Life was enjoyable, but some days I felt that this was not the missionary work that I had hoped to do. Later on the Missionaries of the Sacred Heart would be most successful in reaching out to the vast black population. The first great breakthrough came when the hierarchy of the South African bishops, at the behest of Bishop Rosenthal, set up a missiological institute whose purpose would be immense help in solving the difficulties which the overseas missionaries encountered in their endeavours to understand the vast indigenous non-white population. Without a sound knowledge of their psychology, their language and customs, their traditions and history, their art and music, our missionary labour would be in vain.

Aware that John Durkin was most enthusiastic about this project, Michael O'Leary, the then Provincial of the MSC, was happy to respond with personnel. Sean O'Riordan had gained an Honours degree at Rhodes University and was currently lecturing in the Xhosa language. He had boundless energy and set up language laboratories in the new institute called Lumko in the Eastern Cape. Other MSCs joined him – Tom Nicholson, Paddy Whooly and later Hugh Slattery. They were joined by two German priests, Fritz Lobinger and Oswald Hirmer.

Many a new missionary got the tools of his trade at Lumko – language, customs, art and music. Much later it moved to Johannesburg under the leadership of Dick Broderick. This has been a wonderful contribution to the missionary effort in South Africa by our Irish Missionaries of the Sacred Heart.

The second important breakthrough was the opening of a catechist training centre by Fr Michael Crowley. The catechists followed a two-year course and were housed with their families at the centre. The trained catechist was of inestimable value to the missionary priest.

Twenty-three years later I was asked to return to South Africa. I was so proud of the amazing progress and outreach to even the remotest part of the newly created diocese of Tzaneen. This was despite all the slings and arrows of the outrageous apartheid laws limiting black education and freedom of movement. But that is another story.

* * *

In early 1961, the Dutch province of the Missionaries of the Sacred Heart asked the other provinces for help. Diplomatic relations between Holland and the now-independent Indonesia were at a low ebb over West New Guinea. Indonesia was claiming this as part of their country. Missionaries going back to Holland for holidays were not allowed to return. The Irish Provincial gave the offer of at first three men, with two to follow in 1962. I was asked to volunteer, and so were Jerry Riordan and Dan Shine. There was a silver lining, as we were offered a holiday in Ireland before leaving for Indonesia. I said farewell to South Africa.

The journey home was most interesting. There were still no commercial airlines so Liam Long, Paddy O'Connor and I took an Italian liner from Durban, up the east coast of Africa. We stopped at Maputo, Zanzibar, Mombasa and Aden. When the ship was going through the Suez Canal we went through the desert by large taxi to Cairo. We visited their most ancient museum, some items going back to Alexander the Great, as well as the famous Tutankhamun. We went by camel out to see the famous pyramids. Some Irish girls riding on camels started to scream when the Arab drivers tried to hurry the camels into a gallop. Getting on and off a camel is not for the faint-hearted. It is hard to describe the vastness of the desert, with its miles and miles of sweet damn all. Poor Lawrence of Arabia!

Back on ship again, our final stop was the southern port of Italy called Brindisi. It was the month of May and everything in the countryside looked so green after Africa as we went by train to Napoli (see Naples and die!). Our train journey was paid for as part of a deal with the liner. It was late when we arrived at Napoli and we had difficulty getting a B&B. But it did not stop us getting a taxi out to see Pompeii, which was floodlit. The next day we were in luck when some kind people asked us to join them on a visit to the Isle of Capri. It is quite a historical place. I will never forget the boat trip to see the Blue Lagoon. I began to think, 'I have hardly started my missionary life and I am seeing all these places!' The next stop was Rome. We stayed at the MSC house for one week. It is the only time that I have been to Rome. I can vividly remember so many sights and experiences. Tim Cahalane and Mick Maher were students in Rome and generously gave some of their time to be our guides. They got us tickets for a papal audience at St Peter's – right up front. The sight of Pope John XXIII being brought in on the Papal Chair was something to be treasured. The Second Vatican Council was due to start the following year.

Our train ticket was prepaid to London. Next stop was Venice, where we stayed for a night. St Mark's Church and Square stand out in my memory. It was a long overnight journey to Paris, where we stayed one day. Going up the Eiffel Tower and seeing all of the city was truly breathtaking; also the Church of Notre Dame and Montmartre.

Next stop – London. You won't be surprised that my pocket money had run out. I was broke, and it was not a nice feeling. Fortunately, my brother Frank had gone to London to work at Ford's. He gave me more than I needed for the train and boat journey to Cork.

It was a very warm feeling to see all my family again. My mother was doing well, in spite of her age, in rearing her grandchildren Ita and Donie. Michael had started his own farm and had married Anne Donovan, and she was expecting her first child. Mary was a nurse in Bantry Hospital. Joe's family had doubled with the advent of Andrew. I helped on the farm as the three months went by fast, but the day of departure was looming.

That day was painful. I was going to Indonesia, 12,000 miles away, for at least five years. Would I ever see my mother again? I still remember one incident that cuts me to the heart: little Donie had grown fond of me while I was at home and I remember the look of sadness and tears in his eyes as I said farewell.

Michael and James went with me to Cork. There I was joined by Jerry Riordan, first on the Innisfallen and then the train to Milford Haven, north Wales, where we joined a cargo ship going to the Far East. At that time, cargo ships took a few passengers, who dined with the officers. Life was quite different to the luxury liner. There was not much to do to pass the time. The officers, mostly Catholics from Liverpool, were friendly. But the captain was something else. At the start we noticed that he was missing from the dining room. Eventually, the first mate confided in us, telling us he had a serious drinking problem. Later, when he was missing, sometimes for days, they used to joke that he had 'gone into orbit'. When he used to return with a red and flushed face, he wanted to play deck tennis. After a day or two he was back 'in orbit'. We were few passengers, one of whom was a young lady on her way to Singapore. She was much admired by the officers.

Having gone through the Suez Canal again, our first stop was Aden, a duty-free port. We purchased the most important item ever, a small transistor radio, which would be our only contact with the outside world in the far-flung Moluccas Islands, where we would be for five years. We also bought a gramophone player. We had with us some records of Irish singers. One I remember was Bridie Gallagher. Many a time we played them in the long evenings in our make-do presbytery.

We had a long sea journey to our next port of call, Singapore. It was memorable for the wrong reasons. We sailed into a terrible tropical storm that lasted for two days somewhere in the Indian Ocean. Being the poor sailor I was, I retired to my bunk. A

Chinese steward brought a few cream crackers and apples, the only food while the storm lasted. When it got calm and I went up on deck, I was amazed at some of the damage to cargo on deck. I was curious about what cargo we were carrying and the officer confided it was mostly ammunition for Indonesia.

When we came to Singapore, the ship had to stay a mile out while a barge took us ashore. It was one of the hottest places I have ever been, as well as being humid. It was so interesting to see what is mostly a Chinese city. They seemed to be keen to be businessmen. A tailor made a light white soutane and some light white trousers which turned out to be necessary in the poor mission we would work at. The tailor measured you one day and all was ready, a perfect fit, the next day.

We went to see a Good Shepherd Sister working as Head of a Catholic secondary school. She was from Kilcrohane.

There is a world-famous colonial hotel in Singapore, the Raffles Hotel. Jerry Riordan and I thought we would go to see it. Unfortunately, we did not have a tie and we were not wearing our collars. We were refused admission – the first and only time this has happened to me.

We then set sail again for the final leg of our journey. We sailed past Sumatra Island, the largest and most thinly populated in Indonesia. It was here that the greatest volcanic eruption happened – Krakatoa in 1883. It was also the epicentre of the recent tsunami of 2004, which wreaked such havoc in villages on Sumatra and in neighbouring countries. We disembarked at Jakarta (at that time it was spelt Djakarta), which is the capital of Indonesia, on the island of Java.

Indonesia stretches from Singapore to northern Australia and New Guinea. It is made up of thousands of islands, most of them uninhabited. Java, although not very large, is extremely fertile, yielding two crops of rice a year. About 70% of the population resides there. Before colonisation, all of these islands were separate entities with their own languages and customs. The Portuguese sailed past all these islands and straight to the Moluccas, islands of spices, which they found in abundance there.

Later, the Dutch came and sent them packing. They called all these islands the Dutch East Indies and imported the Malayan language as an administrative language. This also became the only language for schools. Later, after Sukarno declared independence, it was called Indonesian.

Java had the most ancient language and culture, and became the centre of all political life. Jakarta was the capital. More about its history later.

We were met by Fr Sol, who was the Provincial. He tried to help us through customs, but even he was unable to stop them confiscating our precious radio, gramophone and my real treasure – a 35mm camera. Examining our visas and passports, they asked if we were English. We tried to tell them our country was near England, but was called Ireland. There was an immediate reaction as he said, 'Oh, you were the first country to recognise Indonesia as a new state.' This was news to us, but we heartily agreed. Later that week, Fr Sol managed to redeem our precious goods, having to pay some money.

One of the great cultural shocks was living in Jakarta for three weeks, the time it took to get the necessary papers to progress to our mission in the Moluccas. The river that ran through the city was where they got household water; it was also the place where they bathed, and was possibly used as a toilet. Fr Sol's house and church were on a street called Djalan Kemakmuran. When I asked what it meant and was told Prosperous St, I thought what a misnomer it was.

The first night in the presbytery, I found that many mosquitos found me attractive, or at least that my blood was tasty. We had nets over the bed but they found any tiny hole in them. The next morning I went to the room which was the toilet and bathroom. But there was no shower or bath; instead, in the middle, was a concrete container of water. Puzzled as to what to do, I got into it and later pulled the plug, releasing all the water. Fr Sol was so annoyed that he had forgotten to tell us that you stood near the container, poured a basin or two of water over you and then used some soap. You washed it away with another basin or two of water. Clean water was so precious. This was my first lesson in personal hygiene.

Fr Sol's congregation was made up mostly of Chinese families, very pious and generous. One family had brought in the evening meal and left it on the table. As I went into the dining room later I saw a big rat leisurely going up the wall having stolen some of our meal. There are few things in the world I hate more than rats.

We went by bus to our diocese in central Java, on roads with potholes so big you could bury not only a rat but a dog. 70% of the Indonesian population lives in Java. Seeing the paddy fields for the first time, they looked so exotic. There were ponds of water with hundreds of ducks in them. We passed through village after village with high densities of population. It was the first time I saw water buffalo; these are used to work in the paddy fields.

The day before Jerry Riordan and I were due to take the local cargo ship for the long trip to the Moluccas, we were shocked to see Fr Dan Shine. He came from South Africa and had left on a cargo ship for the Moluccas. As we were to discover ourselves, there were so many deprivations that it was understandable that Dan had a nervous breakdown before he reached Ambon, the first big post of the mission.

The Dutch priest decided that the sooner he got help the better. He was able to get him on an air force plane going to Java. Dan, who was usually so solemn and serious, was giggling like a child; asking him to be leader was not an inspired choice! There were some airlines starting long haul flights, among them Quantas (the Australian airline). They were able to get him to London quickly. While Dan was in Jakarta he had written an article for our magazine, which he posted to Cork. Fr Dan Casey was in the dining room of Sacred Heart College, reading this and thinking of Dan Shine 12,000 miles away, when he walked into the room. For a moment, Dan Casey was speechless and thought he was seeing an apparition!

All this was a morale-sapping experience for Jerry Riordan and me, but it did prepare us for the toughest three weeks of our lives. I can only give a rough description of conditions on the cargo ship. We had no cabin. There was a huge number of people on the deck, with all sorts of goods and chattels. We had only learned a few words of Indonesian. The captain, who was Polish, took pity on us and allowed us to use the only cabin, called the Sick Bay. We were travelling along the equator line with the climate hot and humid. All meals were the same: a plate of boiled rice, with the occasional bit of fish. It also contained something else which was like dynamite. There were hot bits of chilli and very hot peppers. We tried to pick most of these out before eating a few spoons of insipid rice. Fr Sol had anticipated this and given us large containers of toasted bread, which we rationed to two slices a day.

The boat stopped at many islands delivering cargo. Some passengers left, to be replaced by others. One of the islands was Sulawesi. I had two cousins who were in the British Navy, one of whom was in a Japanese concentration camp during the war. He died with many others from malnutrition and dysentery a few months before it ended, in April 1945. His mother, my aunt, cried for days when she got the account of his death. His name was John Fitzpatrick. Before I left, she gave me details of the war graves in Indonesia where he was buried. It was on this island. I can't remember how I got transport to get to the war graves, which were kept so beautifully by the Australian government. After searching for some time I found his grave. I took photos, which I later sent to his mother. She cried with joy that I was able to kneel at his grave.

We stopped at Bali, which has since been developed into a world-famous holiday resort. It is the only island in Indonesia whose inhabitants are Hindu.

One night, the Polish captain invited Jerry Riordan and I to his apartment. He offered us a drink of whiskey; I was a Pioneer (teetotaller), but I thought if it helps to keep me sane I will have it. It did not taste very nice. I think he might have belonged to the Polish Communist Party, but he told us how he had discovered that on every island he served with cargo, the only people who were helping the local poor people were the Catholic Church. They ran the only clinics and small hospitals, as well as schools.

When we arrived at the big island of Ambon, which is the administrative capital of the Moluccas, we were taken ashore by Fr Strater, a Dutch MSC. We had our first good meal in two weeks, as well as the availability of washing Indonesian-style. The inhabitants of Ambon Island were the favourites of the colonial Dutch East India authorities. They mostly belonged to the Dutch Protestant Church; most of their army were recruited from them. They were most apprehensive when Indonesia became independent under Sukarno. A large number were taken to Holland for protection.

It was to these islands that the Portuguese came to take back with them the exotic spices which Europe craved. It was also the first mission territory of the great St Francis Xavier, with the advent of the then very Protestant Dutch, St Francis went on to Goa and Kerala in India.

There was one more stop before our final destination in the Kai Islands in the southern Moluccas. This was the best-known spice island, where the Portuguese built a large fortress – and then on to Tual in the Little Kai. The mission boat took us to the main centre of the diocese, Languar. The bishop resided here. There was a large hospital – but only Sisters and nurses, no doctors – and also a large school.

There was a wonderful turnout at the pier to welcome us, with children singing and dancing. The elderly Bishop Grant and some priests led us to the priests' house, where some welcome food awaited us. The Dutch Missionaries of the Sacred Heart who came to evangelise many years before were the most wonderful missionaries. They now staffed four large dioceses. We were surprised that there were so few indigenous vocations after all that time. It would appear that the insistence to learn Latin was a huge hurdle. Things have changed radically: Indonesia is our biggest province now, all seminaries are full and most want to become MSCs rather than join the secular clergy.

We started immediately on the language, which happens to be one of the easier ones. I found that with a dictionary in my hand I would try to speak with some children. When I got things wrong, which was very often, they laughed heartily. This was not good for my pride! But I persevered. I soon got some oral Indonesian. Reading the gospels in Indonesian helped as I knew what they said in English. It was like learning to ride a bicycle – you soon get confidence.

They were so short of personnel that after six weeks the bishop asked me to go to the Great Kai Island next door and take responsibility for about ten villages, each with its own church and community. In Languar there was a large warehouse, where items of food and other basic necessities were stored – all of them from Holland. Unfortunately, many of these goods were stolen on the local cargo ships. The mission boat took me over to Kai Besar (Great Kai) and I was literally thrown into missionary life at the deep end.

In my 'parish' there were two good presbyteries; in all the rest it was less than basic, with roofs made of palm leaves, which often leaked. Mass was still in Latin, even the words of absolution. The usual programme was to start at one end of the parish and spend one or two days in each village. When you were there, that was their Sunday Mass. There would be baptisms and marriages. Each village had an Elder who was responsible with others for all the normal running of the parish. Every Sunday they had worship where the Elder presided, with scripture reading and much music.

When the priest visited, all matters would be discussed and problems solved. Having gone through all the villages, I would take a long walk, which meant climbing a hill to meet the Dutch priest and Jerry Riordan, who was put in charge of some novice Brothers. There would be a few days' rest to collect necessary supplies, before starting all over again. I was more than amazed at how quickly I became fluent in the language.

Indonesia is 90% Muslim; the other 10% of Christians are concentrated first in Flores, where the Divine Word missionaries have over two million Catholics. Our islands were about one-third each: Catholic, Protestant and Muslim. A village was of the one religion when the chief converted and brought all the villagers with him. They rarely intermarried and usually they took spouses from their own village. There was a great problem:

I don't know why, but there was a caste system. There were three classes who lived and worked together, but when it came to marriage you could only take a spouse from your own class. Over the years, many missionaries tried to break this with not the slightest success. The village leaders were from the Mal-Mal, the top class.

The biggest surprise I got was that there were only two seasons. For six months the wind blew from the south, bringing hot dry weather. Then one night it changed and blew from the opposite direction and this brought tropical rain and sometimes severe thunder and lightning. The sun rose at 6 a.m. and went down at 6 p.m. every day. The whole island was jungle and they cut and burnt different areas every year to grow their crops of yams and taro and sweet potatoes. There were some wild banana trees. There were also sago trees, which demanded lots of work to harvest the sago.

No one owned private property; it was all communal and the chief decided how much and where you could use to till for your family. The two seasons made a huge difference to our lives. When the wind blew from the land and the sea was calm near the shore we could use canoes to go from village to village. Also, when the sea was calm they had a unique way of catching fish, of which there were a great number and variety. They used a bamboo fence which was wide at the opening and narrowed to a corral from which the fish could not escape. A family member went to this corral and speared what fish they needed. This went on for six months until the season changed. It was either feast or famine.

We all had a man, whom I would not like to describe as a servant, but maybe cook and cleaner. Ladies from the village took the clothes to be washed and sometimes starched and ironed. I don't know how they did it with primitive equipment, but it always came back so beautifully white and clean. The cook would not be up to the standard of Jamie Oliver, but he would get ladies to do some nice fish dishes with rice – when fish was available. On the island, there were no cattle, sheep, goats or horses, but there were lots of wild pigs. They went to hunt them with spears and dogs and were sometimes successful. All dead meat had to be cooked on the same day as there were no fridges. Even people who died had to be buried the same day, before decomposition set in. They were good at cooking pork with their own spices. The only milk was in powder from mission supplies, which helped with cups of tea. Sweet potatoes I never liked, but some yams were a little like a potato.

What about bread? We used to get some flour from the mission warehouse, but the humidity was great and lots of weevils appeared in it. We sieved them out. We had no yeast, but by using liquid from palm trees with sugar it sometimes worked like yeast and we had a loaf of bread, all baked in a makeshift oven. When we were on visitation to other villages, food was more sporadic. I had days when I had only fried bananas; that is why when I returned to Europe I didn't eat a banana for years.

The only source of cash for the people was dried copra. The palm tree nuts were left to dry in the sun. There were no roads, so they had to hump bags of copra for miles before selling them to Chinese traders. I suspect the traders made most of the money when they exported shiploads of copra. The people were very poor but they had a few garments which they kept clean and neat, especially for Sunday Mass. We used to get bales of second-hand clothing from Holland. It was a mixed blessing because it was so difficult to help everyone. Some of the clothing was not suitable for the tropics. Ladies were puzzled by some of the ladies' items. More than one turned up in church with an ornate bra outside their dress!

* * *

The following year, we were joined by two young priests, Joe Hanley and Martin Rabbitte. Joe was appointed to the Little Kai, where he worked with boundless energy and enthusiasm. Joe did not like to go the extra mile – he wanted to go ten extra miles. Unfortunately, he got cerebral malaria, which set him back for a few months.

Martin joined me for a few months. I helped him with the language and he began to settle down to missionary life. He later took over a big parish. We met every month in the main station for a few days' break. We used to play a kind of adapted bridge with only three players. While he was with me one day, the cook brought in what looked like a brick, but was actually an unsuccessful loaf of bread. He said something to me in Indonesian, which Martin asked me to translate. It was, 'Master, it is less than perfect.' This is the kind of great understatement which is common among Eastern peoples. Martin thought it was hilarious.

In 1962, Bishop Grant was replaced by Bishop Sol. He was the Provincial who was so helpful to us in Jakarta. I once asked him what faculties I had for dispensation and he said, 'I don't know but whatever I have you can have.' Contrast this to much later, working as a parish priest in England, when there was so much unnecessary red tape and bureaucracy, wasting time and money sending away requests to the diocese for dispensation which was always given.

When he came to Kai Besar, I accompanied him around the island, where he administered confirmation in so many villages. We got to know each other very well. Later, he came to visit me at St Albans.

In 1963, Jerry Riordan, who had never really settled down and was getting paranoid about little things, was advised to return to Ireland. Like the crew of the Irish Rover, we Irish were reduced down to three.

The only communication we had with the outside world was our little transistor radio. I could get Radio Australia very well, as we were only 200 miles from the Northern Territory of Australia. Sometimes in the evenings, the children would gather around to hear this miracle box play music. They had no idea what a radio was.

Getting news from Ireland was a problem. The post took months; Christmas cards arrived before Easter. My brother Michael used to send the *Sunday Independent*. I would get a few copies together, but it kept me in touch. Once I thought that a paper was only two months old, but when I was putting it down I realised that it was a year and two months.

My aunt Nora died in New York, leaving me $1,000. The letter said it must be countersigned by an American consul. The nearest was 1,500 miles away. I thumbed a lift with the Indonesian Air Force, who had built an air base on Little Kai, and flew to Sulawesi. They later gave me a free lift back. When they eventually got my signed and countersigned reply in the New York office, it caused such amazement that it could have taken six months.

In the past, there were quite a few Dutch Brothers who were of the most wonderful help in building churches in the large villages. The best timber was available everywhere in the jungle. They provided saws to cut it down and make it into planks. Some of the churches were large. I had one which could hold the entire village of around 1,000. The smaller villages made their own constructions, which were just about functional, but there was always a problem with leaking roofs, which were made with palm leaves. There were no glass windows or doors.

It may come as a surprise to the reader that I was still saying Mass and administering the sacraments in Latin, a language that not one of the congregation would understand. Only a few missals were available in Indonesian. We also said Mass with our back to the people of God who, because of their baptism and confirmation, were participating with us in the offering of Mass.

The people of the Moluccas were famous in Indonesia for their incredible talents at singing and music. It would appear that all the Dutch MSCs were able to sing. Now, here was this new priest who could sing all the notes but rarely in the right order. Those who were literate had this music book of Gregorian chant. They spent hours practising the Mass for the Sunday that the pastor would be in their village. Every Sunday they expected a *Missa Cantata* – a Mass with all the Gregorian music. This was one of the most painful and humiliating experiences for me. I still had my back to the congregation, but I could hear the stifled laughter at my efforts. One Sunday is forever etched in my memory. When I turned around to sing '*Dominus Vobiscum*' there was an immediate response from a nearby cockerel: 'cock-a-doodle-do!' There was pandemonium among the congregation and I continued Mass without further music.

So you will understand how ecstatic with joy I was when Bishop Sol returned from the final session of the Vatican Council and told us that we could now use the vernacular in the liturgy, and the further news that we could now face the congregation. I cannot produce any record to prove what I did, but I must be one of the first priests in the whole world to change every altar around. There would be no more *Missa Cantata*, as Mass would be in Indonesian. People would know for the first time the wonderful prayers in Mass. They could have all the singing they wanted in their own language.

* * *

The Dutch Provincial was getting very concerned that the basic necessities were not being delivered to many MSC islands in the Moluccas. They took the brave and expensive step of buying a small ship. One of our priests, with a licensed captain, went to Holland to sail it to Indonesia. It was an incredibly brave undertaking and had some very scary moments, such as the storms of the Indian Ocean. I forget how many weeks it took them. With a few more crew the priest stayed on to manage the movement of personnel and goods to the islands. After two years he asked for a change and Martin Rabbitte took over his managerial role. It was reported that he wore a captain's hat and was happy when people thought he was the captain.

I very soon began to love and admire these people. Fr Sol told me that I would find them hard-headed and stubborn. That had helped them during the War when the Japanese put all the Dutch priests and Brothers into concentration camps. Without a priest they continued to baptise their babies, assist at weddings and hold Sunday services every Sunday. They prayed night and day that their beloved pastors would come back to them again. When the Japanese were told that churches had sacred vessels of silver and gold, they demanded that the Elders hand them over. They had already buried them in the jungle together with the baptism registers. They beat the Elders, but these so-called stubborn Catholics would not give in. They hung them up, tied to the tree by their hands. They continued to beat, but it was no surrender till they died.

In all cultures, marriage is a rite of passage that has so many human and emotional connotations. There are many cultural imperatives that have to be negotiated. The dowry system, because it involves money, goods or chattels, is a recipe for family rows. When a boy and girl fell in love after clandestinely seeing each other over a period of time, they forced the issue by running away for a time to the jungle. The two families involved made lots of noise, blaming each other. But I think it was a kind of ritual. They came to a mature agreement and I was asked to marry them in church. Very often, it was a simple affair, with none of the trappings of weddings that we have in Europe. For those who were slightly better off there was a feast. After Mass, some tea and biscuits with some speeches. Then I returned to the presbytery to await the main meal. I knew things were beginning to happen when I heard the pig squealing as they killed it. In about two hours, someone came to accompany me to the wedding table. It was nice to celebrate with them. One very interesting custom was that the bride and groom ate off the same plate. This was the public symbol that they were man and wife.

I did not attend many funerals, as the dead had to be buried the same day they died and I was rarely in the village when the death occurred. The Elders would conduct the funeral rites. It was still the time when we could only say Mass before noon.

But I did have one of the most extraordinary funerals that any priest ever had. Years before, this bishop decided to have an opportunity for Catholic girls to try their vocation in diocesan congregations. Their main convent was in the central mission station on Little Kai Island. One of the first candidates was from my main village of Haar, at the very end of the parish. She later became the Reverend Mother and was looked on as their founder. She was Mother Teresa. When she was very elderly and realised that death was near she got permission to go back to her family in Haar to say goodbye. I believe she had her own agenda and was hoping to die and be buried there. If so, she got her wish. I was in a village two hours' walk away when a delegation arrived telling me. I went immediately to Haar to deal with the funeral of Mother Teresa. When I got there, we had a meeting. What were we to do? We had no motor boat. We could not take the body back to her convent for burial.

We started preparations. Some started making a coffin. Others dug a grave outside the church and lined it with bricks. I started preparing for Mass at 4 p.m. Many came to the church and wanted confession. There was an air of extraordinary excitement. As usual, the Mass and singing were excellent – they had some Gregorian chant from the Mass for the dead. My homily was about the consecrated life of a nun. There was the Final Commendation and procession to the grave. When all the rites were finished, they filled in the grave.

I remember returning to the presbytery totally exhausted. At about 7 p.m. I went to bed and fell asleep. Probably an hour later I was slowly woken up – it seemed the veranda of the presbytery was full of people. There was hushed conversation, while some were knocking at the door of the presbytery. I had to investigate. Having put on some clothes, I went to open the door. There was a sea of faces in the dark, slightly lit by a tilley lamp. In the forefront were some nuns from the convent on Little Kai. They said they had come to bring back the body of Mother Teresa. I tried to tell them that we had buried her some hours previously. As I found out later, they started to tell me some lies. 'The bishop has told us to bring back her body even if she is buried.' Looking back, I have no possible idea how they knew that she had died. What was I to do? Send them back without the coffin and maybe incur the displeasure of Bishop Sol? I thought of a compromise. We would get the coffin back up, and if there wasn't too bad a smell they could have their wish. It was the most macabre experience I have ever had. The spade and shovel clashed as they lifted the earth from the coffin with the dim light of the tilley lamp. We said the rosary. They got to the coffin and I still have no idea how they lifted it out of the ground. The nuns, with a few men who came with them in the motor boat, said, 'We are taking Mother Teresa.' It was out of my control now. We took the coffin into church for more prayers while the visitors had some refreshment. Then there was a procession down to the shore with the little tilley lamp guiding them. I stayed on the presbytery veranda. After some considerable time they started the outboard engine. It spluttered into life only to stop and die. This happened about five times. Finally, it got going and it faded into the dark night.

Months later, I met the bishop and he was embarrassed when I told him about the demand to get the nun back. He had given no such instruction. We both understood why they did it. When the body arrived the next morning, it was taken to the cathedral where another requiem Mass and burial took place. Much incense was used to counteract the inevitable decomposition which had set in. Two burials, two different islands, in two days. There was still some drama to follow!

The sacristan had been so busy with the greatest day in his life. Like me he was exhausted and went to bed early. Early next morning, as he passed the church on his way to the beach for the morning ablutions, he apparently almost fainted when he saw the empty grave, being totally unaware of what had happened during the night. Strangely, he did not run to the presbytery nearby but to the village headman. I was puzzled by what he said. I would have thought that he might think Mother Teresa had risen from the dead. What he actually said was that Satan had taken the body of Mother Teresa.

* * *

I forgot to mention that there were no roads on the island. I am told things have changed since. For the six months that the sea was calm I used a canoe that was hewn from a large tree. There was only one seat about 1 foot high. I sat on this while holding onto the sides of the canoe. My helper had only one paddle, which he alternated from one side to the other. In calm waters we moved fast. All that we needed for ten days away were taken in the canoe in aluminium boxes.

When the sea was rough we had to walk along the paths near the seashore. Helpers had to come and bring the boxes to their village. I wore only a T-shirt and shorts with tennis shoes. I became quite a fast walker. It would be unsafe to quench your thirst from the many streams so I would ask my helper to climb a coconut tree, which he could do like a spider. They always carried a machete, or Parang. He would cut a coconut, which would fall with a great thud to the ground. Having come down, he would cut away the fibre and make a hold in the coconut from which I could drink the cool liquid. He then split the coconut in two and made a little spoon so that I could eat the soft delicious white inside. You might ask, 'Were you not stealing?' There was no such thing as private ownership of land. All travellers could do what I did. It was the hospitality of nature.

When I arrived at the destination I would have a wash. There would be a makeshift enclosure of bamboo and palm leaves, with a container of water in the middle. You soaped and washed yourself as best you could. One day, I heard some children nearby. One of them was able to peep through a hole and I heard him say, 'The pastor is white all over.' They must have thought it was only my hands and face that were white.

Lemons were plentiful, and with water and sugar would help quench a thirst before a pot of tea, followed by a rest.

There was one dramatic journey that almost cost the lives of myself and my helper. When the wind was blowing from inland, it was calm along the seashore. Further out, it got rough. I did not realise that my paddler was taking a shortcut, which meant going out a good bit from the shore. I soon realised that we were in trouble. Fortunately, he was very strong and although the wind and waves were pushing us out he strained every muscle to keep the bow of the canoe towards a spur of land. I was holding on for dear life with one hand and trying to bail water with the other. Somehow we got into calmer water and land. That morning, I had got a chicken as Mass stipend – it was at the bottom of the canoe, drowned. If the canoe had capsized he would have tried to save me – but that would only have meant that we would both have drowned. Some shark would have had a lucky day tasting Irish meat for the first time.

This brings me to Joe Hanley's adventure. There were some small islands within fifty miles which had small Catholic communities and which hoped that a priest might call during the course of a year. Joe set off with a crew on the Mission sailing boat. They were due back in two weeks. There was great concern when each day went by over the two weeks. The Mission motor boat went to search, but could not go very far. After a week, the sailing ship limped home. The mast had been broken in a storm. They drifted to an island where they patched it up enough to get home. Joe was a good sailor – unlike me.

The one port where the cargo ships could anchor was Elat. There were some Chinese shops with limited goods for the locals. We had difficulty getting razor blades. One day we got some in the Chinese shops, and to make matters better it said 'Made in the Republic of Ireland'. They wouldn't even cut butter.

Nearby was the mission station, where we would meet the other priests when we took a few days of rest every three weeks. Near to that was the only hospital, run by the Dutch Daughters of Our Lady of the Sacred Heart. The hospital tried to serve everyone, irrespective of religion, with the few resources they had. The Sister served as dentist. When Martin Rabbitte had a severe toothache she asked him to open his mouth wide while she yanked it out – she could not use anaesthetic. It got rid of the toothache!

During my time in Indonesia, my sister Mary married Anthony McCarthy and Michael married Anne Donovan. I got some photographs of their happy day which I could not share – the sacrifice of being a missionary.

We were busy, but there were some dull moments. When we arrived at a village we were busy with confessions in the evening, and next morning Mass with baptism and possibly a wedding. The rest of the day there was nowhere to go and nothing to do. Fortunately, Martin Rabbitte managed to get boxes of books from some Americans in Jakarta. We read everything, even though they were not my cup of tea.

* * *

Are there any memories that I am ashamed of? Yes. The first one is about the carrying of the boxes that I needed as I moved from the main presbytery to the smaller villages where the presbytery was only a shack. This village that had a weakness for the beer from the palm tree kept me waiting for hours to send men to carry the boxes. Eventually I had to ask a few of my villagers to volunteer to get me to this village. To put it mildly I was angry with the villagers when I arrived. Two weeks later, as I was passing their village, they came to me kneeling. I had no idea what had happened. It transpired that on the day I was angry with them, they presumed that I had cursed them. A woman villager walking by the shore was swept out to sea by a wave and was drowned. They were convinced it was my curse that had caused it. I tried my best to explain to them that I did not curse them and a curse could not have caused her drowning. I don't think I had much success. I prayed and blessed them with holy water and realised it was a lesson to me.

I cringe when I think of how unchristian and dogmatic I was in confronting the only man in one village who did not go to church, and how I ranted and raved when one family killed a chicken on a pagan altar as a sacrifice. The Old Testament is full of stories where people returned to idolatry.

I feel bad at the memory of one evening returning from a long session hearing confession to find that the egg I was to have for supper was already cooked. I had many times told my helper to wait till I returned before cooking. When I tried to put the spoon into the egg I knew that it was impossible. Getting angry again, I threw it at him, just missing his head – it was like a stone and would have done damage.

The missionary church has always brought a trinity of values wherever they went: gospel values, values of education and values of caring for the sick. So too in Indonesia. Every Catholic village had a basic school to help children to become literate. We had the only hospital on the island, albeit without a doctor.

When we were on our way to another village, we often had to pass through Muslim villages, as well as some Protestant ones. It was often embarrassing passing through Muslim ones. The children were always on the street, with sometimes little or no clothes. My passing was treated like a circus. They followed us in large numbers shouting '*Belanda*', which was a derogatory name for the Dutch (they presumed I was Dutch). We never engaged them in conversation but got through as fast as possible. When the Japanese invaded the island, they captured all the priests, nuns and the bishop. It is alleged that a Muslim told the Japanese that the bishop had a radio transmitter and was in communication with Australia. When he did not produce something he never had, they beheaded him and threw his body into the sea. At night, the Catholics recovered his body and buried it.

The last three years, the bishop asked me to go to a parish with some very large villages, but not too far apart. The vivid memory I have of this is my first Christmas there. Because they were so religious, they were always vying with one another as to who got midnight Mass or Mass on Christmas Day. In my slightly misguided youthful enthusiasm, I decided that all four would get Mass. I started off with midnight Mass in the first one. At about 2 a.m. we set out for the main village of over 1,000. Travelling with only one torch through a path in the jungle was slow and dangerous. We arrived at 5 a.m. I rested for two hours before Christmas Day Mass. They had prepared so much music, and the fact that we did not have a eucharistic minister meant that the distribution of communion took about forty minutes. This was the most energy-sapping part as one hand was always outstretched. Giving communion to a leper who had lost his nose was a shock. There were none of the trappings of our Christmas. I rested for a few hours before setting out for the third village, where I did the third Mass. After a night's sleep I went to the fourth village, where we celebrated Christmas for them.

* * *

There was a major national political upheaval in 1965. There was a Communist coup, which did not succeed. With the advancing Japanese invasion and the fall of Singapore in 1943, all the Dutch withdrew to Holland except the priests, nuns and Brothers, who were put into concentrations camps. Most survived. During the war, Sukarno had the opportunity to gather millions of followers in a movement for independence, presuming the Japanese would lose the war. After the war, the Dutch, with the help of UK forces, tried to regain power, but soon realised that the game was up and withdrew. Sukarno was a colourful character and showed his gratitude to the Dutch missionaries who had befriended him by giving each bishop a cask of altar wine and, despite great pressure from the 90% Muslim population, he declared freedom of religion. Islam would not be the state religion.

He foolishly wasted most of the GNP on building up the army, navy and air force. Through political pressure he got possession of West New Guinea, which he called Irian Jaya, against the strong wishes of its indigenous population. He created lots of national slogans, one of which was 'Nasacom'. This was the crazy political philosophy of uniting nationalism, religion and communism. The Communist Party, made up of mostly Indonesian Chinese, were happy with this. It gave them national respectability. They belonged to the very violent type of communism in mainland China. They were very clever in their political organisation and in 1965 they believed that Sukarno was in poor health. They managed to invite all the generals of the army to some sort of party. They tried to assassinate them all, but somehow Suharto managed to escape through a window. He rallied all the leaders of the army, who are all pro-West. The coup was ruthlessly put down. Much later I read in an issue of *TIME* magazine that perhaps as many as a quarter of a million communists were killed. The Muslims realised how close they had been to becoming a communist state.

During this time, the army sent a few soldiers to every island in case there were any problems. Two came to Kai Besar. They were a law unto themselves and Catholics came to tell me that one soldier was raping some of the girls. They begged me to do something. They got a large sailing boat and took me to the small Kai Island where the commanding officer was. I reported the soldier to him. He was very concerned and told me he would deal with it, but it took a few weeks. When I returned, the soldier got word of what I had done and was trying to get me. The villagers had to look out day and night, and when he was coming they whisked me off to hide out in the jungle. It was a very nervous two weeks before he was taken off the island and to Ambon. The sad sequel to this was that when some people from my island heard that he was after my blood they found out he was in Ambon and killed him. The pastor was on the same footing as chief, and he had humiliated their flesh and blood.

Suharto had some great success for many years, helped by the Western powers. The price of crude oil hit new heights. But there is a saying: 'All power corrupts. Absolute power corrupts absolutely.' Suharto clung onto power for far too long with the usual nepotism and corruption. But I am sure I would not recognise Jakarta and many cities in Indonesia today. Even the village of Elat may have shops that sell most things, even razor blades that shave.

* * *

It may come as a bit of a surprise to most people that there are two quite famous books written about the Spice Islands. The first is by Alfred Wallace, a contemporary of Darwin, who lived and did his research in the Spice Islands, particularly Kai Besar, where I worked. Tim Severin calls his book 'one of the most remarkable travel books ever written'. It was called *The Malay Archipelago*. The other, a very modern book, is by Tim Severin and is called *The Spice Islands Voyage: In Search of Wallace*. Tim has written so many travel and adventure books, among them one about sailing in a leather boat across the Atlantic in the wake of St Brendan. He has travelled on horseback with the nomads of Mongolia and sailed the Pacific on a bamboo raft to test the theory that ancient Chinese mariners could have travelled to the Americas.

Alfred Wallace was a brilliant and intrepid naturalist like Darwin, with whom he had much correspondence. Darwin said this of him: 'That you have returned alive is wonderful after all your risk from illness and sea voyages, especially the ones on the Spice Islands.' Tim Severin felt that the contribution that Wallace made to Darwin's book on the theory of evolution was never recognised. Wallace founded the science zoogeography.

Tim Severin set out to restore Wallace's reputation by retracing the explorer's journey through the Spice Islands. Navigating through sparkling coral seas to remote shorelines, especially to Haar in Kai Besar, Tim and his crew of Westerner and islanders encountered red birds of paradise, flying foxes and birdwing butterflies. When Tim went ashore in Haar, he discovered the unique great birdwing butterfly in great numbers. Severin recalls Wallace's account:

> This is one of the most magnificent insects the world contains. I trembled with excitement as I saw it coming majestically toward me and could hardly believe I had really succeeded in my stroke till I had taken it out of the net and was gazing, lost in admiration, at the velvet black and brilliant green of its wings, seven inches across, its golden body and crimson breast. I felt it struggling between my fingers, and to gaze upon its fresh and living beauty, a bright gem shining out amid the silent gloom of a dark and tangled forest.

Tim Severin went into the jungle where Wallace discovered the great variety of butterflies. On his way back to the village of Haar, he describes a phenomenon which I often admired:

> Right towards the end of our walk was a never-to-be-forgotten sight. We emerged from the wall of blackness

and there, slightly on one side of the track, was a small, open tree about the size of a tall holly bush. It was a plant of the bean family and an attraction for fireflies. Dozens upon dozens of these insects had settled on its branches, outlining the shape and structure of the tree in points of luminous green which pulsed randomly as Nature's electric illuminated Christmas tree. The phenomenon stopped me in amazement, and I stood watching the vivid green specks glow and fade and occasionally shift a detail of their pattern as insects changed position on the branches.

Tim Severin has tried to prove that Wallace, in June 1858, wrote an essay entitled 'On the Tendency of Varieties to Depart Indefinitely from the Original Type' and sent this to Darwin. He posted this letter with another to a friend in the UK. His friend got this on 3 June. Darwin said he got Wallace's letter two weeks later, on 18 June. It was between those two dates that he discovered the keystone of his theory on evolution. Most acknowledge Wallace's contribution makes for uncomfortable reading.

I would like to finish my story on Indonesia with a couple of unforgettable memories. First was seeing the coral reef with a snorkel. The Australian Great Barrier Reef extends to Indonesia. You will have seen it on TV, but to see it a few feet away is something else. The different shapes and colours of the coral are breathtaking, but what is most clear in my memory is the hundreds of little fish with combinations of blending colours forever darting here and there through the coral.

The second was listening on my little transistor radio in the middle of a dark night, ensconced in my mosquito net, to the funeral of John F. Kennedy on the other side of the world, hearing the clatter of the hooves of the riderless horse, and the recording by one of the Kennedys of 'There is a time for everything'.

The last one is sitting on the veranda in one of my good presbyteries on a bright moonlit night, overlooking the Indian

Ocean. Some of the village fishermen were a distance away, each boat with a lantern. They were swordfishing. So dangerous. They can fly 20 metres or more, attracted by the light. As they do so, the fishermen must try to catch them in a net. If they miss, the sword of the fish, which is long, narrow and sharp, would pierce them through and through. Just beneath me in our village huts, the young men are singing their love songs with self-made guitars. My gramophone is playing some Irish records for the thousandth time. I so often reflected that they have nothing, and yet they have everything. They seemed so happy. In contrast to the youth I have met in the UK, who can have everything and yet have nothing because they seem angry and unhappy.

Part III

In May 1966 I was feeling quite unwell. I went across to the Little Kai to the main mission station to see Bishop Sol. He advised me to take a holiday in Ireland as soon as he could get the air force to give me a lift to Jakarta. I spent a few days in the hospital. The matron gave me some antibiotics. It took two days to Jakarta, as the plane stopped a few times on other islands. The Australian airline Quantas had opened a travel route to Europe via some Asian cities. I got my return ticket to London. The plane was only one-third full and the hostess gave me five seats where I could lay down and sleep. We stopped in Singapore briefly. As we were on the flight to Karachi, the plane was struck by lightning and it jolted so badly we nearly hit the roof. The hostesses turned pale and sat down on seats. The pilot gained altitude as we flew over the storm. This phenomenon is very rare I believe. It took a while to sleep again. We also stopped at Cairo and Athens before the last leg to London. We had been flying away from the sun, so it was a long night. The pilot flew very low over the Alps to give us a sight of the snow-capped hills and valleys.

Having arrived at Heathrow, I went to our parish of St Albans. As there was no room in the presbytery, Fr Roach asked the Loreto Sisters to give me a bedroom. I remember the luxury of sleeping on a good bed between two sheets. How we take simple things for granted. We had to arrange to get a ticket to

Cork – commercial flying had started while I was away. I was feeling very unwell.

When I met my mother and Michael and Fr Breen at Cork Airport I believe they were shocked at the way I looked, but they did not say so then. The following night I got the most severe headache, mostly at the back of my neck. I did not want to disturb my mother and I tried tying a cloth around my head to see if I could diminish the pain. The next morning, we sent for my sister Mary, who was a nurse, and she advised me to go with her to Bantry Hospital. The Sisters of Mercy were so kind in giving me a private room with a bathroom. The consultant physician was Barry Murphy. By some incredible stroke of luck, he had done his consultancy thesis on meningitis. He was an expert on this often fatal disease. It is the inflammation of the covering of the brain and spine. He immediately diagnosed my problem, but to make sure he told me he would have to carry out the painful procedure of a lumbar puncture. I lay face downward on the bed with my tummy on a pillow. He put a needle in between the vertebrae and extracted some fluid. This was sent immediately by car to Cork University Hospital. It was thereby confirmed that I had meningitis. After the lumbar puncture I had to remain very still for a few hours. They started injecting me every six hours with antibiotics. This meant waking me up in the middle of the night.

I would be six weeks in Bantry Hospital. The sisters and staff were so kind. Every morning there was a full jug of milk on my locker, 'We want to build you up again,' they used to say. After a week or so the headache began to subside. Apparently Barry Murphy was in contact with Fr Breen and told him I was very seriously ill. When I had MSC priests visit me every week, I asked them why. They said they happened to be passing through Bantry. I soon realised that this could not be true. I had lost a lot of weight and the preventative malaria tablets we took once a week did not stop the malaria, but stopped it becoming a fever. The malaria affected the haemoglobin in the blood – the red blood cells. This did not help my situation. But I was very fit because of all the walking I had to do. After three weeks there was another lumbar puncture. It confirmed that the huge doses of antibiotics were doing the job.

I saw TV for the first time when they brought a set into my room. Wonder of wonders, the World Cup was on in England. Every night I had a match. I remember Eusebio of Portugal and Bobby Charlton and so many of the greats of that era. The final at Wembley with Germany was more than dramatic. I never realised that one day I would become a soccer fan in the UK, first following Stoke City before my conversion to the best team in the world: Man United.

Thankfully, Mary spared my mother by not telling her how ill I was. And although Mary had two very young children, Declan and Imelda, she managed to bring mother to see me a few times a week. Visitors brought me lots of goodies that I had not tasted for five years such as chocolate and grapes. I was most happy to share these with the nurses, who were so kind. They were giving me all these injections in my bum; I asked them to use my arms for a few days.

After three weeks, Mr Murphy told me I could get out of bed and go to the bathroom. When I told him I had never stopped going on my own, he looked at me with such disbelief. I said no one had told me not to. He shook his head and realised it was not my fault.

I had brought a very good 35mm camera to Indonesia and taken some rolls of film over five years. These I sent to Hemel Hempstead in the UK to develop. I got them back while in hospital and, with the help of a little viewer, was able to show something of missionary life to the nurses.

There was a very lovely medical student who followed Mr Murphy to get some practical experience. She asked me to let her be her guinea pig and allow her to take blood and give injections, which were new experiences for her. She had lots of time on her hands in the evenings and used to come and sit with me for a chat and chocolates. I was rather amused that in the public ward was a Capuchin priest at home on holidays from the USA, and who, according to the nurses, never stopped complaining. I was compared very favourably with him.

After five weeks I got permission to go out and enjoy the summer sun, but Mr Murphy insisted I use a wheelchair. After a week he told me I could go home. He warned me that I could experience severe headaches and maybe some impairment of sight and hearing. None of this happened, and I put on three stone in a few months.

Fr Michael Crowley and Hugh Slattery were home from South Africa on holiday. All three of us went up to Connemara and Donegal for a few days. We stayed in Ballybofey with Colum Mulligan's family. I enjoyed helping James on the farm. I did supply for the local priest when he was away.

Donie and Ita were now in the early teens and their grandmother had done a wonderful job in rearing them so far. They were due for confirmation in Durrus parish church. The parish priest, Fr Walsh, invited me to lunch with Bishop Lucey. I have never in all my life suffered such humiliation. The bishop may have given me some slight acknowledgement at the start, but for the whole meal neither he nor Fr Walsh spoke one word to me. I was just a bit of furniture. I had spent time in Africa and on a difficult mission in Indonesia, just escaping with my life. It did not apparently have the slightest interest for Con Lucey. Is there any way that you can justify such arrogant disrespect for a fellow priest? When I compared him with Bishop Sol in Indonesia they were light years apart. I have often thought it is no wonder things have gone so sour in our beloved Irish church. The big sign of Christianity in the early church was: 'Look at those Christians; how they love each other.' I did not expect love from either of them, but I did expect respect and basic human courtesy. I often thought if I were the presbytery dog or cat, I would have at least got a pat on the head, and even a few friendly episcopal words.

I had a meeting with Fr Breen, who was the Provincial. He told me emphatically that I would not be using my return ticket to Jakarta. He asked me to do a temporary job in Ireland. I would be Vocations Director, based in Cork. This would mean visiting secondary schools where the bishop gave permission. I got a little Wolseley car that was as sturdy as a tank.

Fr Tom Healy got tickets for the international rugby between Ireland and France in Lansdowne Road, Dublin. I drove to Dublin and found my way out to Lansdowne rugby ground, parking on a road some distance away. From the Irish point of view, the game was a disaster – the only bright spot was an interception of a pass by Mike Gibson, who ran the length of the field to score their only try.

What happened next was, as they say now, a learning curve. I did not realise that there were five very similar roads running down to the rugby ground. I could not remember which one I had parked on. To make matters worse, I could not remember my car's registration number. I was up and down the wrong roads for forty minutes before I tried another in desperation. Exhausted, I found my little Wolseley.

The Bishop of Ferns gave me permission to visit secondary schools there. I had a slide projector and some interesting slides of Indonesia. There were several Vocation Directors doing exactly what I was doing. The bigger and more well-known missionary societies were in contact with boys who had an interest in becoming missionary priests.

I remember one incident. I arrived early for an appointment. I was told to wait outside the classroom till the Brother came out. I could not believe my ears when I heard the sound of a rod or stick being used on these seventeen-year-old boys, who were obviously failing to give the right answers. I thought, how can I face these boys after such physical abuse?

We also got permission from the Bishop of Down and Connor. Most of the schools were in Belfast. The Good Shepherd nuns were very happy to give me hospitality for the two weeks I was there. Fr Bill O'Connell's sister was a nun there. It was early 1968 and the political tensions could not have been more tense. Whitehall had knowingly turned a blind eye to all devious political gerrymandering – all the social injustice. The RUC could do what they liked. The Catholic population, because of the Brothers and Sisters, had some extremely good grammar schools. The Protestant population did not seem too interested in education. There was no need. They were assured of jobs in shipyards and elsewhere. Catholics with excellent A-level certificates had not a chance and few could afford to go to Queen's University. The rest had to emigrate.

Bernadette Devlin was to emerge later that year like a young Joan of Arc. The rest is sad history, with the high point of inhumanity occurring on Bloody Sunday. I was told that going from place to place I should avoid streets like Shankill Road. One day, I completely lost my way. I stopped and went into a shop to ask if they could tell me where I was and how to get to a certain place. He looked at me for a few seconds as if to say, is this clergyman for real? 'You are on Shankill Road. Come with me and I will show you.'

I got a few boys who went to our novitiate but left later. The headmaster of the diocesan minor seminary was Fr Cahal Daly. He was pleased to meet a clerical namesake and let me speak to the final year. He later became Cardinal Daly.

The streets of Belfast were like a graveyard on Sunday. Sport was forbidden on the Lord's Day. When I had finished, I was glad to be on my way south. Having gone through the border security, I went into the first pub I could find. As I reflected, I had been to Africa and Indonesia, but I have never felt such tension as in a part of my own homeland.

Back in Cork, I was asked to help Fr Willie Clarkson to collect the proceeds from missionary mite boxes. It wasn't easy work. Some shop owners had the money counted and had notes in envelopes. Sometimes they would invite you into the kitchen for a cup of tea and a chat about the mission. I would call them the salt of the earth. The rest expected you to count the money there and then and they would give you notes for it. The pubs were the worst of all. There were 240 pennies to the pound, and having emptied the box of bronze onto the counter you tried to count them, some of them sticky from beer. There were usually a few elderly men slobbering over their pints and keeping a beady eye on you. Occasionally, in a moment of reckless generosity, one would get up and while walking towards you would toss a penny – maybe two – while saying, 'Have that, Father.' Being a priest made me bite my tongue and say a polite thank you. There were other sentences that came to my mind!

For seventy years or more our little Sacred Heart College, later with the addition of the Old House in Carrignavar, produced a number of vocations every year. Many of these became missionaries, first in Papua and the South Sea Islands and then the South African missions; later going to Venezuela and a few to Indonesia. In 1960, the provincial administration decided to build a new college in Carrignavar. I remember when I was at home in 1961, Fr Paddy Sheehan was the lone whistle-blower and said, 'Other big orders are pulling out of schools – it is the wrong thing to do.' The whole field of education in Ireland had changed. There was now free primary and secondary education for all. Schools were built or extended. Fleets of school buses worked in rural areas to carry children to school.

We spent a lot of money on the school and then we asked many priests to teach in them. In my mind, there was no need for priest teachers any more. There were plenty of lay teachers who were as good, if not better. I said that boarding schools were once a necessary evil. They were no longer necessary, and in hindsight have brought a lot of disrepute because of child abuse, both sexual and physical.

Having built the new college, there was the problem of getting pupils to fill it. Fr Tim Gleason, the headmaster, asked me to go to primary schools in Kerry to promote the school. We had permission from the bishop. I used to do an average of six schools a day. The few I got helped. In fifty years we have had only one or two vocations. It is now a community day school for boys and girls.

I got the most wonderful surprise when Fr Breen asked me to go back to parish ministry. The auxiliary Bishop Cleary of Birmingham had asked our congregation to take over the parish in Stoke-on-Trent. I would go to the nearby parish of Birches Head to get experience of English parish life in preparation. Fr O'Leary was earmarked to be the parish priest.

Stoke-on-Trent was the first conurbation in the UK. Six towns were amalgamated to form Stoke-on-Trent. The main one was Hanley, where there is a statue to Stanley Matthews – one of

England's greatest footballers. Previously it was the hub of all the pottery industry; that is why it is sometimes called 'The Potteries'. There were huge coal mines near the city, now closed, with the vast black mountain of waste from the mines. All in all, it was not a salubrious place, but the people could not have been nicer.

The parish priest of Birches Head was most welcoming and helpful. I would be his curate for at least a year. I was also chaplain to the Catholic secondary modern school. These schools were for pupils who failed the dreadful 11-plus exam and could not go to the much-desired grammar schools. Things were to change later. The 11-plus was stopped and most schools became comprehensive schools.

Doing Sunday Mass for an English congregation was a new experience. Some of my friends told me, 'You Irish priests speak too fast – slow down.' It was a lovely experience visiting families in their homes; this was appreciated very much. Sometimes families would say, 'There are a few more houses you may not have on your list – they don't go to church any more.' I usually called on them just to say hello. They nearly all told me the same story of why they stopped going to church. It went back to their days in primary school and the catechism – 'It was beaten into us,' they would invariably say. Those who created the primary catechism meant well, but all the language was adult and dogmatic. Those who were intelligent could get it off by heart and maybe understand some of it. The rest killed themselves to memorise something they did not understand. They said to me that they swore that once they left school they would never see the inside of a church again!

How sad that getting children to have a relationship with Christ and with his lovely gospel stories found no place in their religious education. Sometimes they said that if they missed church through no fault of their own they got beaten on Monday mornings.

There were slow attempts to put Vatican II recommendations into practice. Dioceses started to have resource materials, as well as personnel to advise schools, and sometimes parents, as they prepared their children for first holy communion and confession. A new series of books to replace the catechism was available to teachers.

Many parish priests were less than enthusiastic about implementing any changes. Progress was slow. There were still no parish councils or finance committees. The parish priest decided everything.

From priests who visited Fr O'Reilly, I gleaned some of the hardships that curates endured under many tyrannical parish priests. For example, when the curate arrives at the new parish to share the parochial home with the parish priest, he is told to be in by 10 p.m. every night; otherwise the deadlock will be on and he won't get in. A very strong curate warned, 'If you do that I will bust the door in,' which he did that night. Somehow the parish priest got the message. It was said that a curate was a mouse learning to become a rat.

Another clergy phenomenon that I became aware of was the rivalry between secular (parish) clergy and religious clergy. The parish clergy were very happy to have a religious order like the Dominicans and Redemptorists give parish missions. They could also have city churches, which parishioners could use for Sunday Mass and confessions. But they did not want them to have parishes where baptisms and the other sacraments were administered, and no funerals allowed. When some bishops started to ask religious orders to run parishes, there was mighty antagonism from parish clergy. When I went to Stoke, the clergy realised that I might get a parish, and I was rarely spoken to at deanery meetings. The dean never acknowledged me or introduced me. I heard it said that Archbishop Dwyer was losing his marbles because he gave a parish to a religious order in Coventry. The parish priest whose parish we were to have was encouraged to resist being moved.

The Catholic children who passed the dreaded 11-plus could go to the two very good grammar schools run by Brothers and Sisters. The rest, who now felt they were failures, went to the secondary modern. As chaplain, I had problems relating to the apathy of the staff and pupils. A few times, I offered to take the

RE lesson. Imposing silence was impossible. I compromised by taking about ten who were interested into a corner, where I tried to have some relevant discussion on some topic; the rest did what they liked, but they did try to keep the noise level down. They were eagerly awaiting the day when they would be sixteen years old and could leave, hoping to pick up some apprenticeship or even a job.

On Saturdays, I learnt to become a soccer enthusiast. I became a follower of Stoke City Football Club. I got a season ticket to the Victoria Ground. Stoke were high up in the First Division. We entertained the great Leeds, Liverpool and Arsenal teams. England's Gordon Banks was their goalie. He had just made a miracle save from Pele in the World Cup group stage. England as champions could not defend their title.

That year Stoke went to the FA semi-final against Arsenal in Sheffield, which was a draw. They were beaten in the replay at Villa Park and Arsenal went on to win the double. The following year, I went to see Stoke beat Chelsea at Wembley in the only cup they ever won, the League Cup.

The great shock I got in going to see Stoke play at home was to see some of the away followers being shepherded like animals by the police, with dogs and horses, from the station to the ground, where they were corralled into one corner of the ground. From there they shouted slogans and obscene abuse at all and sundry. They were shepherded back again some time after the match was over. I thought how different it was to go to a Gaelic match in Ireland, where everybody mixed and there were no police (Gardaí) present. What caused this section of the English to be a disgrace to their country?

I was forever being told of the great feats of the legendary Stanley Matthews, born in Stoke, who played for them and Blackpool as well as being the star of the England team for so many years.

Before I finish with my time in Stoke, there is one small interesting thing I would like to mention. The diocesan school chaplains met a few times a year. One of them was Fr Tolkien, son of the famous J. R. R. Tolkien, writer of *The Lord of the Rings*.

He was still getting royalties from his father's books and insisted on paying for a very good lunch from these.

* * *

I had a telephone call from the Provincial, Fr Paddy Breen, asking me to go as parish priest to St Albans. Fr Jack Roche's term of office was up and he was anxious to go immediately. He had spent the past few years carrying out major extensions to the church and it all got too much for him.

I drove down to St Albans in my VW Beetle car. The parish fair was on the following day in the town hall. Parishioners were anxious to get a look at the new parish priest. It would appear that I was young to be a parish priest and they were hoping I would be able to cope.

St Albans is a very historical city. It is really a large town, but if you have a cathedral you can claim the right to be called a city. It started off 2,000 years ago as a Roman city. Some of the Roman walls are still there, as well as a Roman amphitheatre called Verulanium. The local population at that time were Celts. Alban was a Christian Roman who was murdered when it was discovered that he was a priest. He became the first Christian martyr of England. When the Benedictine Order built a huge monastery, the city became St Albans and there were large pilgrimages both to St Albans and Canterbury. Henry VIII looted and destroyed the monastery but the abbey church was left intact. They whitewashed all the paintings on the walls and all of the statues were destroyed. It later became the centre of the Church of England diocese of St Albans. It is the most beautiful building, with Romanesque and Gothic architecture side by side. The tomb which contained the bones of St Alban was broken; the monks had taken the bones to some unknown place in Europe.

About 160 years ago, a dean of St Albans wrote to the Archbishop of Canterbury boasting that there were no papists in his territory except one, and he was of no consequence because he was a beggar. Migrant Irish farm labourers came to work, and they used to meet once a month for Mass in the pub. A priest came in a pony and trap from 25 miles away. Eventually, they built a small church.

At the end of the nineteenth century, a Fr Michael Tierney, who went to Australia to join the Missionaries of the Sacred Heart, returned to England and was given the parish of St Albans and surrounding towns. He later came to Cork to found the MSC there in Western Road. He was a man with extraordinary vision. He built the present church, which must have been about ten times too big for its needs. Gradually, many Irish came to work there, some to nurse in the five mental hospitals and others to labour in building and road construction. Over the last hundred years, many MSC priests have worked there. Other parishes were started and given over to the diocese and to secular clergy. Schools were built; the Mercy Sisters came to teach there and the Loreto Sisters came in the 1920s to begin a secondary school for girls, and it is impossible to overestimate the contribution they have made to the Catholic life of St Albans.

With that short overview, I start my ministry in St Albans in 1971. Fr Roche left almost immediately and I felt thrown in at the deep end. The other MSC priests were Fr Jerry Buckley, who semi-retired the following year, Fr D. Desmond, who was transferred to Yorkshire, and Fr S. Moran, ordained seven years previously and moved to Liverpool. We had a complete new team of priests: Fr M. O'Leary, who was a former parish priest, Fr J. Fallon and Fr D. O'Rourke.

The church had just been extended and two new aisles added, as well as a new church tower. The second part of the building programme was to knock down the old presbytery and make a new one out of two large semi-detached houses next door and create a small church car park. The architect, who was a parishioner, advised me that it would be impossible to create a presbytery out of the two houses and that it would be better to knock down all three and build a new presbytery. I spent many hours with him, drawing and redrawing the plans for the new presbytery. I did not know how the parishioners would react when they saw this new parish priest knocking three houses down. The Loreto nuns gave us temporary accommodation while the new presbytery was being built. It was built facing into the quadrangle to minimise the noise from the railway line and noise in Beaconsfield Road.

We started to form the first parish council. There were few models to base it on, but it was most helpful to us. We had a core group of very committed people. Fr Roach had lots of people involved in fundraising. This was most necessary with all the building being done. One novel way was something called 'Armchair Bingo'. Probably seventy or so volunteers sold these tickets with their list of winning numbers for each week. Occasionally, people tried to cheat by altering the number on their ticket, but we had a master sheet and they felt sheepish when told.

At that time a marriage programme called Marriage Encounter, which was aimed to make good marriages better, was started in the parish. I got very involved in it as I found that those who were brave enough to go away for the weekend – Friday evening to Sunday evening – came away so full of enthusiasm to put more time into sharing and communicating their feelings for each other. Some of the couples we had became leading couples in running these courses. I had one reservation: they never allowed any evaluation. It was imported from the USA and should have been free to adapt to English culture. This eventually led to its demise.

We started a new programme for preparation for first holy communion, taking it out of school and running it with lay catechists and some of the parents. It was an uphill struggle to get parents involved in the children's preparation, but was worth it in the end.

Parish visitation was still considered a very important part of a priest's work. This was time-consuming. We all had our own areas to visit. At that time, most mothers were at home, especially in the late afternoon. People appreciated these visits. It was a problem trying to refuse too many cups of tea. I remember one funny incident when on a warm summer's day, as the lady of the house kept chattering on, I fell asleep, maybe for a minute or two. When I woke up, I made some irrelevant remark not knowing where I was. The poor lady looked rather puzzled.

There was a very favourable climate for ecumenism in St Albans. Priests and lay people met with their counterparts. Pulpits were exchanged during the Week of Prayer for Christian Unity. Bishop Runcie was the Anglican Bishop of St Albans then and he came as a guest preacher a few times. On Good Friday, he and I carried a cross through the marketplace.

We had ten Masses on Sunday – seven in the church, one in a school, one in the convent hall and one in the chapel of a mental home. Many people did not have cars. Most Masses were full. The last morning Mass on Sunday was a sung Latin Mass with a very good choir, but it soon became clear that only a select few wanted it. It was eventually discontinued.

As is well known, there was a very anti-Irish and anti-Catholic attitude among a big majority of English people. This had gradually been improving, but even in the fifties it was still there. When the Sacred Heart Brothers came to open the high school in St Albans in the late 1950s, two of the American Brothers went to shop in St Albans for some requirements for their new home. They wore Roman collars and the shopkeeper asked them if they were vicars. When they said they were Roman Catholic Brothers, he refused to serve them. They could not believe it and banged the door on their way out.

What was my ordinary day like? It usually started with early Mass in one of the convents. I did not have a parish secretary like nowadays. I was in the parish office most mornings, answering mail and making phone calls. I paid the many bills and kept the finance books up to date. On Mondays, we all helped with the counting of collections and the banking. People would call at the presbytery and the priest on duty would attend to them. We had two primary schools where one of the priests would be chaplain and two secondary schools, which also needed chaplains. Fr Fallon did the local hospital. I was on the board of all of the schools, which meant many evening meetings. We tried to do our parish visitation in the late afternoons. In the evenings after tea there were couples getting married and we each did the marriage preparation. I also had individuals who wished to be instructed in the faith before becoming Catholics. All that has changed now, thank God. Most of these duties are done by lay people; some paid, most voluntary. But that was what I inherited.

Did I have time off? Yes. A most wonderful thing happened to me. Fr Jerome O'Hanlon came to see me from Liverpool, and he invited me to go for a game of golf. I told him I had never played but I would walk around with him. He let me hit a few iron shots. I thought, 'I could get to like this.' I bought a half-set of clubs, got a few lessons and started to play on the municipal course. Fr O'Leary joined the community, so we went together on Monday mornings. There was one dramatic Monday when we were crossing the road from one hole to the next and a car came screeching up and halted. The lady got out and said, 'Fr Daly, you have a wedding today!' I had forgotten they were a rather elderly couple who wanted a quiet wedding and had chosen Monday morning! She took me back to the church with my golf shoes on and I got Joe Fallon to do the wedding while I did the books in the sacristy. The civil books take some time. I don't think that poor couple ever spoke to me again!

What serious problems did I have? The Troubles in Northern Ireland were at their height and there were some horrendous bombings on the streets of London and Birmingham. The majority of our parishioners were first- or second-generation Irish, but the rest were English, some of them converts. All of the clergy were Irish. I must say the English Catholics never gave me any trouble. I always preached against violence from whatever source, including the State.

There was one very explosive situation when some hot-blooded Irishmen had placards and collection tins asking for donations to help the victims of British murders. I went to the presbytery and called the police. I never told anyone, even the priests. They confiscated the placards and collection tins. One Christmas Eve, at about 10 a.m., I got a phone call from a lady telling me to cancel the midnight Mass as there was a bomb in the church. I did not tell the other priests. I went out myself to the locked church and searched every corner. It was a hoax call. I went ahead with Mass, but I worried all through it.

I mentioned having to build the new presbytery. Fr O'Leary, when he was parish priest, was most astute in buying future sites for schools and churches with the help of a Catholic estate agent. One of the sites was a large building where they once grew the most exotic orchids. We sold this to the diocese for the site of a new junior school. It was a nominal sale. The diocese got a government grant to build the school on it. This the diocese refunded to the parish, which enabled me to pay for 15% of the new building. The government paid the rest. I had money left over to build a new hall on stilts at the back of the presbytery. We now had an almost-new church, the new presbytery and the new hall, with a car park for forty cars.

During my first year I got a phone call from a Bill Farrell. He was one of our priests who had a problem with alcohol in the forties. Nobody realised then the nature of the disease. He left the priesthood and went to Northern Ireland. Here is an article that I wrote, which sets out his life:

HE HAS COME BACK TO LIFE
An Appreciation of the late Fr Bill Farrell
One day when talking about Fr Bill Farrell, a young MSC present asked: who is Bill Farrell? So I decided that I would put something on paper about the life of Bill.

In the early seventies when I was working in St Albans, Fr Michael O'Leary was one of the priests with me. He often spoke about Bill Farrell and wondered if he were still alive. Some time in the past there was a rumour that he might be in Leicester. Michael made some enquiries and asked some clergy if they might know a Bill Farrell. There was no positive information so it was presumed that he must be dead. Then, in the summer of 1971, we heard that Bill turned up at Moyne Park – subsequently he told me how he was visiting Galway and he decided that he would visit Moyne. He got the bus as far as the gate and walked in the long avenue. A few times he got 'cold feet' and was about to turn back. He thought that the priests in Moyne Park might never have heard of him and if they had they might only be embarrassed to meet him. But he decided to keep going. He was overcome with the wonderful reception he got from the late Tommy McGeough. Having broken the ice, he began to enquire about all his classmates and the older MSCs. It was a great shock to him to discover they were all dead. Having spent a few hours there Tommy asked him to promise that when Bill got back to England he would go to see Michael O'Leary at St Albans.

After some months Bill turned up at St Albans. Joe Fallon and I met him. He spent a few hours with us. Before he left, we went to the church to say a prayer together. There, I invited Bill to come and stay with us in the presbytery. I told him that we were to build a new presbytery and there would be a room for him. He said, 'I have left the priesthood for so long now, how could I live with you?' I suggested that he could just be a lay person living with us. He had told us about all the work he was doing for AA.

He said that his only ambition in life was to help other alcoholics. Again, I suggested that there was plenty of opportunity to do this work in St Albans. He was still unconvinced about coming back. He would not give us his address at Leicester – he said he was living as a lodger. When he left, he said: 'I will think about it.'

It was over a year later that one day I answered the phone. He said, 'Jerry, I am Bill Farrell and I am coming back. I will come and stay with you as a lay person.' I told him they were the most wonderful words I had ever heard. After a week he arrived with a few suitcases. The first night we did all the wrong things. We were all going to Loreto Convent for a meal. Michael O'Leary suggested that Bill wear a Roman collar. He was very unhappy about this and when we got back to the presbytery he tore it off and threw it into the corner of the room. Eventually, he calmed down when we said he would not have to wear it again.

When I got news that Bill was coming to live with us, I phoned Paddy Breen, who was the Provincial. He was amazed at the coincidence that, only the day before, Bill's sister, who was a nun in Australia, had arrived in Cork and was asking if there was any news of Bill. When she heard that he was in St Albans she came over immediately. They spent a fantastic week catching up on all the family news. Bill had cut himself off completely from all his relatives. He felt that as an alcoholic priest who had left the priesthood he was a scandal and disgrace to them. I will always remember the sight of Bill, a white-haired elderly gentleman, walking locked-arms with an elderly nun up and down Beaconsfield Road, totally lost in conversation. It was forty years since they had spoken to each other. There were so many relations that Bill had never seen or heard of. So many had died; some from the same problem that Bill had – alcoholism. The Providence of God is wonderful. This reunion with his sister was a most healing process for Bill. She had never stopped praying for him. Her hope was so strong that she would one day see him again.

As soon as Bill arrived, he made contact with the local AA. He started attending meetings a couple of times a week. Then, he started going to other towns to attend AA meetings. We gave him the use of a car. Gradually, he began to tell us about his life from the time that he first went into a pub in Cork with Fr Clarks. He said the first time he had a glass of whiskey, he realised that he had some extraordinary affinity for it. It was not too long before he found his own way to the different pubs where they would invite him into the kitchen and where he often got free drink. Soon, drink was a problem. He began getting drunk. Getting back to Sacred Heart College was a problem. When he found the right bus one night and being very heavily under the influence, he was annoyed when the bus conductor suggested that he alight at Sacred Heart College. He told the conductor that he was a Capuchin and demanded to be taken on further! Another night, when he got into the college drunk, he saw a statue of Our Lady in the corridor. He embraced her and took her for a dance. Unfortunately, his legs were not up to dancing and he fell, breaking a hand off the statue. Fr John Toomey was the Superior. John was very kind to Bill and was trying to find ways to help him. They took him to Mount

Mellory a few times to dry out. But Bill said that he had no motivation to give up drink. This was an age when there was little enlightenment about the disease of alcoholism. Even some of his MSC brothers said, 'Why can't you give up that drink? If you are a drunkard, it's your own fault! You just need a bit of willpower and to say your prayers.'

Gradually, the tension of being a priest teacher and living in a religious community became too much for him. If there must be a choice made – then it would be for drink. So Bill decided to pack his little bag and leave the college and the priesthood for good. He walked down the Mardyke with his bag and he took a train for Belfast – he wanted to get as far away from Cork as he could. He got a job in a factory. He went to night school and eventually got a diploma in engineering. Now he could indulge in all the drink he wanted. There was nobody to nag him. He said that when calculating his wages, it was not in pounds and shillings, but in how many bottles of whiskey it would buy. Whiskey was his currency. Once, on a visit to Dublin, he accidentally bumped into Fr Willie Byrne, who unfortunately was not very keen to engage in any brotherly conversation!

After a few years, he moved to Leicester and changed his name to Bill Read. The drinking got worse. He said that he often put a full bottle to his lips and never took it away until he fell down in a drunken stupor. He might wake up in a police cell. Once, he woke up in Dublin without any idea how he got there. When he left Cork, he also gave up the practice of religion – he felt that he was a lost soul, so what was the use. He never thought of getting married. He said he had one wife and that was whiskey. But although he had given up all practice of the faith, he would vehemently defend it if any of his working mates were to attack it. Once, he recalled that he challenged one of his mates to a fight outside the factory gate because he had insulted Our Lady. 'It was the worst fight I ever had.' This was interesting, as some of Bill's pupils at Sacred Heart College could recall how eloquently Bill used to preach on Our Lady.

When Bill was over sixty, and having lost some jobs because of drink, he decided to phone the Samaritans one night when he was drunk. They said they would visit him next day, which they did. But he was drunk when they came. He was touched that they were interested enough to come to see him, so he consented to go with them the next night to an AA meeting. This happened to be the great miracle in his life. For the first time he was in the company of men and women who were fighting the same demon that he was. They were so genuine in supporting each other; they were open and honest about their shared problem. What they were saying made sense – together they were strong, they could live day by day, taking one day at a time. The Supreme, or God, would be on their side. Somehow that very night was born in his heart a light and hope that would never go out again.

These men and women had fought the battle against their common enemy and had regained their dignity. One man in particular took Bill 'under his wing', and arranged to pick Bill up every evening and bring him to the AA meetings. Bill often talked about this man with tears in his eyes. This was the best friend he ever had and what was so bitterly sad for Bill was that this man broke out one day and started to drink and died from alcohol poisoning. Bill would say, 'He helped me so much and I wasn't there when he needed me.' It was a new experience for me to listen to Bill because all his conversations were about AA and the problem of alcoholism. Drink had destroyed so many cells in his brain that he never realised that I heard the same stories so many times. I don't know how often he told me about the member of AA called Dick who went to the theatre with his wife who had unwittingly bought some liqueur chocolates, which they were both eating until the interval when Dick excused himself 'for a few minutes' and went to the bar and was drunk before she realised it. So, Bill's constant dictum was 'a thimbleful is too much and a barrel is not enough'.

Bill often repeated another story which was a startling revelation to him. One night he was giving a talk at an AA meeting (and I gather his talks were excellent). Afterwards, while they were having a cup of tea, he heard a group of men discuss him and one said, 'I bet you Bill is a defrocked priest.'

Bill had forgotten that he was ever a priest and here were people who saw something of the priest in him!

The months were going by in St Albans and we moved into the new presbytery, where Bill had a nice room of his own. He started to put on quite a bit of weight as the food was better than he had received from his landlady. He was attending more and more meetings. He had one extraordinary 'convert' – a parishioner and Irishman called Mick Brophy. Drink had wrecked havoc with his building business and his family life, and as he said to me later, 'It was like having a devil on your back and you could not shake him off.' Bill and Mick became bosom pals and many a night they sat talking in the car after returning from a meeting. Becoming sober again changed all of Mick's life, so much that one day he said to me, 'If I met Jesus Christ and Bill walking up Alma Road, I would salute Bill first.'

Bill told us that he had not been to the sacraments since he left; the problem was that he felt that God could not forgive him. Even coming to Mass was a new and strange experience; everything was now in English. But gradually, with some gentle persuasion, we suggested that he go to confession. I told him about the Jesuits on Farm Street, London. One morning he took the bold step and went and had a talk with one of them. He came back full of emotion at how kindly they were to him. They had also fixed a date for his 'first confession'. Another big step was taken and it was such a joy to see him come up for holy communion. There was something else that was the source of great astonishment to Bill. It was the very enthusiastic welcome all MSC gave him. He was embraced by the Provincial, Paddy Breen, and when the Fr General paid us a visit, Bill was left speechless at the welcome Fr Gus Kelly gave him. Later, the General said to me that in all his travels, he had not seen such a saintly face as Bill's. Deep down, Bill was anxious to visit Cork – he had not been there for thirty-three years. He used to say, 'How can I go back there, I gave so much scandal there!' With the help of Paddy Breen, we convinced him that he must go and see all his new-found relatives, who were longing to meet him. One day, I took him to Heathrow and he flew back to his native

Cork. There must have been some very emotional reunions. Bill was a most sentimental person and would cry easily.

One evening Bill and I were talking, when he returned to us and his work with the AA. I suggested to him would it not be nice if he came back to being a priest again. I gathered from what he said that he had been giving it some thought. There was no canonical problem. But he expressed the one insurmountable practical problem. How could he say Mass without the wine? And he was not prepared to take 'even one thimbleful'. I wrote to Cardinal Hume about the problem and asked for a dispensation so that Bill could use non-alcoholic wine. This the cardinal gave. Bill was pleased and he agreed that he would practise a few 'dry Masses' first. So, on Christmas Eve 1973, Bill said his first Mass after so many years. It was a difficult and emotional experience as he cried quite a bit.

Now, he used to go to the convents to say their community Masses – they loved him dearly. One Saturday, I asked him to go to the Brothers of the Sacred Heart to say Mass. It was only that evening during supper that he said, 'Jerry, this has been one of the most difficult days of my life.' It was a shock to me when he told me what had happened. On his way out in the morning, he had forgotten to take his non-alcoholic wine with him. When he arrived at the Brothers' he discovered that there wasn't time to go back. He decided to take a thimbleful of ordinary wine. This apparently set up a whole lot of incredible craving for drink. He said that the one thing that helped him through the day was that, as it happened, we were very short of priests that Saturday and I had asked Bill to do a few sessions of confession. But, thank God, he survived the day. It was one more lesson for Bill on how vulnerable and fragile he was.

One evening during our regular conversation about alcoholism we discussed this problem in Ireland. We had heard that a nun had set up a clinic for alcoholics in Ireland. I suggested to Bill that this might be a golden opportunity for him to help some other Irishmen. Paddy Breen thought it might be nice for Bill to end his days in Ireland. Having consulted the Sister in charge, it was agreed that Bill move there and be a counsellor and advisor to these men. It did not work out so well. As Bill explained later, this Sister was one of the most marvellous people in the world, 'but she had one fault – she was not an alcoholic, and will never understand alcoholics'. He felt she was doing all the wrong things, all out of the goodness of her heart. Bill was unhappy and the tension, plus the fact that he had put on a few stone in weight in St Albans, caused him to have a heart attack. After hospitalisation, he went to live at Merrion Avenue. He found abundant work to do. He attended a great variety of AA meetings in Dublin. In the few years he lived there, God alone knows how much good he did. One thing was certain: Bill would spare not one ounce of his strength to help another alcoholic.

Considering his life history, Bill lived to the ripe old age of eighty-one years. I went to his funeral in Cork. It was wonderful to see his older sister, the nun, who had come from Australia for the funeral. She did one of the readings. She was as lively as a bee. All her prayers were answered in a way she could hardly have hoped for. On a bright sunny day, 24 April 1983, we buried Bill in the MSC plot. As I looked at the gravestone a thought struck me – Bill is lying now beside other MSCs who had to do battle with drink: John Burke and Hugh Patton. But they are at peace with God. It was wonderful to see all the friends of Bill, especially the large extended family who had come to know and love the man so much.

'He was dead and has come back to life.' Now he is enjoying eternal life forever. May his memory never be forgotten in our MSC family.

* * *

Although St Albans is in Hertfordshire, we belong to the Catholic archdiocese of Westminster. When Cardinal Heenan died after a painful illness in 1975, Basil Hume, the Abbot of Ampleforth, became the new archbishop, later cardinal. Shortly after his new appointment, he came to St Albans on a parish visitation. He spent the whole Sunday with us. He was such an extraordinary man – profoundly learned, with an aura of sanctity and also beautiful humility. He was so naturally charming and put everyone at ease. His pastoral letters were gems: very short sentences containing profound and simple meaning. I kept one on the topic of suffering for years. How upset he would be with the new translation that we have to suffer with every day. More about that anon.

I mentioned the Anglican Cathedral or Abbey and how beautiful it is. It is a great tourist attraction. The paintings that were whitewashed over are now painstakingly (and very expensively) being slowly restored. It is very 'High Church' and all its liturgy is very like ours. On the Feast of St Alban in 1973, the dean of the cathedral gave us permission to say a Catholic Mass near the tomb of St Alban. There were about fifty parishioners present. It was the first Catholic Mass since the Reformation. Now there is a Catholic Mass every Friday at noon in the Lady Chapel, attended by Catholics and some Anglicans. We use their vestments and sacred vessels. Not all the priests in the presbytery were keen on any ecumenical outreach.

There was an Anglican priest who had a severe stroke; his speech was impaired and he was constantly in a wheelchair. He lived in a little flat some distance from us, but his daughter-in-law was a member of our congregation. She and her husband used to wheel the Rev. Vicar to our Sunday Mass. One day I asked him if he would like to have holy communion during Mass – even in spite of his speech impediment he gave such a good 'Yes'. I told him I would ask for permission. I wrote to Cardinal Hume and he answered me by saying to 'follow my conscience'. I used to give him communion with the rest of the congregation. The Sunday after I left St Albans, the other priests stopped giving it to him. It must have been sad – a heartbreak for him.

One other very welcome change was taking place. We could now have lay people commissioned to help distribute holy communion and take communion to the sick on Sunday. Steve Pickard was chosen as the first one. It took the people a little while to get used to the Eucharistic Minister. Some will resist any change at all cost. I thought of the effort in giving out communion on Christmas Day in Indonesia to nearly 1,000 people.

Another change that came in was that cremation was now allowed. It took a while before Catholics felt comfortable in having their loved ones cremated, even though the deceased had made this their wish. I had one Italian man who was so indignant with me for doing a cremation. Some time later, I was surprised that he had his own mother cremated. I think he realised how much cheaper it was to take her ashes to Italy than to have her body taken there!

The biggest and most welcome change of all was that for some time we were allowed to give a general absolution with special permission from the bishop. Before Christmas one year, the cardinal gave all priests permission to have a general absolution service before Christmas. Of all the services I have ever done, that was the most memorable one. Many came but could not get into the church. We had a service of readings, prayers and a homily, followed by the general absolution. It was followed by Eucharistic Prayer Two and the giving of holy communion. There were so many faces I had never seen before. Unfortunately, in spite of all that Cardinal Hume could do, this permission was withdrawn.

We had many people calling at the door looking for help. Most had drink problems. We gave them tea and sandwiches. Sometimes their stories sounded half-plausible and we gave them some money. There was a man from Co. Clare who had a problem with binge drinking. Once every few months he would appear at the door on Monday morning looking very much the worse for wear. I used to help him with some food and I would also try to advise him. Then for years he didn't turn up. One day I got a tatty letter. It was addressed to Fr Daly, St Albans, England. Inside was a little note: 'Dear Fr Daly – I am doing well now in Co. Clare. Thank you for your help. Steve.' I was a little amazed that the letter got to me.

Fr O'Rourke, who was a great communicator and related well with the youth of the parish, volunteered to go to Africa. We missed him very much. He was replaced by Fr Dan Joe Maguire, who was just ordained. Fr Joe Colbert also joined us as a semi-retired priest. Fr Joe had never worked in parishes, being involved with teaching and also as a bursar. He had never baptised a baby, assisted at a marriage or done a funeral. He asked if he could be at a funeral. The next one he did. All went well in the church. Then, he put on a cassock and white surplice to go to the cemetery. We were building the hall at the time and there was a big muddy puddle which he foolishly tried to jump over – only to fall head first into it. He came into the presbytery crying. I went to do the committal at the cemetery.

We had an excellent relationship with the local clergy. We had some very good deanery meetings, held in Maryland Mercy Convent, with their usual wonderful hospitality. Some of them said to me how they envied the community life that we MSCs had. I think they found life lonely in the presbyteries. One of them had a drink problem. Having consumed some whiskey one morning, he went out in the car and crossed the reservation on a dual carriageway and got killed. Celibacy was beginning to have an effect on some, and a few high-profile priests left to get married. It was not difficult for some to drift into relationships with women which were not platonic.

St Albans Abbey got the new wonderful Dean Rev. Peter Moore. He decided the Abbey, with its many visitors, needed basic amenities. When he proposed to build on its land to provide a much-needed tea room, toilets and other facilities, he got such a bad press from those who could not accept any change. They called him a philistine, among other things. Nevertheless, he went ahead and provided all that was needed. When he was first installed as Dean of St Albans Cathedral, the Queen Mother was the special royal guest. I once put it to him that in the event of our two churches becoming one the Catholic Church might demand conditional ordination. He replied that it was a 'small price to pay'.

I have left the most painful memory to the end. In 1975, I went to Ireland for a summer holiday. I knew my mother had not been well. She was now eighty-six years old. Her birthday was a few days before I arrived and with one thing and another I overlooked sending her a card. The first thing she said to me was, 'You forgot my birthday.' That sentence will haunt me forever. Mary told me that mother had a very advanced stage of leukaemia. They did not tell her. She had a few bad hours of intense pain but otherwise she was up and around every day. Having met our Superior General on the plane to Ireland, he, Fr J.J. O'Brien and I planned to go to Ballybunion to play golf the following day. Before I left to go to Cork that evening, I took her over to see Mary and left her there. Early the next morning there was a phone call to Cork saying she had died peacefully during the night. Being in Ireland and not being with her when she died was too difficult to bear. I drove back to Kilcrohane; at what speed I do not know.

As priests, we are called on so often to be with the dying at home or in hospital. This is when people are at their lowest ebb – sometimes too numb to talk. Elisabeth Kübler-Ross wrote a wonderful book about coping with grief. She talked about the five stages we go through: denial, anger, bargaining, depression and finally (and hopefully) acceptance. It is important that we name and own our experiences during grief and bereavement. Journeying through these stages of loss, grief and bereavement can eventually bring us to acceptance. Journeying through loss, therefore, puts us in touch with our own mortality. Someone said that it is only when I come to terms with my own mortality that I have arrived at the door of my authentic self.

The wake took place in her own bed in her own room. I have never ceased to be amazed how good people are to respond in so many little ways to families in grief and mourning. I had two days to compose myself and prepare the funeral liturgy. We laid her next to my father's grave, who had died twenty-eight years previously. May they rest in peace.

Two years later I had to do my first sibling funeral. Michael, who returned from the USA to take up farming had four boys and two girls with his wife Anne. Michael contracted MS and before he had to get into a wheelchair suffered a massive heart attack. It was so sad to see his wife and children – the youngest was only nine years old – without a husband and father. Anne remarried. In hindsight, all got on well and have families of their own now. Three of the boys are in San Francisco.

* * *

If I had to look back on my time in St Albans, I would remember some wonderful happy times and celebrations. Perhaps the consecration of the church was one of them, and the meal in the town hall afterwards. We were a happy community of MSCs. I remember the half-hours after lunch doing the crossword together and watching *Match of the Day* on Saturday evening.

But one Christmas Day stands out. Mrs Nora Doran and Mrs Donovan, who were always helping at the presbytery, prepared a wonderful lunch. Pat Donovan also joined his wife with us for the lunch. Pat's one sadness in life was that a younger brother was ordained a priest for an Australian diocese some fifty years previously; on the five-week boat journey to Australia he fell in love with one of the passengers and was never heard of again.

The one outstanding regret is that we did not have the collaboration that is now so common. We priests tried to do too much – we did things that we were not too good at. I had done six months more than the six years we did as superior or parish priest and I was due for a change. My new appointment was at Tamworth. There was a wonderful farewell party for me. I said that as MacArthur said to the Filipino people, 'I will return one day.'

Around this time our order, among others, decided that priests needed a sabbatical. Time out for some renewal; time to reflect; time to catch up on new developments in theology and scripture; time to read some new books. Most of all, time for some spiritual renewal. Those with over twenty years in ministry got first choice. I got permission to join a renewal course run by the Carmelite priests in Gort Muire, Dundrum, Dublin. It was a happy choice. We could share in the liturgy of the Carmelite priests and students for Divine Office and evening Mass. With many talented students, the music and liturgy were very uplifting.

We had some very good lecturers. There was time for spiritual retreat. We felt we were topping up all the batteries again. Our own wells can easily run dry. It was very interesting sharing with priests from different orders and ministries in so many different cultures.

There was ample time to relax. Some polished up their golfing skills on the nearby course; some went mountain walking on the Dublin Mountains; some ventured into the Wicklow Mountains; some took the opportunity to go to the Abbey Theatre. The course was extremely well run by its director, Fr Griffin, who could only have come from Cork.

* * *

The Archbishop of Birmingham, Dr J.P. O'Dwyer, asked our congregation to staff a parish in Staffordshire – Tamworth, twenty miles from Birmingham. It was a small market town that had changed very little over the years, with about twelve villages in the parish. In the 1970s, Birmingham ran out of sites to build new council estates. Tamworth gave them permission to build huge estates for 60,000 people nearby.

Fr Lane, the parish priest of Tamworth, could not cope with this new influx of people. Three of us MSC priests were to form a team ministry, trying to get away from the model of parish priest and curate. Sean Moran, Pat Duffy and I made up the team. Pat Duffy had no experience of parish ministry, as he was in charge of the farm and bursar in Carrignavar College. He found it very hard at first to adapt to life in England. He talked about looking out of the window of the presbytery on a sea of chimney pots. But he soon adjusted and took like a duck to water to all aspects of parish ministry.

It took us almost a year to get started, and by that time Sean Moran was unwell and went to the USA, where he was diagnosed with a rare disease. Fr Pat and I had a different MSC to come to help. We decided that some building was necessary. At the same time, we did a census and discovered over 7,000 Catholics, most of whom where nominal. Many of those who came to the council estates from Birmingham were on second marriages. It was 'my children, her children and our children'. Many were unemployed.

We started a new way to get people involved. In the early church there were all sorts of ministries as well as priesthood. We had many meetings trying to empower people to take active roles in the church. We had some success. After the second year we had over 200 people who were really active in one or other aspect of parish life. We were beginning to grasp the importance of collaboration and delegation.

In the northern part of England, every town had social clubs – many of them. The Catholic Church also had one. In hindsight, I don't know if I should describe them as a necessary blessing or a necessary curse. There were so many things to go wrong when you had alcoholic drinks. To get honest stewards was a problem. We had St John's Club. We had it refurbished, as Fr Pat wanted it to be a place for dances and where Catholics would find community. He got the brewery to put money into it. For a while it worked well.

It was important to build a church and community centre where all the newcomers from Birmingham were. A priest in the diocese who was involved with building before he became a priest had started helping parishioners with a team of builders. He and I drew up plans for the new church, social centre and hall, as well as a convent. Fr Pat was involved in raising money.

Many people were now unemployed. Money was scarce as inflation was very high. It was 15% to borrow money. Without going into detail and with some sleepless nights, we built the Sacred Heart Church and centre with convent. We were fortunate to get three nuns – Daughters of Our Lady of the Sacred Heart – to join the parish pastoral team. Before we had the convent, they were staying in a council house. The neighbouring children would never have seen a nun before and were intrigued by them. One morning a child asked them, 'Have you got baby nuns in the house?'

During the summer, we had some of our deacons come from the House of Formation to get work experience. It was a great learning experience for them to visit the homes and see some of the social problems of urban society. We let them do the homilies on Sunday and asked them to make them relevant to the lives of the people they encountered. Fr Kevin McNamara said how he was helped by the constructive evaluation of his homilies.

Before we built the Sacred Heart centre, we had four Mass centres – two of them in Church of England churches, which they were more than willing to let us use for Sunday Masses. We stopped all of them with the opening of the new church.

Fr Pat tried everything to get the newcomers to come to the centre – he had snooker tables and games and every weekend a band for the dance. Gradually, he had some success. We had two primary schools and mingling of the old and new parishioners began to bear fruit. He also got some youth clubs going. All this took much time and effort, but it also got so many lay people involved in active ministry.

In 1979 I went to Ireland to assist at my niece's wedding in Newbridge, Co. Kildare. When she picked the date she never foresaw that it would be the day that Pope John Paul II was to say Mass for a million people in Phoenix Park. There were papal flags and bunting everywhere. That Sunday evening, another nephew, Donie, and his fiancée and I drove through the night to Galway, where the pope would have the youth Mass. I don't know how many hours we waited at the racecourse where the outdoor Mass was to take place. But the youth, led by Fr Michael Cleary, tried to keep everyone entertained until about 11 a.m. when the papal helicopter appeared and the pope went into the Popemobile and went around blessing the large congregation. It was difficult to describe the enthusiasm of the youth, their exuberance and joy, which we only associate with pop festivals. The pope seemed to be in his element. They clapped every sentence of his homily, sometimes bursting into impromptu song. In hindsight, I reflect that the two Irish clerics on the stage with the pope were Bishop Eamon Casey and Fr Michael Cleary. It became a startling revelation later that both were having problems with the vows of celibacy. As a church, we had become adept at sweeping unpleasant truths under the carpet only for them to come out again to haunt us.

* * *

I would like to reflect on how authority is exercised in the church. The model is the one of a pyramid. The pope is top of the pyramid; then cardinals and bishops; then parish priests and priests; and underneath these heavyweights are the people of God. Women can feel especially squashed. I mentioned the tyrannical use of power that was often exercised by the parish priests towards curates and people. Unfortunately, parishes run by religious orders followed the same model where parish priests decided everything.

Fr Pat and I decided that if we used a team we would make decisions by consensus. This is not always easy and takes time and patience. The diocese demanded that one of the priests would be the canonical parish priest, but this made no difference in our everyday exercise of parish authority. Consensus, as I said, can sometimes be painful, and I must respect the feelings of others and sometimes agree to do something which I would see as not the best way forward. So there is always some compromise, in the good sense of the word. I believe we got over-involved with social clubs, but they did help us for a time. They became a problem later and are now no more.

It is imperative that a priest takes some time off – if you try to burn a candle at both ends it will end in burnout. Fr Pat rarely took any time off. Eventually, it caused severe health problems, ending in his premature death. I was lucky that I took up golf. Next to our parish, a new golf enterprise opened called the Belfry, which later became famous as a venue for the Ryder Cup. We could play there for £10. Later, I used to join some Birmingham priests at the Sutton Coldfield Golf Club on Mondays. It was such a wonderful feeling walking down the first fairway, knowing that for a few hours there would be no phone calls – this was long before the mixed blessing of mobiles. One Monday morning, a Holy Benedictine, another priest and I were on the first tee. The skies were ominous with clouds laden with rain. I suggested we go back to the clubhouse, but the Holy Benedictine said that we should say three Hail Marys and our

Blessed Lady would help. This we piously did. After two holes the heavens opened with thunder, lightning and a deluge. We made a quick, sodden, silent retreat back to the clubhouse.

I also kept up my interest in football, going to see Stoke when they came to Villa Park and other nearby clubs. Aston Villa won the European Cup in 1982, beating the German champions Bayern Munich in the final. The supporters brought it to our social club one evening, so I have touched that famous cup.

In 1979, Margaret Thatcher was elected as Prime Minister, and dominated the political landscape for the 1980s. Social division became rife, and unemployment soared. It impacted greatly on an area such as Tamworth. The 'Iron Lady' was going to take on the unions, and she had Arthur Scargill and the National Union of Mineworkers firmly in her sights. The miners had taken on the Conservative government of 1970–1974, winning major pay rises in 1972 and 1974 after industrial action. Maggie was determined that would not happen again under her government, and she mobilised and coordinated police forces all over the country to stop miners from undertaking 'flying pickets' at collieries and steelworks. The bitter legacy of the Thatcher years was still strongly evident at the time of her funeral in 2013, and her very name can bring strong reactions from people (positive and negative) to this very day.

In the early 1980s, it was announced that Pope John Paul had accepted an invitation to visit the UK. There was a whole year to prepare – personally I believe that they overdid the preparation. In Ireland, they had only a few months and they got enormous crowds. It was well managed. In the UK, they started making so many security arrangements that when the pope came, many were deterred from attending. Only one third of the estimated crowds turned up on the day.

Because of the outbreak of the Falklands War, it was uncertain if the pope would come. Up to a week before he came this uncertainty lasted. In the seven venues where there would be celebration of Mass, there would be one of the seven sacraments administered. The first was at Westminster Cathedral and there would be some adult candidates for baptism. They had difficulty finding candidates being prepared for baptism. They somehow found that in the convert class in Tamworth there was a Nigerian man being prepared for baptism. He was chosen as one of the candidates. I was asked to accompany him and his wife to Westminster Cathedral and had a seat up near the front. I was in rather good company – the Catholic Duke of Arundel was next to me with his wife.

As the procession of cardinals and bishops moved up the aisle of the cathedral, the first close-up sight of the pope was one of surprise. I had seen this robust man on TV and at a distance in Galway, but he looked stooped and much smaller than I expected. He had of course survived an assassination attempt and it seemed to have taken a big toll on him. I got holy communion from him on the tongue like the rest of the people of God. My Nigerian parishioner was sponsored by his wife – they looked overcome with joy in the sanctuary. Afterwards, when the papal entourage left, we were invited to the archbishop's house for refreshments.

Afterwards, I had to rush back to Tamworth as the next day there was going to be a big outdoor Mass for all of the Midlands in the airport of Coventry. Although we were only 20 miles away, we had to leave Tamworth in the middle of the night and go by train to Coventry. I think we were bussed to the airport. We waited for hours and hours for the papal helicopter to arrive. We priests concelebrated Mass from some distance and helped with the distribution of holy communion. Again, only a third of the people expected came. During the papal visit, we had the most excellent weather – blue skies and sunshine every day.

It was late afternoon when we returned to Tamworth by train. We saw the papal helicopter fly to its next destination. The pope's visit caught the imagination of all the people in the UK and it got some wonderfully positive publicity. But underneath all this public euphoria there were signs that big changes were starting to happen. There was a drain of priests leaving the ministry, most of them because of celibacy. The same was happening in convents. The Vicar General of the diocese was a great church man called Dan Leonards, who was a west Cork man like myself. He was always solicitous and helpful about our ministry in Tamworth. He occasionally asked me to come to the city and say the noon Mass for him. Afterwards, we had lunch. On one of these days, he told me that he had just attended the election of an abbess in an enclosed order. He was there as canonical advisor. He shocked me when he said it was 'like being in Beirut'. That was a severe trouble spot then. He went on to explain that the outgoing abbess was certain she would be re-elected, but when things were not going her way, she created havoc; she subsequently left the convent. Many nuns entered the convent at a very young age. It was like romantic love in marriage: it is not meant to last. The real love in marriage is made of sterner stuff – it is the love of giving and often sacrifice. With the nuns, many of them crossed this threshold to live fulfilled lives. For others, the maternal instinct became too strong and they wanted to marry and have children of their own. Living in such close communities, there were often lots of petty jealousies and seeking after power in becoming Superiors. For some, the only alternative to save their sanity and humanity was to decide to leave. Gradually, fewer and fewer vocations caused a drop in morale.

Archbishop George Patrick Dwyer, who was both lovable and often irascible and who was bishop of three different dioceses, passed away. The clergy of the dioceses wondered which of the auxiliary bishops or competent priests of the diocese would succeed him. To their utter consternation, Maurice Couve de Murville was appointed. No one had ever heard of him. He was chaplain to the Catholic students of Cambridge and most likely never saw the inside of a presbytery – he is now appointed leader of the many city and rural parishes of the largest diocese in the country. Could this happen in any other organisation? My only encounter with him was not a happy one. An elderly local priest died in a small rural parish. To facilitate the funeral I offered the use of our church and the provision of a buffet in our hall afterwards – all free. When the archbishop went to the hall for the refreshments, he summoned me and asked, 'Haven't you got any soup?' I said no. He peremptorily commanded me to get some. I rushed to the presbytery to get a bowl of soup for his Grace. Coming back with it, I thought, 'I bet he won't say thank you.' I was right.

If I was asked in 1983 what a paedophile was, with my very tiny knowledge of Greek I would have said 'love of children'. If I had looked it up in the *Concise Oxford Dictionary* (1963 edition), I would not have found it there. So it is quite understandable that around this time, when some devastated parents approached church authorities telling them that their children altar servers were sexually abused by their priest, they were quite unprepared to respond appropriately to the allegations. There was almost total disbelief that this could possibly happen. They had no idea as to the nature of this perversity and the denial of the perpetrator. Unfortunately, their first impulse was to save the good name of the Institution. They were as yet unaware about the incredible damage done to the victim. In the Birmingham diocese, paedophile priests were moved to different parishes even after the indisputable evidence of abuse. For years to come, the damage done to the church is almost impossible to measure. The end of this sad chapter is nowhere in sight.

I have mentioned a few times the indefatigable zeal of Fr Pat Duffy and one incident shows him living out the gospel precept of turning the other cheek. One evening rather late, the front door bell rang. When Fr Pat opened the door a young man hit him with his fist, sending his glasses flying. Pat never retaliated. How different it might have been if I had gone to the door – a little war would have broken out. I once heard Fr Pat arguing on the phone that there was no such word as can't – he felt that if we wanted to, everything could be achieved. No wonder his health failed. First were his kidneys. He was on dialysis and later got a donor kidney. I persuaded him, one Saturday in 1996 in Dublin, to go to the hospital. They told him that he had had a heart attack during the night. At the start of the new millennium, the MSC appointed him parish priest in Tamworth. It was the same as signing his death certificate. He was dead within a few months.

In 1982, I celebrated the silver anniversary of my ordination. It was quite a milestone for me. My ministry had been varied and exciting – there was never a dull moment. The parish had a delightful celebration. Mary and Joe came from Ireland and Frank came up from Ilford. I was presented with a gold watch, which I treasured.

There were three suicide-related deaths in my family, all of them late adults. One afternoon, I was fortunate to be in when the phone rang. My nephew Danny from Seven Kings, Ilford, was on the phone. He said he had 'come in from school and found my mum dead'. I told him to phone the police and ambulance and that I would be down there as soon as possible. His mother Kathleen was married to my brother Frank. After Danny's birth some eighteen years previously she suffered from postnatal depression, from which she made a good recovery. Eight years later Angela was born. A few years later, the depression returned, requiring psychiatric care from a mental hospital nearby. She never made any real recovery and often threatened that she would kill herself. Frank and Danny had hoped that it would only remain a threat. But it happened.

On the way down the motorway, I was worried about Angela, and when I got there my first question was, 'Where is Angela?' Danny said she was safe with neighbours. Frank went to work by bicycle to Ford's, where he worked on the assembly line. He told me that he prayed every day that if things couldn't get better that they would not get worse. The worst happened. Danny was doing his A-levels when his mum died. For his age he was amazingly mature and he helped to pull his father through. He did his tertiary education from home.

That evening, Frank, Danny and I were sitting in the kitchen having a drink. There was a terrible thunderstorm, but we were not quite conscious of its severity. Then there was a severe bang as the chimney pot came through the roof of the back kitchen. The lights went out. After a few seconds, I asked if they were okay. It was so difficult to console my brother and try to explain to him that he was not cursed. I never felt so low in all my life. The next day, I took Angela on my knee and told her that

Mummy had gone to heaven. She was quite bewildered. I helped with the funeral arrangements and contacting family in Ireland. All family funerals are so difficult, but this was extremely sad. Frank became mother and father to Angela, with the help of Danny. One day she would repay him with great tender loving care as she nursed him in his final illness. She insisted he would die with love in his own home.

My six years in Tamworth were coming to an end. Before I finish, I would like to thank those MSCs who came to work for a year or two. It was great having Joe Hanley, who had also worked in Indonesia. I was sad to find that his mental health and memory were fading. Some would say the cerebral malaria left its mark. Joe was simply one of the best.

* * *

I would like to mention some happy family celebrations of weddings. For different reasons, I was able to assist at only one of my sibling's weddings. Now I am doing some of their children's weddings. While in Tamworth I went to Bantry to do the weddings of Diarmuid and Marian, Bernie and Liam, Mary and Evin. Martina and Timmy had worked so hard to rear their seven children. It was the pinnacle of happiness for them when these children chose very suitable partners to start their own families.

It was a new experience for me as a priest to be in the house on the morning of the wedding. So much organised chaos. Everyone trying to do two things at once. Things getting lost, like cheque books. After that experience, I am more tolerant of brides who are late. Weddings in Ireland have taken on an affluence which would hardly have been imaginable in former days.

The one thing I have noticed about all weddings is that the father who walks his daughter up the aisle is often more nervous than the bride. I have always tried to meet them at the door of the church, to reassure and calm them. I have said to them that nothing can go wrong; however there was a wedding where this was not true. There was an elderly lady called Frances who had been in a convent most of her life but did not get on with her sisters in the same convent. Eventually she left. She was in an old people's home and when an old friend lost his wife, they decided to get married. She was seventy-four years old and he was seventy-nine. I suggested that they have the wedding on a weekday, with a few guests. I did not anticipate that all the residents in the home wanted to come to church, possibly out of curiosity, and they hired cars. I asked the bride and groom to remain seated during the ceremony. Among the residents from the home was a Mrs Ashford, who was a pious Catholic but unable to be in church for many years. Being totally deaf, she got a little bored and midway through the wedding got up and stepped over to the side altar to light a candle. Having done so, she knelt down and bowed her head to say a prayer. Then there was a shout: 'Mrs Ashford is on fire!', which was not really accurate. Her furry hat was smouldering and a spiral of smoke ascended like incense. There was pandemonium. The Matron ran over and snatched the hat off Mrs Ashford and, having thrown it on the ground, jumped on it. Mrs Ashford was totally unaware of all the commotion, and said to Matron, 'Why have you done that? I always wear my hat in church.' It wasn't easy to continue with the ceremony after all that excitement. Did they live happily ever after? Well, in a few weeks the husband had to go to hospital and for some short time Frances was more nurse than wife before she became a widow. If there are any elderly single ladies reading this and if they are getting some romantic feelings, it might be wise to remember the old adage: 'Marry in haste, repent at leisure.'

It was also a great joy for me to assist at my nephew Donie and Teresa's wedding in Carrick on Suir.

Part IV

———————

Fr Michael Curran, our Provincial, asked me if I would be willing to go back to South Africa. The first thing that came into my mind was the beautiful weather there – our memories are selective and I thought of the blue skies every day. We had just had a bad winter and poor summer. I said yes. After a couple of months' holidays, I left from Heathrow to go to Amsterdam in January 1984. The flight from Heathrow was in doubt up to the last hour because of snow. I met up with Fr Dominic Duffy, who was our Director as well as a kind Superior in Moyne Park. He was now sixty-four years old and very bravely volunteered to work in South Africa. He was with a newly ordained priest, Fr John Finn. Fr John looked nervous as he smoked his cigarette. We boarded a KLM flight for the eleven-hour flight to Johannesburg. After the meal and late-night film, the lights were dimmed as everyone wanted to sleep. As we flew over the Sahara, I woke up and raised the blind. I seemed to be the only one awake. For a whole hour I witnessed one of the most amazing scenes. We were at the first sign of dawn. The sky gradually took on the most indescribable range of reds and oranges – first very delicate and then growing into more bold colours. It was all so subtle, like some great artist in the sky painting. Eventually, and rather suddenly, the great red orb of the sun appeared. This was one of the greatest displays of nature's bounty I have every witnessed.

We were met at Jan Smuts airport, Jo'burg, by several MSCs. There was now a house of formation for indigenous vocations at Mid-Rand between Jo'burg and Pretoria. There was a great welcoming party for us there. The number of priests available for mission was decreasing and to have three of us was cause for celebration. Many of them had been students of Dominic as professor or Superior and they were so proud to welcome him to Africa. Having been there some twenty-three years earlier, I was a sort of veteran. It was suggested that I would give Dominic a quick tour of our mission up north. They gave us the loan of one of the little pick-up vehicles that are so common in South Africa.

The journey up north through the little towns they call *dorps* brought back so many memories – the houses with red corrugated roofs I had forgotten. Our first stop after passing the Tropic of Capricorn was the Dwars River Mission, started by Fr B. Fleming in 1951. It has developed into the biggest centre of the diocese, with many outstations. Here, Fr Mitchell was our host. Later, Bishop Slattery would get funding to build a large secondary school for African boys. This was my first experience of the great advances our MSC missionaries had achieved in spite of all the hindrances of apartheid. Fr Jimmy was fluent in two African languages. It was here that Fr Michael Crowley and Sr Monique Stubbe started the school for the formation of catechists that did so much to further the evangelisation of the African people.

We next headed into the African hinterland and arrived at Saint Scholastica Mission, where the German Dominican Sisters had a school and orphanage for African children. Here we had our first taste of mangoes. Fr Terrence Mooney was our host. He told us he had thirty-three outstations. With the help of paid catechists, they had made advances into huge territory. Fr Terrence had at least two African languages and did so much for the upliftment of Africans – he seemed to get bursaries for the brighter ones so that they could pursue their studies. Later, many of them rose to positions of responsibility and authority – they owed so much to the generosity and extraordinary zeal of

Terrence. It was a shock to Dominic to hear the tumult of the monkeys on the corrugated roof of his bedroom. After a night of rain, we were fortunate to get out as the road was covered in slippery mud.

We headed for Louis Trichardt, which was a large European settlers' town of mostly Afrikaans-speaking people. Fr Donie McCarthy was in charge. He was one of the first MSCs to arrive. He became so proficient in the African languages that he and a Protestant minister translated large parts of the Bible into them. This was a wonderful resource for catechists and people.

I had difficulty believing all the progress made in twenty-five years as we headed for Vendaland. Because of the apartheid laws that meant that whites could not live in so-called African homelands, the MSC built a mission station on the border. Here we met Fr Tom Plower and Fr Jimmy Stubbs. Also nearby were the Holy Rosary Sisters, who ran a very important clinic.

The MSC had started many mission stations in Venda, although they could not stay overnight there. A catechist who worked there is now being put forward for canonisation. He was stoned to death because of his stance against witchcraft. Fr Jimmy Stubbs had built a beautiful church in Thohoyandou, the capital of Venda. But all would agree that the great founding apostle of Venda was Fr Paddy O'Connor. Venda became his second African language. He was supported by family and friends in Ireland, who gave generously to Paddy to help build a church and money for bursaries to help young Africans pursue their studies.

We were very venturesome the next day as we went through Vendaland to get to Nzhelele. We got detailed instructions on how to get there. It was mentioned several times about crossing a rickety bridge. However, we soon found that every bridge was rickety. There was worry we might get lost and with lack of knowledge of Venda, we might be in trouble. This was real Africa; the landscape and villages would have changed little over the centuries. There were the many plots of maize which are so common now in Ireland. Rain was scarce here and their main vegetable seemed to be spinach. The women were hoeing the plots as most of the men were away working in the mines of

Jo'burg. The women had their children with them. Some of the landscape was covered with the ubiquitous anthills and mole heaps, the bush mainly acacia interspersed with the aloe with its tubular bright flowers. There was the occasional tree, giving shade in the midday sun to the boys herding their goats.

And then there was the occasional baobab tree – my favourite African tree. These are found in a few countries, but always near the Tropic of Capricorn. The most magnificent specimens are reputed to be very ancient – some as old as 1,000 years. When the tree gets old, it becomes hollow. In Africa, as elsewhere, they are associated with many myths and legends. This is the tree that many African people believe to be the home of their ancestral spirits. In the creation myth in which each animal receives it own tree from the Great Spirits, it was originally given to the hyena, who threw the tree down in disgust. It landed the wrong way up and so it became the 'upside-down tree' with its roots sticking up like branches. The bark can be stripped from the trunk and harvested to make cork without killing the tree. Pound the bark and you make rope; weave it and you have bark cloth to wear; flatten it and you have tiles for your roof. If I may go on, not far from where I would work in the eastern Transvaal was one of the finest baobabs. It is called the Leydsdorf Giant. During the gold rush in the 1880s nearby, the hollow in the middle served as a bar.

Dominic was getting worried as we had made more than one wrong turn. I have a kind of inbuilt compass (not boasting!) and somehow we found landmarks that helped us reach our destination. Dominic was amazed to see the women on the road carrying such huge loads of firewood, probably walking miles to and fro. Some were carrying large containers of water, also for long distances. The odd baboon would cross our path. We got a very warm welcome from Fr Sean Horgan and the nuns – Daughters of our Lady of the Sacred Heart. The convent was made up of different large conical huts with thatched roofs, all connected. Fr Sean had a small house nearby. The nuns ran a clinic, which was so badly needed in a highly populated area with no such amenity available.

Over a lovely meal with Sean and the Sisters, we discussed the small Christian communities now being encouraged and organised for the new converts to Catholicism. Groups of about twenty or so would meet every week in one of their huts for reading and reflection on the scriptures, prayer and singing. Like the early church, they would be concerned for each other's welfare on a practical level. When all these small communities met for Mass whenever Sean visited their area, there would be a great feeling of Christian solidarity. The paid catechist would have several volunteer helpers to prepare candidates for baptism on a two-year course. This Easter coming, there would be ninety adults who would gather in one of the larger churches to celebrate Easter. On Holy Saturday night, the vigil would go on through the night with scripture, singing and many impromptu prayers.

Before the dawn of day, all the congregation would process to a nearby river. As the sun appeared, the baptism would be administered. Great shouts of joy and prayer would arise as each was baptised. Then they would head back to the church, where the Easter Mass would start. Confirmation would be administered after the profession of faith. All the candidates would receive communion with the rest of the congregation. There would be some refreshments and celebrations afterwards. Fr Sean would spend the rest of the day catching up on some sleep.

As I lay in bed before sleep, the noise – or was it music, or cacophony – from the numerous cricket-like insects was soporific. The pale light from the full moon made me think that this same moon was shining over Dunmanus Bay in West Cork. It is the same Planet Earth, but worlds apart. The distant beat of an African drum left no doubt as to where I was.

We said Mass for the nuns and mission helpers in a beautiful small chapel. The African ladies were singing that haunting African hymn 'Nkosi Sikelel' iAfrica', which is now the song sung at Springbok rugby matches. As we left for our next destination, there were clearly crowds building up outside the mission clinic. We headed for the main tar road going to Messina and Southern Rhodesia, as it was then called.

We turned left and descended into the most scenic valley before reaching Louis Trichardt and then down to the Low Velt. Immediately, we felt the temperature rising as we passed many white farmers' houses with the usual African huts nearby to house the farmworkers. We came to the valley where I had worked some twenty-three years previously. A quick visit to Duivelskloof presbytery and Fr D. F. McCarthy, with promises to call back again. We moved on to the centre of the diocese of Tzaneen, where the newly consecrated bishop had his modest house. It was great to be able to congratulate my classmate and friend who had travelled with me to South Africa the first time in 1958. Hugh had gone to Witwatersrand University in Jo'burg to study African languages and worked at the Lumko Institute, helping new missionaries with African language and culture. He was the Religious Superior before his appointment to succeed Bishop John Durkin. It was nice to spend some time with him as we enjoyed the hospitality of the Daughters of Our Lady of the Sacred Heart convent. The Sisters had a large mobile clinic which they took to the different mission stations nearby. We visited the local presbytery and Fr Sean Laffan. He was jack of all trades and master of all of them. He was a most experienced missionary and was also involved in formation as Novice Master. He spent a year in charge of the Mission Forum. He attended the same national primary school in Kilcrohane as me, and his early vocation would have been nurtured by Mr and Mrs Hurley, his first teachers.

Nearby there was a small cathedral built with modest means, but which was a trusty architectural beacon to the work of the MSC fathers.

The next day we travelled along a tar road skirting a very large African homeland. There were white-run farms which should have been incorporated into the African territory, but no political pressure was put on farmers to leave. The Africans were left with land that was less than arable. We passed the road to the mission at Ofcolaco and went on to Olifants River Mission. The Olifants is one of the great rivers of South Africa. The land for the Jimmy Porter Mission was donated by an English settler and pioneer of the Low Velt. He came to South Africa in 1900 to work as a policeman, but bought himself out for £5. During the gold and emerald rush nearby, he became a hotel-keeper, miner, butcher and farmer. His future mother-in-law, Ma Carroll, insisted that Jimmy change his religion before she would agree to give her daughter's hand in marriage. 'Small price to pay,' he said. Before we turned off at the sign for the London Mission (after the name of the farm), there was a hut where a lady was selling some beautiful African wall carpets to tourists. These were made at the mission. We had to negotiate a river without even a rickety bridge.

We passed through a forest of marula trees with women collecting the ripe fruit into sacks to sell to an enterprising businessman who had started to make marula liquor. Not all these bags of marula found their way to the businessman; some were used to make African beer. It was not unusual to see some tipsy men and occasionally tipsy women. Even the elephants in neighbouring Kruger Park, when they hoover up large quantities of ripened fruit which ferment in the stomachs, can find themselves if not dancing, then doing a good Muhammad Ali shuffle.

We were welcomed at the mission by Fr Pat Galvin and the Holy Rosary Sisters. It was quite a large complex, with a school, a clinic, a church and a very large shed where they make the carpets. The art of spinning and weaving traditional African carpets was started by Fr Jerry Riordan and improved on by Fr Galvin and others. They found markets for these in Germany and the passing tourist trade. Fr Pat believed in getting people to help themselves. You can give a hungry man a fish, but better to give him a fishing rod so that he can catch his own fish. He helped people to make and bake bricks. Most of all, he found funding for boring holes for water and pumps, the most necessary commodity of all. He brought in heavy machinery to make a small dam so they could enable irrigation for vegetable gardens. The Sisters were involved in community development, catechetics, the clinic and healthcare, as well as teaching.

Fr Bill Flemming came to visit us from the next-door mission, still going strong after all these years. He thanked me for giving him my tennis racket on leaving Africa twenty-three years previously, and introducing him to tennis at the ripe old age of thirty-five. It was a great uplift for him to play tennis once a week. He took me to task for not having the necessary missionary first aid kit, which consisted of a spade, a rope, a container of water and a toilet roll. The rope was to help with being towed in the event of breakdown; the spade to help dig out of mud; water necessary for hydration in the hot African sun; and the toilet roll was for emergency needs from tummy bugs, and was needed as the African grass was rough on the whole.

We left for our last destination, Phalaborwa. This is one of the gateways to the Kruger National Park, one of the great tourist attractions in the world. We passed through Leydsdorp, where the giant baobab tree is. It is hard to believe that thousands of gold-seeking miners once flocked to this place. Malaria and black water fever were the great killers. It was a waterless inferno in summer, with temperatures in the forties. It was known as Death Valley. Malaria was eliminated with the application of DDT and pyrethrum drugs. Nearby is a present-day mine where antimony is found – a rare semi-metal used in the hardening of steel.

We arrived at Phalaborwa, a town that did not exist forty years previously. Rio Tinto started developing a very rich vein of copper and other precious minerals. It was open cast, with a vast hole ½ mile across and ¾ mile deep. This town would be my home for ten and a half years, after my short stay in Cape Town. Fr Michael Kelly was our host; he had an extraordinary talent for building and could turn his hand to every aspect of the trade. Many churches and presbyteries are landmarks to his achievements. He did a very interesting barbecue for us.

Early the next morning, we went to the gate of Kruger National Park, named after President Kruger of the Transvaal Republic. We paid a small fee to enter for the day. The park came about through the efforts of an Irishman, Colonel James Stevenson-Hamilton, who in spite of opposition from farmers, miners, hunters and poachers, and even some politicians, won the approval of the government to set aside this area the size of Wales for all the wildlife of South Africa. It is now one of the greatest parks for the presentation and management of wildlife in the world.

It is one of the great tourist attractions of the world. There are tar roads from one village reserve camp to the next, with key dirt roads giving access to most parts of it. We saw thousands of impala deer and kudu, as well as fat zebras, giraffes and wildebeest. It was a little frightening when a herd of elephants started to cross the road. There was a vast herd of Cape buffalo, with their huge horns. As I was to discover later, it is all a matter of luck when you see any of the great cats – they like to keep a low profile and they sleep a lot during the midday sun.

Dominic was getting hot in the car and as it is strictly forbidden to get out except in the village reserves, we sought what seemed a safe high spot to get out and stretch our legs. I suggested to him that in the event of a lion attack, I would have the most to lose as they would find me more tender and succulent. We had lunch in one of the camps (internal villages), protected with electric fences; these are often near one of the large rivers and it is possible to see the wildlife coming to drink. There are always hippos making lots of noise.

We had to make our way home as the gates close at 6 p.m. There is a speed limit of 35 mph patrolled by the usual traffic cops. We stopped to admire a large troupe of baboons ruled over by a massive patriarch. One of the little ones was chastised by his mother for some misdemeanour – his cries were just like a baby's.

Fr Kelly wined and dined us and invited us to an outdoor cinema night in the bushveld – you drove the car in and got attached to sound. It was surreal to see Hollywood images on a screen surrounded by the shadows of the African bushveld.

The next day, we made the long journey back to Jo'burg. On the way, Dominic expressed how proud he was of all those students whom he had taught and helped with their formation to become Missionaries of the Sacred Heart. For the next few days we joined the Annual MSC Assembly, where discernment was sought on how best to consolidate the work so generously begun. When it was over, Fr Michael Crowley and I boarded the plane for the two-hour flight to Cape Town. We were met by Monique Stubbe, a good friend of the MSCs, and taken to our parish in Goodwood, a suburb of Cape Town.

I would be here for eighteen months before returning to our mission in the North Transvaal. It was a nice easy time after many years of hard parish work in the UK. There was time to study South African history and culture.

I decided to go to Cape Town University for two mornings a week to learn Afrikaans. The course was set up for students from Rhodesia who hoped to get work in South Africa, as they would have to have basic Afrikaans. The university is on the side of a hill overlooking the city and is a most impressive building. It seemed strange sitting at a desk with all these young people. Our lady tutor was most helpful and gave us homework to do. We had to sit exams at the end of the year. It brought back all the negative memories of exams and I swore it would be the last exam I would ever do. I got a good pass. As it turned out, it was not any great practical help to me, but I could understand the news on TV in Afrikaans. Once, an Afrikaans couple, both doctors, insisted on taking their marriage vows in Afrikaans. It went off quite well.

We had a large congregation of white people – some of them were from Madeira and had come to settle in Cape Town. Many of them had large fishing boats; others ran what they called cafés – a South African name for a corner shop open twelve hours a day. They were very devout Catholics with great devotion to Mass. I spent a few evenings every week visiting their homes, which they greatly appreciated.

The Portuguese were good explorers. At the end of the fifteenth century, they sailed down the west coast of Africa until they reached the Horn of Africa, where the Atlantic and Indian Oceans meet – they had found the route to the East Indies. In 1488, Bartolomew Dias rounded the Cape of Good Hope, disproving the view that had existed since Ptolemy that the Indian Ocean was separate from the Atlantic Ocean. Strangely, they did not look on it as a future colony, but instead found a route to the East Indies where they discovered all the islands that now make up Indonesia. Their goal was the Spice Islands, from where they brought back the most sought-after spices. They settled there until the Dutch drove them out. The Dutch followed the trade route pioneered by the Portuguese and found the Cape of Good Hope to be a suitable refreshment station to take on meat, fruit and vegetables. They discovered that when sailors had fruit and veg they did not get scurvy. In 1652, Van Riebeeck arrived to start a colony in the Cape peninsula. They called the local inhabitants 'bushmen' and shot them as if they were not human. They feared them because they retaliated with poisoned darts.

With the persecution of Protestants in France, the Huguenots found refuge with their Calvinist brothers in the Cape. They brought with them the knowledge of growing vines and the making of good wine. The Afrikaaners welcomed them but discouraged them from speaking French. They became more Afrikaans than the Afrikaaners themselves. They all got the name 'Boers', meaning farmers.

With the advent of the British, there was a great clash of language, religion and culture, so the Afrikaaners took to the veld and moved gradually north, calling it the Great Trek. They upheld the old custom of family prayer, reading the Bible every day and little else. They looked on themselves as people of the Old Testament in search of a promised land. When gold was discovered in the Transvaal and diamonds in Kimberley, the British found new interest and, with the leadership of Cecil Rhodes, wanted this new wealth for the British Empire. This led to the Boer War, which the British finally won but which left a deep and lasting hatred in the heart of the Boers.

We Irish spend a lot of time talking about the weather. The Cape peninsula and the coastal region to Port Elizabeth have a different climate to the rest of South Africa. They get their rain in the winter, with only sunshine in the summer – the opposite to the rest of South Africa. This is why the region is ideal for vineyards. Some of the best wine is produced in the well-known vineyards, of which there are many, some more famous than others.

In the winter, you can get some beautiful days of sunshine, but also lots of wind and rain. They say it is like a baby – it is either windy or wet. The population is made up of white people, black people and coloureds. (In South Africa the term 'coloured' was used as an ethnic label for people of mixed ethnic origin, including African, Chinese, Khoisan, Malay and white.) The latter came about because the first Dutch settlers did not bring women with them from Holland and so took concubines from the African population. When eventually Dutch women came, they disowned the progeny of mixed race. These increased and multiplied and became a large section of the population today. There was a famous area in Cape Town called District 6 where many of the coloured population lived. It was vibrant and was attractive to tourists, especially sailors, who were sometimes entertained by attractive ladies for monetary considerations.

In the ethnic cleansing and forced removal of black and coloured people, they were moved to housing estates many miles away. All their homes were bulldozed, leaving only the church, now boarded up, as a monument to what Mandela called 'an orgy of social engineering'. In this orgy, coloureds suffered the most. In being classed as non-white, they lost the opportunities for employment reserved for whites only. Sometimes siblings were divided, one classed as white and the other as coloured. In Port Elizabeth, coloured people will tell you that when Churchill was a young war reporter for the Boer War, he generously left some of his genes with the coloured population. Some of them boast about their name Churchill!

Michener, in his book *The Covenant* (1980), sums up the lot of the coloured people: 'They would be preached against by the Predicants because they would be living testimony to the fact that in the beginning days whites had cohabited with brown and black and Indian slaves – the land of their birth would be the home of their sorrow and they would be entitled to no place in society, to no future they all agreed on, but they would forever be a testimony.'

One of the most sensible weddings I ever attended was a Madeira Portuguese couple. Shortly after the marriage ceremony, we went to a large community hall for the reception. It was an extremely hot day so air conditioning was very welcome. In our weddings in the UK and Ireland, there is a long, boring wait between the actual ceremony and the wedding meal – sometimes four hours – when there is nothing to do but drink and make small talk. This wedding was different. We all sat down and with a short prayer the first course was served. Then there was one speech. There was time for dancing and music. After fifty minutes the second course was served, followed by a short speech and more music and dancing. This went on for the whole afternoon and evening, with coffee served at 11 p.m. People were drinking good Cape wine and having food at the same time – what a civilized way to do a wedding!

There were two outstanding South African clerics who fought fearlessly against apartheid: Archbishop Denis Hurley and Archbishop Tutu. The latter was appointed to the vacant Church of England See of Cape Town in 1984. The Instalment (investiture) took place in an open-air service in Goodwood Show Ground, just beside us. After my Masses, I went to join the vast congregation of all races. Just at the entrance I recognised Winnie Mandela, dressed flamboyantly and surrounded by a large number of black youths, like bees around a honey pot. She wisely did not go in to join the congregation, as it would have been an unnecessary distraction.

There were many provincial Anglican representatives from overseas, including the new Archbishop of Canterbury, Dr Robert Runcie. Desmond Tutu continued to be a thorn in the side of the nationalist government and was the spokesman for many black leaders who were banned or in prison.

Around this time, Nelson Mandela was moved from Robben Island to a prison on the outskirts of Cape Town. Before he was moved, they brought him to the mainland to see a dentist. Afterwards, they left him alone in a car, hoping that he might try to escape. He was too clever – he knew it was a trap. If he tried to get away, he would have been riddled with bullets.

In the great apartheid plan, all races must be kept apart. There would be new homelands where the different ethnic African tribes would have to live. Like the coloured people, some millions were forcefully removed to their homelands and their former dwellings destroyed. Generally they did not provide new homes for them and, as the whites had taken over the arable land, making a living was now impossible. If they went to work in mines or elsewhere, they had to carry a special pass and identity documents. If they failed to have these, they were put in jail. Fr Michael Crowley MSC, in his book *To Cape Town and Back*, talking about this Group Areas Act 1960 and the forced removal of 3.5 million people, calls it 'man's inhumanity to man'. He personally witnessed some of it:

> I will always remember the removal of some of my African people. The mud huts crumbled under the bulldozers; mothers with babies on their backs were crying; old men standing silent, afraid and helpless as their few belongings were flung onto the back of army trucks to be dumped in the dusty homeland. I, too, stood there, helpless and scared. 'Where was God now?' I asked. 'We cry inside,' an African confided in me one time. But the might of Afrikaaner power was hell bent on pursuing the evil engineering of apartheid. It was reminiscent of what happened in history in my own land.

Many thousands of black people came to work in Cape Town in all sorts of menial jobs. Some would be legal; many were not. They formed huge shanty towns with houses made of corrugated iron and tarpaulin. It was impossible for the government officials to control the mighty influx of disenfranchised and needy humanity. It was the law of the jungle, the survival of the fittest, and crime was rife. To protect themselves, white homeowners had all of their windows secured with burglar-proof bars and security alarms, as well as guard dogs.

There were a few controlled residential areas for black people, with some basic needs like electricity, water and sanitation. One of the priests who worked in one of these areas was a Fr

Desmond Curran. His father was the Protestant Lord Chief Justice for Northern Ireland. Desmond became a barrister, but before starting work went to Africa to take some time out. There he became very friendly with some Irish missionaries. His eyes were opened to the wonderful work of empowering people through the gospel, schools and hospitals. He became a Catholic and soon after decided to become a priest. After ordination, he went to the Cape Town diocese and spent all his priestly life working in the black townships. Because of his degree in law, the police began to fear him as he tried to defend the rights of helpless people. He was a very tall man with a short temper and there are many stories told about him. His father disowned him when he became Catholic and a priest. On the father's deathbed they were reconciled.

Most tourists want to see Table Mountain and Cape Point, where the Indian and Atlantic Oceans meet. Table Mountain is probably the most famous and unusual mountain in the world. It is nearly 1,110 metres high and is completely flat at the top, where you can walk for a few miles. At one end, lower down, is a formation of rock called Lion's Head – from a distance, it looks just like a resting lion. The mountain breaks into a series of gable-like peaks called The Twelve Apostles, overlooking Hout Bay. The mountain is famous for its flora and fauna – occasionally during the hot and dry summer there is a fierce fire, but it always recovers. Many intrepid mountain-climbers try to get to the top by various routes. It has its casualties every year. The least challenging and one of the most interesting ways to the top is in the cable car, which offers dizzying views across Table Bay and out to the Atlantic. The cable car rotates on the way up and down. You want to close your eyes as it slowly edges its way to the top ledge. There is a top-of-the-range restaurant at the peak. You can spend the whole day walking to different parts to get the most beautiful views I have ever seen. It is the most incomparable spot to watch the sun go down. The little animals that scramble between rocks are not rodents and are called dassies – apparently, they are related to the elephant. It stretches my imagination.

There are many very scenic golf courses around the Cape Town peninsula. About a dozen clergy met every Monday morning for a game; some were Salesian, others Capuchins and MSCs. Royal Cape Golf Club, underneath Table Mountain, was our favourite. It was a great opportunity to relax after the week and exchange some clerical news. We had meals together, with the winner buying some drinks. Because there was so much unemployment among the non-white population, we used to hire a caddy. It helped them some little bit. This brought its own problem. One day, as we finished and were walking to the club house, Fr Michael Crowley's caddy disappeared with his clubs. Fr Michael was not amused and had some unkind things to say. On another occasion, one of them stole my watch that I had got as a going-away present from the congregation in Tamworth. This story has a sequel, which I will tell you later. When I started to play there first, some of the scenery was almost distracting from the serious work of winning a game.

There was an Irish family from Mallow in the congregation. Their only son had an extraordinary experience. When his mum was pregnant, she contracted German measles. As a result, her son was born profoundly deaf. As a teenager he became a very angry young man because of his serious disability. One day, while crossing the main road, he was knocked down by a drunken driver. The ambulance was called and shortly after he was brought to the hospital he was pronounced dead and taken to the mortuary. At that time his mother arrived and she screamed and screamed that her son be taken back to the theatre. They relented and did so. Some time later, he started to breathe again. As a result of the accident, he was paraplegic. Even his speech was impaired. However, his mother could understand him. He told her of his near-death experience. He told her how his soul had left his body and was drawn to a tunnel of light. This experience completely changed his life.

I used to take him holy communion on First Friday. I never saw him without a smile. He seemed so happy in spite of all his desperate handicaps. He always tried to thank me as I left. It helps us to reflect on the mystery of life and death, and its dividing line.

* * *

Gradually, the outside world realised that they could defeat apartheid by economic and sporting sanctions. Not every country would cooperate in these sanctions. It was wonderful when we heard about these brave women workers in Dunnes Stores in Dublin, who refused to handle South African goods, for which they paid a big price in earnings. But little things like that made the world realise that this was the only way to bring the South African regime to the negotiating table. The sporting sanctions hit them hard as they were a great sporting nation in rugby, cricket and golf.

This brings me to their famous wines. There are so many Winelands estates. The most famous are Stellenbosch, Paarl and Franschoek. European countries started sanctions against South African wine. This was a painful loss to their economy. It did make wine very cheap for South Africans however – we could buy a five-litre cask of the best wine for a few pounds.

Our parish comprised many white South Africans, as well as many Portuguese from Madeira. They had big celebrations for baptism, first communion and confirmation. They were always inviting us to their barbecues on Sundays. Because there was so much poverty and unemployment among the non-white population, there were lots of house burglaries. Outside the main presbytery door was another steel door made of steel bars. When you opened the door, you could see and speak to the person outside. All the windows had security bars. One night when alone in the presbytery, I was woken up by a burglar trying to get in. I phoned the police and hoped they would get there before the burglar got in. Fortunately, they arrived in time. When they arrested him, they caught him by the legs and hands and threw him into the back of the police van. Everyone lived in a certain amount of fear. When you returned by car at night, you had a zapper to open the garage door. You entered the presbytery through the garage's back door.

We had lots of people looking for help. We tried to give them food. One African amused me by saying there was a fly in his

Ordination, 1957

Indonesia, 1962

Family at ordination, 1957

Ordination day with Bishop Lamont and Frs Duffy and Scriven

One of our plays in Moyne Park

Classmates in Moyne Park Seminary

Picnic in Sligo

On liner to South Africa, 1958 with Hugh Slattery, Bishop of Tzaneen

Blessing of new school with Bishop Butler OSB, St Albans, 1973

With Fr Tom Nicholson R.I.P. before
leaving South Africa for Indonesia

Retired Abbot/Bishop whom
I helped to look after

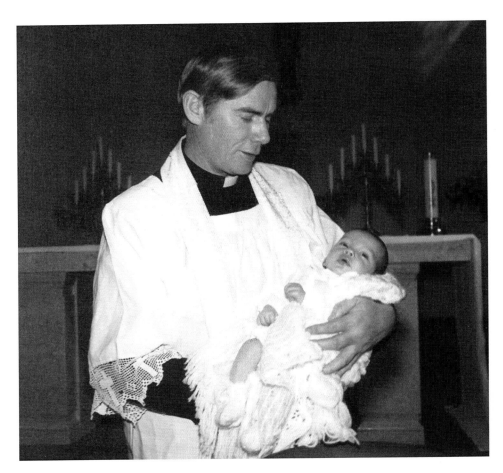

Baptism, St Albans, 1973

ointment – this fly needed money, which I gave him. A few mornings later, the doorbell kept ringing at five a.m. Eventually, I went to the door, where the same man told me once more about the fly in his ointment. I can't tell you what my response was.

We had a rather elderly man in charge of the Cape Town Archdiocese, Cardinal Owen McCann. When asked by a charismatic person if he had received the Holy Spirit, he petulantly replied, 'I give the Holy Spirit.' He had done his best to fight apartheid policies. When he celebrated his twenty-five-year jubilee as bishop, he told us priests a rather unusual story. One Saturday night, he got a phone call from a man who wanted to speak to the cardinal. He told him that he was out. The man then asked who he was and the cardinal said, 'I am the secretary.' The man then said, 'If you don't mind me saying so, you sound as if you are pissed,' at which point he dropped the phone. The cardinal then went on to tell us he was making this public apology to his secretary!

Around this time, Mandela was moved from Robben Island to Pollsmoor Prison in Cape Town. The apartheid regime felt that his influence on other ANC prisoners was too great. Also, they were hoping to start some possible private talks with him about his political ambitions. Newspapers were banned from mentioning any news about him.

* * *

My good time in Cape Town was coming to an end. I was asked to go up north to the very opposite side of the country to our diocese of Tzaneen. Fr Michael Kelly had been the first parish priest in Phalaborwa and had ministered there for over twenty years. I was to replace him. I would first have to travel about 1,000 miles to Johannesburg. I could do the two-hour journey by plane, but I decided I would travel by train. If I had been a rich man, I would have taken the famous Blue Train. It is said that train journeys rarely come more opulent than this. It bills itself as the world's most luxurious train service, with one butler for every three passengers, and it compares with the Orient Express and Trans-Siberian Railway. It has an observation car with massive windows covering all wall space. It is like an exclusive hotel on wheels, with the best cuisine and most desirable South African wine. But I also remember another side of the Blue Train: it is a play in which a group of poor black children scrabble for scraps of food thrown from the train by rich passengers. It casts a different perspective and reminds us of the gospel story of Dives and the poor man Lazarus.

So I took an ordinary train to Johannesburg, which took over twenty-seven hours. I got a two-person berth with wash basin and seats that converted into sleeping bunks at night. When I got on the train, I found that I had the luxury of having the berth all to myself. There was also a very fine dining carriage, with the best South African food and wine.

I will always remember the first part of the journey as the train slowly climbed the first ridge of mountains. It took extraordinary skill to build this railway line – quite a lot of Irishmen came to work on it. We left the rich Winelands behind us and we passed one deep gorge after another in the craggiest of mountains. I was spellbound by the vegetation. I cannot describe its colour and beauty, and I have no idea what the rich variety of plants were. It was like seeing the land version of the coral reefs. But when we reached the summit and started to descend, there was a dramatic change. We soon reached the semi-desert called the Karoo. For most of the daylight, we travelled mile after mile of bushveld. The only vegetation was a small bush, and the only animals were little sheep that thrive on this little bush. It took a couple of acres to support one sheep. One farmer would need thousands of acres. The Karoo lamb is famous in South Africa and is most succulent. The little towns were few and we passed through most of them with their Afrikaans names. We had a super lunch in the dining carriage, which we dragged out a little over nice wine and conversation with some English tourists.

Our first long stop was at Kimberley, famous for its diamond mines. In the 1870s, it became known that diamonds were to be found in the area. The famous De Beers had possession of most of the land. One day, a few pioneers were scratching around at the base of a koppie (a little hill) on the De Beers land. The story goes that they sent one of their cooks to the top of the hill as punishment for being drunk, telling him not to return until he had found a diamond. The unnamed servant returned with a beautiful diamond peace offering. Within fifty years, there were 50,000 people in the area, frantically turning the koppie inside out. As with the gold rush, each day saw lives lost and fortunes either discovered or squandered. They started to dig a shaft underground, which went down 800 metres. This was done with picks and shovels, and was for many years the largest man-made hole in the world. It all came to an end in 1914. Cecil Rhodes played his part in the diamond industry.

Sundown in the Karoo was spectacular. This has been the subject for many artists, who give lots of technical, atmospherical reasons. Following an interesting dinner on wheels, I retired to my apartment. Soon an attendant brought sheets and blankets and changed my bunk into a comfortable bed. Before I got rocked to sleep by the rhythmic movement of the train, I reflected on my life's journey as a priest. I was now fifty-four years old. I was probably the only person alone in a train compartment speeding through Africa. But if I weren't a celibate, I could not have done the things I did – go here and there at the drop of a hat.

I had some serious worries about this new adventure. The whole apartheid climate was changing fast. The Soweto uprising of 1976 signalled the transfer of protest from the workplace to the townships as black youths took to the streets to protest about Afrikaans being the medium of instruction in their schools. Many of them were killed brutally by armed police trying to restore order. Then there was the Black Consciousness Movement, with its martyr Steve Biko. Whenever they banned an African organisation, a new one started up. It became obvious that apartheid wasn't working. When the political bully P. W. Botha became prime minister, he adopted a two-handed strategy of reform, accompanied by unprecedented repression. He had extended conscription for all white males. He was preparing for

135

war. The possibility of a bloodless and peaceful solution seemed remote. We missionaries would be caught between a rock and a hard place. Catholics, as well as blacks and communists, were still high on the list of the dangers for South Africa. With a little prayer to the Sacred Heart, I fell asleep. When the train stopped a few times, the noise inevitably woke us up.

When day dawned, we were in a different world. We were passing through the very fertile region of the Southern Transvaal, with its rich farmlands: vast crops of maize and wheat, interspersed with some expansive dairy farms. South African railways have a very narrow gauge, so trains can never go that fast. But we were passing many busy towns with a few stops. It was time for our last meal – a good South African breakfast with lots of fruit. I was glad when we were passing through the suburbs of Jo'burg. We saw the vast black township of Soweto in the distance, then the skyscrapers of inner Jo'burg. I was met by an MSC friend who took me to Midrand, between Jo'burg and Pretoria. After a day or two, they kindly loaned me a pick-up vehicle so that I could drive myself the 200 miles to Phalaborwa. Fr M. Kelly would drive it back to Midrand with his goods and chattels, on his way to take up appointment in Cape Town.

When travelling long journeys by car, we try to stop for a rest and a cup of coffee after 200 kilometres or every two hours. Many of our missionaries here have had lucky escapes from falling asleep or lack of concentration. In very hot weather, I always changed my T-shirt, which was wet from perspiration, during these rest stops. I did feel somewhat anxious travelling this five-hour journey, but this was something I would have to get used to. I finally arrived at Phalaborwa, which would be my home for the next ten years. I was greeted by Bishop Durkin, who had retired there. It would be a great advantage to have his presence in the presbytery.

Phalaborwa did not exist thirty years previously. A German geologist, Hans Merensky, had discovered copper and in the 1950s Rio Tinto had started its mining operations. At the same time, the government started to develop the rich seam of phosphates found nearby. The town of Phalaborwa was for the white workforce – because of apartheid, the big African township had to be built ten miles away. This grew to be a very large township called Namakgale.

It was opencast mining and when I arrived the hole was one of the biggest in the world – over the ten years it got bigger. It was three-quarters of a mile in diameter and went down nearly a mile. Only a small seam was copper-bearing, so millions of tons of rock had to be dynamited and brought to the surface in massive trucks on roads built into the side of the hole. All this rock formed a huge mountain. They discovered not only copper, but also uranium, gold and other minerals. It was a very lucrative enterprise for Rio Tinto. The huge smelting complex spewed clouds of pollution into the atmosphere. Every evening, huge trucks laden with gleaming copper left en route for Durban export ships.

I had a couple of hundred in my white congregation, made up of a few nationalities. Fr Kelly had built a beautiful church and large presbytery, with an open covered space between serving as a hall. The families were most friendly and committed to church. They were very generous with their offerings towards our financial support.

Fr Kelly also built a large church in Namakgale, which I later extended. I soon discovered that this township had the most gifted catechist, Matthew Mokgashi. He and I formed a very good partnership in helping this very vibrant and enthusiastic congregation. I always believed that a missionary should learn the language and this I tried to do. Unfortunately, because I was getting on in years and African languages are very difficult, I made little progress. In my case it wasn't too much of a disadvantage, as most of the congregation were working in the mine and had a good knowledge of English.

On Sundays, the Liturgy of the Word went on for a long time and was in the African language of Soto. Matthew translated my homily. The Prayers of the Faithful took fifteen minutes as many from the congregation joined in. They loved to sing and sometimes almost took the roof off the church. The offertory procession was accompanied by dancing and singing. I did the Eucharistic Prayer in English. The service took about one and a half hours.

Matthew had many volunteer catechists to help him with the preparation of the sacraments for children. One of the most helpful community-building initiatives was the creation of small basic communities. In every few streets, the Catholics would form a small community that met once a week in each others' houses. There would be reading of scriptures, reflection and prayers. There would also be some outreach to others, especially to those in need. There was great concern for any of the members who were sick or had some problem. Matthew had his own house and parish office near the church where meetings were held. He was blessed with a wife, Sara, who was a teacher, and their adopted daughter.

All the houses in this township were built by the mine; they were more than basic and there was only a small rent. This was a most untypical township in the apartheid era.

There was a populated black area near Phalaborwa where there was little missionary outreach. The nearest township, where a few got jobs in the mine and others got work as domestic help and as garden boys in Phalaborwa, was Lulekani. Apart from the occasional Mass in the courtyard of one family, there was little scope to get people into any community of worship.

Matthew and I felt that we needed a church; but before this could be realised, another problem began. When Mozambique finally gained its independence from the Portuguese, it immediately became a divided country, with the Frelimo government challenged by opposition from former comrade rebels calling themselves Renamo. The apartheid government was quick to see a political opportunity. Frelimo were perceived to be pro-communist, so they immediately began to give arms and strategic help to the Renamo rebels. Most of this covert operation took place from a secret army camp near Phalaborwa, where some ex-Portuguese solders from Mozambique, as well as remnants of Ian Smith's army from Southern Rhodesia, disbanded after independence. Gradually, there was outright civil war in Mozambique. Many refugees began to come through the Kruger, in spite of all the dangers from the wildlife there, to find refuge in the homeland of Gazankulu. When I arrived, there was a small number near Lulekani. But as every week went by the numbers grew. The Methodists, Anglicans and our church decided that we must help. We had little expertise and fewer resources. This was the start of my involvement with refugees and I don't think there is any more distressing work than to see these vulnerable people without food, clothes or houses. Many of them brought their starving children with them. They arrived totally traumatised. Some lay on the bare earth for a day or two. Some lost family to wild animals in the Kruger Park. The Missionaries of the Sacred Heart in Ireland made an appeal for us, raising a million pounds.

As we slowly got organised, we got land from the chief and we called it *Humulani* – 'place of rest'. Bishop Slattery asked the missionary Sisters of the Assumption to help. We would first have to build them some simple convent. The South African apartheid government would not allow the UN Refugee Department to enter the country. One of South Africa's greatest philanthropists, a Jewish lady called Ina Pearlman, got assistance for us from the foreign embassies in Johannesburg. She also begged for money from big corporations.

The refugees immediately started to build little mud huts. The mud they mixed with ground-up dust from the many anthills – this had some of the properties of cement. They put on grass roofs, so they were shielded from the hot sun. We managed to get some piped water from Lulekani. Ina Pearlman started to send huge truckloads of maize and some peanut butter. We had to build a big shed to hold the maize till the weekly distribution.

The sisters helped us to get funding to build a convent. We were grateful to get a free site from the chief. When it was completed, Srs Bartholomew, Ancilla and Brenda came to be our most-treasured helpers. Sr Brenda felt that the very little children were the most needy. At the same time, a white lady from

Phalaborwa called Pat McDougall offered to help. I got a second-hand pick-up truck, which she used to great advantage. She was forever scrounging leftovers from two local supermarkets. She and Sr Brenda began to organise to build some crèches for the little children, where they fed them some nutritious food. With the help of local volunteers, they started little classes of music and simple lessons. In a few months, those children were transformed and they could smile, play and dance again.

While all this was happening near Phalaborwa, even greater numbers came across the Mozambique border to Giyani and Malamulele, some sixty miles away. The same process of help had to take place there too. The MSC appealed for lay volunteers to help. We got some wonderful lady volunteers, who spent two to three years helping with crèches, working in gardens growing basic vegetables, as well as helping with the many social needs. We provided transport for them. My niece Imelda McCarthy came for a few months and stayed in the presbytery with me in Phalaborwa.

Matthew, my catechist, was one of the most indispensable people in helping the refugees. Because he knew their language, he was able to pick and train some leaders who would help control the dispensing of the food. The volunteer helpers went from hut to hut to count the occupants and give them cards with the number of people requiring food. On the day we dispensed food it was bedlam. The maize came in bags of twenty and forty kilos. Big queues were formed and controlled by leaders with rods. Slowly, they all got their ration of maize and peanut butter. Our volunteers helped to provide seed for vegetables, especially spinach, which was so badly needed in their diet. Each had a little garden near their huts.

Sr Bartholomew, who was in her sixties, decided to help some of the men to acquire a bit of English. Without it their chances of getting work were nil. She had some success.

At this time, the great AIDS epidemic had started. Bishop Slattery asked Sister Ancilla to start a programme in the diocese to create awareness and, in the simplest possible way, to explain the dangers of unprotected sex. Many of the rural men who migrated to Jo'burg to work in the mines and were miles away from their wives and families for months acquired AIDS – often without knowing it – and returned to infect their wives. The ANC were in denial about AIDS and said it was another example of oppression to stop black people having sex. Even Mbeki, who was a very learned man, when he became president, made the most naive and embarrassing remarks to minimise the scourge of AIDS.

Eventually we managed to get funds to build a church near the convent in Lulekani. Through Matthew's zeal and work, we started to build up a new community of Catholics. I have always admired the moral strength and spiritual courage of African women. They seemed to get so much fulfilment from gospel values and the liturgy, as well as belonging to sodalities. My long-time MSC friend Fr Dick Broderick, who had ended a much-deserved sabbatical, decided to spend some time working with the refugees in Lulekani. Dick had done trojan work as a missionary in the diocese before joining the Lumko Institute, which he transferred to Jo'burg. He was also Regional Superior. He was going to live in a hut with the refugees, but we persuaded him to compromise. He lived in the sacristy of our church, which we adapted with a shower and toilet. He had his main meal with the Sisters.

He spent many hours just talking, listening to and befriending the refugees. Only a very small number were Catholic. Dick and I spent time discussing the Portuguese colonisers. It seemed to us they came at the very bottom of the lot. They spent hundreds of years in Mozambique without in any way empowering them with the gospel message, or even basic hospitals and education. Only a few of the refugees were literate. Those they did baptise they made take Portuguese names, as they said their own names were only fit for dogs! When eventually they were forced to give independence, they sabotaged factories and burnt their homes. What a disaster our so-called Catholic European countries have been in bringing the good news of Christ to poor nations. After a year, Dick returned to Jo'burg to start a new ministry to empower people.

Sundays were very busy. I drove to Namakgale for Mass at nine a.m., a journey which took one and a half hours. After a cup of tea with Matthew, we drove 8 miles to Lulekani, which was at the end of a different homeland, and the locals spoke Shangaan. It was wonderful to see this community grow. When we got the site for the church and convent, there was one massive round boulder which we rolled into a corner, and we got an outdoor statue of Our Lady to place on top of it. The people planted bougainvillea around it. After Mass, the whole congregation moved to this grotto to sing a hymn to Our Lady.

While the bishop was alive, I drove back to the presbytery and we often went out to parishioners' homes for barbecues or lunch. He loved company, conversation and friendship. After a rest, it was time for Sunday school for the white children. With the help of volunteer catechists we prepared them for the sacraments. I usually took the confirmation class. We had evening Mass at 6 p.m., followed by tea and little refreshments, all prepared by the congregation. It was a great opportunity to meet all of them. It was early to bed on Sunday nights.

A word about the climate. I do not know what the meteorological reason was, but we had the hottest climate in South Africa. After the evening news on TV, a lengthy weather forecast was given for the whole country. Nearly always, Phalaborwa was top of the pops. During the height of summer it soared to over 40°C. Fr Kelly had a second-hand air conditioner in the bedroom and one in the sitting room. Unfortunately, they made as much noise as a tractor. I used to put it on before I went to bed but had to turn it off to get to sleep. In the middle of the night I woke up sweating, even though I had an overhead fan and nothing on. I sometimes put the air conditioner on for half an hour before trying to go to sleep again. But the good news was that during the three months of winter it was perfect. If I had control of some thermostat in the sky, I could not improve on it.

Rainfall was most important to South Africans, especially the farmers. We got the minimum. One year we had drought with not a drop of rainfall for nine months. The poor Africans lost their cattle, their most treasured possession, and they could not grow their vital maize crop. Drinking and household water came from sixty miles away, from a lake near Blyde River Canyon. It was released into Olifants River, which brought it near Phalaborwa, where it was purified. One day it rained. Everyone stopped to look at this precious element fall down from the sky. When I returned to the UK, I often spoke about this during baptism – water, the source of life, and the pouring of it, the symbol of Christ's life.

Shortly after I came to Phalaborwa, Bishop Slattery asked me to be his vicar general. Although we were still only an infant diocese, with a small number of priests, it meant more responsibilities and work. This was mostly meetings with his consultors, and he asked me to take responsibility for all transport of priests. When he was away from the diocese, I had to spend time with his secretary in the diocesan office. If priests had a problem with the bishop, I was the one who tried to help.

In 1983, President Botha came up with a new idea to shore up the failing apartheid system. There was a so-called New Constitution in which coloureds and Indians would be granted the vote for their own racially segregated – and powerless – chambers.

Around the same time, 15,000 anti-apartheid delegates met in Cape Town to form the United Democratic Front. This UDF became a proxy for the ANC, and two years of strikes, protests and boycotts followed. The world watched the government's reaction on TV as apartheid troops and police beat and shot unarmed Africans. An increasingly desperate Botha offered to release Mandela 'if he renounces violence'. Mandela replied: 'I am surprised by the conditions that the government wants to impose. I am not a man of violence. It was only when all forms of resistance were no longer open to us that we turned to armed struggle. Let Botha renounce violence.' At the same time, the ultra-right Conservative Party was winning support; also a neo-Nazi movement called AWB was darkly muttering about civil war.

The political scene took a new turn when South African businessmen, mostly Afrikaaners, flew to Senegal to meet an

ANC team headed by Thabo Mbeki. A joint statement said they wanted a negotiated settlement with the ANC. In 1988, Mandela was rushed to hospital suffering from tuberculosis. When he got better, he did not return to Pollsmoor Prison but moved to a prison warden's cottage in a small prison in Paarl. It was from here that he was released on that famous Sunday.

I was most lucky to have for four years the company of retired Bishop John Durkin, MSC. Having been ordained a priest in 1937, he volunteered to work in New Guinea with German MSCs. The War had started when he and Bill and Michael Murphy set sail on 8 December from Liverpool on the Mauritania – a brand new ship that was being taken to the USA for troop transport with only a few passengers on board. They spent Christmas in the USA and met in San Francisco to get a liner for Sydney, then to Port Moresby and finally Rabaul, New Guinea. In 1942, the Japanese invasion of New Guinea took place. John Durkin, Bill Cadogan and Bill O'Connell were taken into a concentration camp. Fr Murphy was beheaded and Fr Culhane was shot. The only items they were allowed to take with them to prison were a Bible and a complete works of Shakespeare. As John said to me, 'This gave us a great love for scripture and the literature of the Bard.' They were half-starved and if it were not for some Sisters who brought some food and left it near the wire where they could get it, they would not have survived. He said to me once, 'Who would have thought that we would have come through the prisoner-of-war camp? For a few years our families had no account of us. All the odds were against us. But we never gave up hope.' On 15 August 1945, the war ended and they were released and returned to Ireland to convalesce.

We had started our missionary effort in South Africa in 1950, and both Bill Cadogan and John Durkin were seasoned missionaries to lead it. John Durkin was the first Prefect Apostolic, and ten years later was consecrated the first bishop of the diocese of Tzaneen. I have already mentioned some of the great work of our missionaries under the leadership of Bishop Durkin for over twenty years.

In the early 1980s, John was diagnosed with cancer and resigned and came to retire in Phalaborwa. He got up every morning at 6 a.m. and spent time in meditation and Mass. In spite of the heat in Phalaborwa, he used to like to go to Namakgale to hear confession. He wrote in his diary, 'I have always found the confessions a great joy, a source of profound humility when I hear people pour out their hearts begging God for mercy. And the many things I did not hear or understand correctly, the good Lord did and I was able to assure them that with effort and God's grace they could do better in future.' In a lighter vein, one person said to him that he did not have any real big sins, only trashy ones, so he said, 'All trash must be thrown into the rubbish bin.'

He loved celebrations and jubilees and had this to say about them: 'They are good and fulfil a human need to affirm and be affirmed on the pilgrim way. They fulfil spiritual need in making us climb the mountain, survey the countryside and look into the horizon and even strain our vision. It is good to be alive on such occasions.'

I have always been very vocal in my conviction that priests should take time off. The busier the life of a priest, the more necessary this is. In his early years as a bishop, Hugh Slattery suffered from what is called executive burnout. It took him some time in the USA to recover. I have been fortunate that I find golf so helpful to unwind, so I was extremely lucky that the Rio Tinto mine created a championship course out of the bushveld. Because of the heat, all the fairways had to be irrigated with waste water from the mine every day during summer. The course shared a fence with the Kruger National Park. There was an electrified fence, but this did not always keep wildlife out. Elephants have no respect for any fence, electrified or otherwise. Warthogs burrowed under the wire and came in. Other animals enlarged these openings and found their way in to eat some grass not available in Kruger Park. Lions somehow made their way in occasionally. Large signs which said, 'Beware of hippos and crocs' were not enough to deter us!

I had a wonderful stroke of luck when Ferghal Purcell from

Ennis came to be manager of the golfing complex, as well as recreational facilities for the mine. He and his wife Helen and their three boys were my special family friends. He had his pick-up truck rigged with powerful arc lights so that at night it was a real treat to drive through the golf course and see so much wildlife. The biggest surprise was the hippos, who left the water for the night's grazing. It was amazing how their little fat legs could carry their huge bodies so fast. No wonder that they have killed so many Africans. In the spring, the very many impala deer started to give birth, with the horrible hyenas not far away hoping for a very nice meal. There were massive porcupines that came out at night. The warthogs had retreated to their burrows, which they entered backwards so they could defend themselves with their dangerous tusks. The many troops of baboons had taken refuge in the branches of trees.

Ferghal and I played in fourball competitions every Saturday. They had a unique facility on the course: every two holes had taps of refrigerated water, so I carried a can and filled it up at each tap. In South Africa, it is customary to stop after nine holes for some liquid refreshments, hot or cold. You take your place for the second nine. After the match there are some social drinks. If you were to neglect this considerable intake of liquid in the 40-plus temperature, it could cause serious problems of dehydration. You also need lots of sun protection on exposed skin. Once, when I got back to the presbytery, I felt that my back was sore. In the mirror I realised that the sun had burnt me through my shirt.

I sometimes tried to sneak in nine holes during the week, but it was difficult to relax when you were afraid a lion or leopard was watching you from thick undergrowth, especially when you saw the impala deer looking quite alert and ready to run. When I got back to the UK, I got a cutting from the paper telling of some Germans who were playing golf, and some others following taking photos. At one green very near the perimeter fence there was an elephant which charged through the fence, killing one of the photographers. They are, of course, one of the most dangerous and unpredictable of all wildlife.

Sporting sanctions hurt South Africa as much as economic sanctions. They started their own golfing tournament called the Sunshine Circuit, mostly for South African and Zimbabwean golfers. A few European golfers broke the sanction. Phalaborwa Golf Club was the most exotic venue for the tour because of its wildlife backdrop for TV. It was there I first saw a seventeen-year-old Ernie Els, who became famous as 'the Big Easy' because of his elegant swing.

After a few efforts to get a suitable person to cook for us, we were fortunate to get a black lady called Maria. She had been working with an Afrikaaner family, so her knowledge of English was poor at the start. She kept the presbytery spotless, as well as doing laundry and cooking lunch from Monday to Friday. Sr Eileen in Tzaneen, who made wonderful soda bread, gave me the recipe, and having got all the necessary ingredients, Maria gradually made beautiful soda bread for the bishop and myself.

You have to live in Africa to realise how much Africans fear snakes – maybe they have good reason. When my niece Imelda was with me she left a plastic snake in my wardrobe, which I only found months later. I should have known better but I played a trick on poor Maria – unusual for me to do practical jokes! Before I went out in the morning, I put the plastic snake under my pillow and left a note in Afrikaans 'Passup vir die slang' ('beware of the snake'). When I returned later, I got a terrible shock. Maria was on the couch saying she was going to die. She had thought the snake was real. She was not as bad as she pretended, but she wanted compensation. I agreed to give her a new watch. She seemed to get better slowly. I learnt my lesson.

Fr Kelly built a very fine presbytery with three bedrooms en suite, and an outside hut which served as a bedroom. We had many visitors who wanted to stay overnight before entering the Kruger Park. I became quite an expert in doing barbecue, which was a way of preparing a meal for them. I was fortunate in having the only Irish woman in Phalaborwa working as manager of the butcher's shop. She insisted on giving me the best. South Africa is famous for its very large sausage, which is called 'boerewors' (farmer's sausage). It made barbecues very tasty.

At the beginning of 1989, Mandela wrote to President Botha calling for negotiations. The intransigent Botha – now being threatened with sanctions by President Bush – had no room left for manoeuvre. When he suffered a stroke, the party rushed to remove him, replacing him with F. W. de Klerk. At first, de Klerk said he was opposed to majority rule, but he started by unbanning the ANC and other organisations. One Saturday afternoon, as I returned from golf and was sitting for a while with Bishop Durkin watching South African rugby, the commentator, speaking in Afrikaans, said there was breaking news. Mandela would be released on Sunday. Bishop Durkin refused to believe me. But it was true: the next day, on 11 February 1990, Nelson and Winnie walked free while the whole world watched. Things began to move fast. There was a backlash from the right wing Nazi-style Afrikaaners, who threatened no surrender and all-out warfare if necessary.

By a strange coincidence, on the day that Nelson Mandela walked out from jail a free man, some African men were hell-bent on murder. A headmaster of a school in Venda was ambushed on his way home from an errand of mercy. He had taken his sister-in-law and her sick son to the doctor. The reason for his murder was that Benedict Daswa was opposed to witchcraft.

Benedict was born in Venda. During school holidays he stayed with his uncle in Johannesburg so that he could find work. He became friendly with Catholic men and became interested in the Catholic faith. When he returned to Venda he was instructed and was baptised in 1963, taking the name Benedict. He trained as a primary teacher, eventually becoming principal.

He was known for his generosity and care for the disadvantaged. Those unable to pay small school fees he let work in vegetable gardens on Saturdays to earn the money. He was always helping priests and catechists in the parish, especially in working with the youth.

In the latter part of 1989 there was exceptional rainfall accompanied by severe lightning which caused some huts to be set on fire. The Africans did not want to know the natural causes of lightning, believing that some human agent was responsible – some witch. The local leader decided that a traditional healer must be consulted. These demand large fees: people must pay five rand each.

Benedict was brave enough to argue against and oppose this burden on poor people. He tried to give a natural explanation for lightning. He tried to say to them that witchcraft could not be responsible. This made the leaders very angry and they decided to murder Benedict. On his way home from the doctor they blocked the road and when he got out of his car they started stoning him. He managed to escape and, though bleeding and injured, he ran across a soccer pitch to find refuge in a hut. When the mob arrived they challenged the owner, indicating that they would kill her if she did not tell them where Benedict was hiding.

Hearing their threat, Benedict came out, and then asked why they wanted to kill him. A man with a huge knobkerrie came forward. Benedict had time to say the prayer that St Stephen said when he was being stoned: 'God, into your hands I commend my spirit.' A fatal blow crushed his skull.

At his funeral Mass, Fr Jimmy Stubbs, John Finn, Donie McCarthy and Fr Thobela wore red vestments convinced that Benedict died a martyr's death.

From the time of his death, local people recognised his Christian heroism and looked on him as a role model and as a devoted husband and father of eight children, the youngest of whom was born after Benedict's death.

About ten years ago Bishop Hugh Slattery had started the formal process to promote his beatification. He worked tirelessly at this, seeing it as a possible spiritual help to fight the scourge of witchcraft that bedevils most African cultures. He has been helped by Fr André Bohas, who spent months in Rome promoting the cause.

It has all been worthwhile. Pope Francis has formally recognised him as a martyr. He was beatified on Sunday, 13 September 2015 at his new shrine in Tshitanini in Venda by

Cardinal Angelo Amato. It was a wonderful celebration with bishops, priests and an enormous open-air congregation.

* * *

Every three years we got a holiday back in Ireland. I always managed to get some priests to do locum for me. However, I had one painful unscheduled trip back to Ireland. One day I had a letter from my younger sister Mary's husband. Anthony said that he had bad news for me. Mary had been diagnosed with an inoperable brain tumour. She had only a few months to live. They had seven children; the youngest was only eight years old. I went back to Kilcrohane to be with her and her family for a month. Imelda, the oldest, had taken on the responsibility of mum to her siblings. When some afternoons I asked Mary if we could go for a spin in her car she agreed. But when I asked her where we should go, it was nearly always a visit to the graveyard. This was so difficult for me. She told me one day, 'I don't want you staying at home and watching me die. I think you should go back to Africa.' This I did. I will never forget the night before I left. Mary was the one who was closest to me. Knowing I would never see her again was beyond human words to describe. She died before Christmas and her requiem Mass was on Christmas Eve. I was not able to be there. I was told it was the saddest funeral ever in Kilcrohane. All the MSCs in South Africa gathered with me later for a memorial Mass.

A few months later, Bishop Durkin began to feel unwell and it was diagnosed that the cancer had returned. He still kept to his routine of getting up early for Mass and saying the fifteen decades of the rosary during the day. He had a lovely sense of humour, telling me one morning, 'As I put my vestments away this morning, a glance at the statue of the Sacred Heart reminded me that I should pray for one of my fellow priests, and, indeed, I did, asking the Sacred Heart to remember him. I must add that the person in question often annoys me no end. And as I was in full flight, beseeching the Sacred Heart to be kind to him, I found myself saying as a conclusion: "and tell that fellow to cut out the codding and stop the jackassing." When I realised how my prayer had ended, I burst out laughing. Lucky for me there was nobody around to hear or see my goings-on. I thought I saw a wry smile on the face of the statue. But that may be the result of my own exuberance.'

The morning came in September when I would take him on the long journey to hospital in Pretoria. We decided to leave at 11 a.m. Normally, he would be ready and waiting a half-hour beforehand, but at 11 o'clock he was still in his room. I then realised what he was going through. Eventually, we set off. For the five-hour journey hardly a word was spoken. Irishmen have difficulty in expressing their feelings, I thought. Tigers don't cry. All sorts of emotions, feelings and thoughts must have been racing through his mind, but he had no way of sharing them. Is this one of the consequences of celibacy? Eventually, we got to the Catholic Hospital run by the Blue Sisters. I left him in their tender loving care. I would not see him alive again.

On the journey back the next day, I began to realise that as Bishop Slattery was away, I would have to start to make the funeral arrangements. My first task was to get permission from the Tzaneen Town Council to have the grave near the little cathedral. Someone I baptised when first in Duiwelskloof, Aldo Rech, who was now a lawyer, helped to get the permission. I wrote to the bishop's favourite niece, Sr Angela Durkin, in Dublin, but he was dead by the time she arrived. She stayed in his room in the presbytery, and it was most helpful for me that she had time to go through his papers and sort out what was personal and family, and what was diocesan. The latter mostly pertained to the selection process of his successor. The first three candidates were rejected and of the second three Bishop Hugh was chosen. I was surprised that he kept these papers and decided to burn them. At a glance, I discovered people's views are so subjective as to who is suitable or not. It helped Sr Angela to start her grieving process for her beloved uncle. I had to inform all of the bishops in South Africa. A few were able to come to the funeral and some sent delegates.

The African Catholics would have looked on the bishop as

'spiritual chief'. Some oxen would have to be slain and eaten after the funeral. All the requirements for this meal had to be organised. The grave was dug beside the grotto at the front of the cathedral church. The bishop's very old and trusted friend, Fr Dick Scriven MSC, came out for the funeral. We received his body into the church the evening before and had a quiet Mass for MSCs, religious and friends. Bishop Hugh returned that evening, and together with some bishops and priests he conducted an outdoor Mass. Some 1,000 African faithful attended, as well as several hundred from the white parishes. As usual, the African people contributed with their vibrant and enthusiastic singing. The bishop had a wonderful reliance on divine providence. He talked about the many times he had no money for all the needs of the diocese. Like our founder, he would immediately have recourse to Mary. He said help used to come from some unexpected quarters. Now his remains would rest near the grotto of Mary. The MSCs and the bishop gave me permission to select some monument for his grave. I have a terrible dislike for those massive headstones so common in front of parish churches in Ireland. The manager of the mine in Phalaborwa got a huge boulder for me. We had the top of it dressed with the bishop's name and motto on it. The bishop was a rock on which Christ helped to build a little bit of his church in this corner of Africa. May he rest in peace.

His successor, Hugh Slattery, took many new and necessary initiatives. One of the most important was to have a pastoral and development centre for the diocese. An Italian man left his farm and big avocado orchard to the diocese. Hugh slowly started to build a centre for the training of new catechists and for meetings and weekend courses to empower the new communities to take on the responsibilities of being the church in their area. Later, he started a new 'Called to Serve' programme. Its special emphasis was on the formation of lay leaders, and it ran over two years. They identified some of the main issues facing the young church. Firstly, one in three mothers is HIV-positive; as a consequence, many children are orphaned. Unemployment is still 60% in rural areas. The indigenous churches offer physical healing and are attractive to some Catholics. Lastly, witchcraft still controls the lives of many who live in rural areas.

Because of the lack of vocations in Ireland, very few new missionaries were available. There were few African vocations, and vocations to the MSC in South Africa were most disappointing. Many who came to the novitiate and seminary left to get jobs. The first two to be ordained worked in the diocese for a couple of years before leaving to get married. Bishop Hugh began to look to other orders to help. St Patrick's Missionaries were the first to offer assistance, sending several priests. He went to Kerala in India, and got some priests and Sisters. The French Province of MSC in Africa sent some very seasoned missionaries; Australia also helped. Later he got help from the SVD Order. He was also successful in getting many orders of Sisters to send volunteers for different ministries.

The negotiating process from 1990 to 1994 was fragile, and at many times a descent into chaos looked very likely. Obstacles included violence linked to a sinister element in the security forces, threats of civil war from heavily armed ultra-right-wingers, and a war of attrition in Natal with the Inkatha Freedom Party.

But in my humble opinion, the negotiations were saved by an Afrikaaner housewife, Mrs Retha Harmse. Communist countries were publicly seen to be more sympathetic to the ANC cause than the non-communist countries. A freedom party formed, calling themselves the Communist Party; it was led by a very charismatic person called Chris Hani. When all the parties were unbanned, he returned to South Africa and took up residence in a white suburb of Jo'burg. On Good Friday, 1993, Chris was returning from the supermarket in his car with his daughter. This is what happened, in the words of Retha Harmse:

As I drove towards Mr Hani's home, I saw a red car pull behind Hani's car in his driveway. A tall thin man got out and walked to the open door of Mr Hani's car. I saw the blond man lift a gun and pull the trigger twice. By that time I had gone a short way past the house. I stopped my car and watched the blond man walk over to Mr Hani as he lay on the ground. He calmly lifted the gun again, and at point-blank range pulled the trigger twice more. I can still hear the ring of the shots in my ears. The blond man returned to his car and reversed and drove away. I do not know what possessed me. I reversed my car and got his registration number. I kept repeating it over and over so I wouldn't forget it. I sped home. I was so upset to see a man shot down in cold blood. I ran up the driveway screaming out the registration number. Within seconds I had told the police the make, colour and number of that car.

Shortly afterwards the police arrested this man with an accomplice. They also found the smoking gun. If that lady had not done what she did, there was no possible way that the African population would be convinced that Chris Hani was not assassinated by SAP (the South African Police). Nelson Mandela was asked to go on TV to calm the situation. Tutu begged, 'Do not let this tragic event trigger reprisals.' The days of mass mourning were mixed with frenzied rioting and massive looting. There were 26,000 security personnel deployed for the funeral, where 70,000 assembled. Singing, talking, with many eulogies, and with a special oration from Nelson Mandela. The peace process was saved thanks to an ordinary Christian housewife.

Life in the presbytery was different after the bishop's death. For the next six years, I would be alone apart from the few visitors that came to stay for one or two nights. As I write this in 2014, there was a news item after Christmas about a priest who went shopping and was found three days later, dead in his car. No one had missed him. Like most secular clergy, he was living alone, albeit in an urban parish. There was an article in *The Tablet* about this. One priest remarked that he had experienced terrible loneliness, especially at times 'after Midnight Mass in my parish – everyone had gone. I cleared up, locked the church then walked to the empty presbytery. I got a cup of hot milk and thought – this is hardly a life.' The child abuse scandals of recent years had made priests feel less welcome to visit local families at home. In the past, they felt respected and looked up to. One priest felt that priests were not prepared in seminaries to handle intense isolation. Many priests felt that mandatory celibacy is the prime cause of priests' loneliness. However it is my belief that only as a celibate could I have done what I did.

During ten years I had only two health problems. The first was rather unusual. One Saturday morning I could not get out of bed. Bishop Durkin was still with me and sent for the doctor. He advised me to go to Pretoria Hospital. Fr Sean Laffan came with his station wagon and a mattress in the back. I travelled the five hours on the mattress. It being Saturday evening, the consultant was on the golf course, and when he eventually entered the public ward, he felt like entertaining the patients by shouting, 'Have you been on the drink again Fr Daly?' He diagnosed my problem as a severe inner ear problem causing acute vertigo. Medication soon enabled me to go home, and after a year the problem disappeared.

The second happened when I was alone in the bishop's house. During the night, I had the most severe pain. I lay on the floor, twisting and turning until after a few hours it stopped. Back in Phalaborwa on Sunday night it happened again. Sister Ancilla said it was a kidney stone. I drove myself to Pretoria and the consultant said the stone was stuck in a duct between the kidney and the bladder. When he said he would have to insert a camera and basket to fish it out, it brought a tear to my eye. Fortunately, I had a general anaesthetic. When I was told that the pain of a kidney stone is like the pain of childbirth and mentioned that to some women, they sort of sneered at me, almost saying, 'How little you know about childbirth.'

I had a phone call from Fr Michael Crowley. He was very excited: he had just met Nelson Mandela. There were quite a number of Portuguese who were worried about the future of their business and commercial investments in the event of a black government. They asked to meet Nelson Mandela for reassurance and Fr Michael was invited to go with them. After a meal in the Cape Sun Hotel, all lined up to meet Mandela, who sat behind a small table. He shook hands with all the guests as they processed along in front of the great man. 'When my turn came – I was dressed in my best clericals – he stood and shook hands. "Thank you, sir," I said, "for being so gracious." "You are a priest," he said. "I will always show respect for a priest." He went on to praise the Church's support in the dismantling of apartheid. Having mentioned several bishops, he went on to mention Fr Brendan Long, who used to visit him on Robben Island. He said, "This man visited when few others did."'

On an unrelated note, one day I received a phone call from Fr Michael telling me that he had located my watch, stolen by the caddy. One of his parishioner's garden boys had a watch, which he showed her. Fr Daly's name was on the back. I told Fr Michael to buy it, which he did. I was reunited with my sentimental watch from Tamworth again. But it was not a happy ending. A week later I jumped into a swimming pool with the watch on my hand. It stopped, never to go again.

In their madness, the apartheid government even passed a law forbidding sex and marriage between whites and non-whites. It was called, strangely, by the name of the Immorality Act. The ironic fact was that most convicted under this act were Afrikaaners. There was one case of one of their ministers, Rev. Odendaal, who while involved in sex with a black woman had his pants stolen and was forced to walk home trying to invent some cock and bull story for his wife.

Archbishop Tutu made a most perceptive remark when he said, 'The Afrikaaners look on us as human but not as human as they are.' They called black people 'kaffirs', which meant 'infidels'. This was the abusive term frequently used. Nadine Gordimer, the well-known South African writer, tells us that when she was a volunteer with the Red Cross in Jo'burg, she saw this white medical officer stitch, without any form of anaesthetic, the gaping wounds of black miners caused by falling rocks underground. He grinned at her, saying, 'They don't feel like we do.'

When Bishop Hugh and Bishop Paul, a black bishop, went into a country café for a cup of coffee with two Kiltegan priests, the owner asked them to leave. Bishop Hugh tried to remonstrate, at which he got down a whip used for beating cattle and threatened to flog all of them unless they left quickly. Near Phalaborwa, a child of a black worker on a farm started to come and play with the son of the farmer. The farmer warned him not to come near his child. The next time he came, he shot him dead. One of our priests, driving to Jo'burg, gave a lift to a black lady who sat in the front with the driver. A police car stopped them and insisted she sit on the outside of the pick-up truck. It was raining heavily. They followed them with laughing faces until she was completely drenched and then they drove away. If I may give one more incident of wanton cruelty: one of our catechists was cycling to Messina to join in celebrating the Holy Week and Easter ceremonies. At the advance of an oncoming car some cattle crossed the road, forcing them to stop for a few minutes. Three young Afrikaaners got out and beat up the poor black catechist. He spent Holy Week in hospital in Messina. These stories give you some idea what it was like to be black during the apartheid era.

When I reflect on my life, I think how gracious Providence has been to me. I have always been fascinated by wildlife. Now, for ten years, I was living next door to the best-maintained wildlife park in the world. A narrow strip of land between Mozambique and South Africa 250 miles long with scores of elephants, all of the Big Five – elephant, rhinoceros, buffalo, lion and leopard – as well as thousands of other game roaming freely across the savannah. It has tarred roads between ten rest camps – all strategic vantage points, most near rivers. There are many dirt roads giving access to every corner of the park. Being a resident, I got in for a nominal fee. I must have visited the park fifty times. I got a present of a camcorder and made some interesting videos. It was like fishing; one day you were lucky and saw many of the Big Five. It was two years before I first saw the fastest animal on earth, the cheetah. The leopard is also a very shy animal, living a solitary life except when they have cubs. But they are high profile when they drag a kill almost their own weight up a tree to be enjoyed at leisure. They also go up trees for siestas. It very occasionally happens that a very sharp-eyed tourist will spot them there. Once one car stops, perhaps a hundred will follow suit. Seeing a leopard gives the same bragging rights as a fisherman catching a big fish!

When South Africa got a new government, black people were no longer restricted and had access to all amenities. They could now visit the Kruger Park. As a special treat to Maria, who came to cook for us, I took her into the park one morning. Shortly after entering, we saw a huge herd of impala deer. These, with the springbok, are the most beautifully structured animals. But to my surprise, I heard her mutter, in her own language, 'nama', which means 'meat'. Beauty is in the eye of the beholder. She only saw them as potential meat.

I had one scary experience when Bill Clarkson and I went into the park. On a dirt road I got a puncture. According to the rules, we were supposed to stay inside until some other car came along. They would have to report this at the next rest camp, where they would come to our aid. This could take hours. We decided to take a chance, so while Bill stood sentry I changed the wheel in record time.

Outside the Kruger's western flank are many private reserves with safari lodges on large tracts of land with most kinds of wildlife. They have luxury accommodation and food. One of them was owned by a Catholic family, who travelled all the way to Phalaborwa on Sunday evening for Mass. It gave the three nuns a great thrill to take them there very early in the morning with the overnight guests. We would start with a walk with two tame elephants and two young lions, as well as a huge dog. After an hour of leisurely walking, we had a big breakfast with the guests on the veranda of the lodge. The tame animals were the result of getting them when they were little and orphaned. One of the lions and a large warthog were bosom pals, having grown up together. When lions are over two years old, they become dangerous, so he was moved to an enclosure where they bred lions for sale to zoos. The warthog was devastated. He smelled his way to the wire perimeter of the enclosure but could not get in. However, he persevered and eventually found an opening.

When he got in, the other lions had him for breakfast. It was a case of identity crisis – he thought he was a lion, but he was only a warthog.

One place in the world not suitable for a wedding is Phalaborwa in the height of summer. One such wedding I did was exceptionally hot. During my homily, I tried to explain the little candle ceremony, which they are not familiar with in South Africa. I said, 'After you exchange your vows, you will light the middle candle as a sign of two becoming one.' As I glanced over at the outer candles I stopped. The wax had got so soft they had dropped, forming horseshoes. First there was a giggle, then loud laughter. I got on with the ceremony of marriage without the candle ritual.

* * *

After intense negotiations for four years, Mandela called for a date for elections. It was fixed for 27 April 1994. There were 11,000 South African monitors, as well as 5,000 international observers to safeguard a free and safe election. Three of these observers from Dublin stayed with us for a week. I don't think they were very gospel-hungry, and going to Mass was not high on their agenda. I took them out to see what we had done for the Mozambican refugees. I also invited them to come with me to Mass in the township. They were amazed at the joyous enthusiasm and singing and dancing of the black congregation. I heard them whisper that the church had helped a lot to bring about a new day for South Africa.

I was so proud to be able to vote in the first historic free election for all the people. Some of the scenes on TV were unbelievable. People waited in queues for hours and hours; some elderly women were taken to polling stations sitting in wheelbarrows. The voting went on for a couple of days. Apart from some logistical problems with ballot papers, it went off amazingly peacefully and well. In the words of Nelson Mandela: 'The images of South Africans going to the polls that day are burnt in my memory. Great lines of patient people snaking through the dust roads and streets; old women who had waited half a century to cast their vote saying that they felt like humans for the first time.'

Dervla Murphy has written some very good travel books and she spent two years travelling into every nook and cranny of South Africa on a bicycle before the elections. She was in Cape Town on 27 April and later, on 28, she wrote:

> Something mysterious has happened within South Africa during the past 48 hours. Extreme tension has been replaced by an extraordinary calm. A deep calm that can be felt as though it were a climate change – physically felt, in the body as well as the soul. And this phenomenon is nationwide. Since 25th April, there has been an eerie lack of crime.

A police colonel remarked to her, 'I've visited all the polling stations. There is so much goodwill going around you can feel it.' Cartoonists and columnists were beginning to mock those whites who crammed their cellars, garages and garden sheds with every kind of food.

Dervla goes on to relate a conversation with a seventeen-year-old white South African:

> My Dad was a racist five years ago; now he is not. Well, what I mean is he can take a black President now. I don't mean he will ever have black friends. Mandela made it easy. Even people who go on about him being a commie really trust him. You have to. You would be screwed up yourself if you couldn't see he is a good guy.

Dervla Murphy went on to say: 'Recalling last year's atmosphere, the Afrikaaners' placid acceptance of change astonishes me – not surprisingly, given its past, present and future, it is the most confusing country I have ever travelled through.' She goes on to quote from a conversation with a former right-wing supporter: 'Now everything is different. We needn't hate each other any more.'

The result of the election gave the ANC 62% of the vote. Mandela was happy that they did not get two thirds, which would have given them the sole right to write the new constitution. It took another two years to bring this about. It was said that it is one of the most progressive constitutions in the world. It incorporates an extensive bill of rights.

I still have regrets that I did not drive all the way to Pretoria for the most historic event, the inauguration ceremony of new President Nelson Mandela on 10 May. The outdoor ceremonies took place with the lovely sandstone amphitheatre background of the Union Building. For decades, this had been the seat of white supremacy; now it was the site of a rainbow gathering of different colours and nations. In his speech, Nelson said:

> Today, all of us do, by our presence here, confer glory and hope to new-born liberty … We who have been outlaws for so long have been given the rare privilege to be the host of the nations of the world on our own soil … Never, never and never again shall it be that this beautiful land will again experience the oppression of one another … The sun shall never set on so glorious a human achievement. Let freedom reign. God bless Africa.

His later reflections display his deeply Christian formation:

> Our deepest fear
> is not that we are inadequate
> Our deepest fear is that we are
> powerful beyond measure.
> It is our light, not our darkness
> that most frightens us.
> We ask ourselves
> Who am I to be brilliant,
> gorgeous, talented and fabulous?
> Actually who are you NOT to be?
> You are a child of God,
> your playing small doesn't save the world.

There's nothing enlightened about shrinking
so that other people won't feel insecure
around you.
We were born to make manifest
the glory of God
that is within us.
It's not just in some of us,
it's in EVERYONE.
And as we let our own light shine
we unconsciously give other people
permission to do the same.
As we are liberated from our own fear
our presence automatically liberates others.

It is no surprise that your siblings' funerals will be time to mourn their loss. My eldest sister Nora got cancer on the eve of her eightieth birthday. I was able to get home and be with her during the last week of her life. I used to watch by night, giving the family much-needed rest. It gave her comfort that I was with her during the long nights. If I were to sum up her life, it would be that she was generosity personified – her whole life was a gift to others.

Later on, James, who started doing man's work on the farm at the age of fifteen and had the tragedy of losing his wife Mary during her third childbirth, died suddenly. There wasn't time to go to the funeral. May they rest in peace.

During my time in Phalaborwa, the Missionaries of the Sacred Heart organised a pilgrimage to the Holy Land. Gus O'Brien, Jimmy Stubbs and I went with them. I have fond memories of the sacred places in Jerusalem, but the memory that stands out most was my first glimpse of the Sea of Galilee and, later, going on a boat across to Capernaum and the reading of the relevant scriptures on the calming of the storm; the reading of the Sermon on the Mount from the place it was first preached; later hearing the gospel proclaimed and explained by the great scripture scholar, Fr Jerome Murphy-O'Connor, as we re-enacted the Jewish Passover meal. But there were also the sad memories of seeing the suffering of the people of Palestine. My mind can never understand that the Jewish people, who have suffered more than any other nationality, should have so little sympathy for the people whose land they have taken over. Any dealings with officials left us all sharing the words 'palpable arrogance'.

Because Matthew, my indispensable helper, had done so much for the people of God and rarely took a break, we gathered money to send him on a pilgrimage to the Holy Land. He had never been on a plane, and on his return he told us that for the first hour after take-off, he never let go of his firm hold on the seat in front. Eventually, the hostess calmed him down and he enjoyed the flight. It was wonderful to hear him tell his people of his experiences in the Holy Land.

One of the great benefits for us of the new government in South Africa was that they invited the UN Commissioner for Refugees to take responsibility for the Mozambican refugees. As peace had been restored in Mozambique, they offered to assist voluntary repatriation. Quite a number took up this offer. The great day came with a fleet of buses, as well as trucks for the little bits of belongings they had acquired, especially zinc for roofing. Sr Theresa and I accompanied them. We went through the dirt road in Kruger Park. In all my life I have never seen such devastation. All the villages were burnt down and there was not an animal in sight, except the odd small wildlife. The countryside was riddled with landmines.

We came to a destination where they were rebuilding some villages and starting some farming. Some had lost limbs from landmines. It was very emotional to see the joy of the refugees meeting family and friends, and their hopes of building a new life again in their homeland. They were proud to introduce Sr Theresa to their friends, telling them what she did for their little children.

* * *

As I approached my sixty-fifth birthday, and after ten years in Phalaborwa, I decided that I had little more to give. The heat was starting to get me down, as was living alone. I told Bishop Hugh I was resigning as vicar general and I would go back to the UK to do parish work.

First, the black township of Namakgale wanted a special Sunday to say farewell. We started with the usual Mass. After a short break, there was an hour or more of musical entertainment. This always involves some African dancing. There were speeches and then each of the adults danced their way to the front to say goodbye. Some of the elderly ladies wanted a hug. I thought they might smother me. Then there was a gift of money from the whole community. It was a lovely heartfelt experience, both sweet and sad. I was involved in doubling the length of the church, for which they were very grateful.

Next Sunday we had a smaller version in the Lulekani church, and that afternoon in Phalaborwa, after Mass. My friend Ferghal Purcell organised this. I did not realise we would meet again in Ireland. But that is another story.

In my homilies, I have often talked about travelling lightly. We accumulate so much unnecessary baggage. Some even suffer from the addiction of hoarding – almost incurable. At sixty-five, I put all my worldly goods into two small suitcases; I had sent some books on by post beforehand. I flew from Jo'burg to London and on to Cork. It is always nice to go home for Christmas. It brings back memories of times and faces long since gone.

The day after I arrived, the news of a terrible murder spread fast. Just three miles across the bay in Dunmannus, a French lady, Sophie Toscan du Plantier, who had just arrived from Paris to enjoy Christmas in her holiday home, was brutally bludgeoned to death. In this quiet and peaceful corner of west Cork, nothing like this had ever happened in living memory. Sophie du Plantier's murder was never solved, much to the grief of her loving parents. Neither motive nor murder weapon could be found, and the fact that she lay on severely frosty ground for so long had a negative effect on the forensic evidence.

It was a shock to the system to go from the heat of Phalaborwa to winter in west Cork. But it was great to walk along the shore of beautiful Dunmanus Bay. It certainly gave you an appetite for Christmas festivities. Strange how memory works. The donation box in the crib in Kilcrohane Church brought back the painful memory of the Christmas Day when I knelt to pray and took what I thought was a penny to put in the box. But it was the wrong coin. I put all my Christmas money in – a half crown. It seemed like a disaster!

I have said previously how South Africans loved their sport. In 1995, the Rugby World Cup was held in South Africa. In the first round, New Zealand played Ireland in Pretoria. It was the first time that my great hero Jonah Lomu burst onto the sporting scene. He scored two tries that day. Four years later, my nephew got me tickets to see New Zealand play England at Twickenham in the World Cup. To my great joy, Jonah dragged three English players over the line to score the try of the match. I wanted to jump and shout, but seeing the sea of sad English faces around me I thought discretion is the better part of valour. For a few months, rugby was the 'beautiful game'. At the final in Cape Town, Nelson Mandela was wearing the colours of the Springboks and 65,000 people were joyously shouting his name. It was a tremendous moment in the transformation from apartheid to multiracial democracy. Who will forget the moment when he handed the cup to captain Francois Pienaar? 'Sport has the power to change the world – it has the power to unite people in a way that little else does.' So said Mandela later. Pienaar recalled: '"Thank you for what you have done for South Africa," said Mandela. I said to him, "No, Madiba, you have got it wrong. Thank you for what you have done for South Africa," and I felt like hugging him.' What a change.

At the end of January, I got permission to have a three-month sabbatical, which I did with the Redemptorists in Dublin. There were nuns as well as priests on the course. Again, it was time to have some good lecturers and time to catch up on some new books. We had one most enjoyable outing to St Kevin's in Glendalough, with talks on Celtic spirituality as well as outdoor Mass. We went to the Redemptorist House in Belfast for five days. This was a great experience to meet those Catholics and

Protestants who had crossed the religious barrier to meet in shared prayer and friendship. Some Redemptorist priests played a vital role in the peace process.

After the sabbatical, I had a few months of very enjoyable holidays. Being asked where I would like to minster next, I requested to go back to my beloved St Albans, near London, where I had worked in the seventies. I slowly got back to parish life in the UK with Fr Michael Fitzgibbon, Sandy Murray and Pat Coakley.

Part V

———————

When I started this book, I did not want it to be about me. I wanted to use it as a vehicle to reflect on the mounting problems facing the church, a church for which I gave my whole life. I have so many strong opinions about what has gone wrong, and even stronger opinions as to where we should be going. This was the only opportunity for me to get an audience. So the rest of the book will be about my personal reflections, with of course some reference to parish life, which I was to be involved with, and life that was happening around me.

Coming back to a parish after twenty years made me a bit nervous. The majority would have remembered me. Shortly afterwards, Fr Kevin McNamara MSC did a short parish mission. I took him around to visit some of the sick. On one of these visits, the lady asked Fr Kevin to visit the man next door, who had lapsed and whose wife was not well. The man was an Italian called Johnny Brumana. I waited in the car while Kevin went in to see them. It transpired that Johnny told Kevin that he knew a Fr Daly. It was very sad, he said, that many years ago he had called to see me and been told that 'Fr Daly is not with us any more.' He took this to mean I had died. For twenty years I was in his little book with names to be prayed for. When Fr Kevin told him that I was still alive and in the car outside the house, he would not believe him till he came out. His words were, 'Oh my God.' I told him what they should have told him was that I had moved to Tamworth. Johnny and I became great friends and I did both his wife's funeral and, later, his. For many years, he took holy communion to a few people every Sunday on his bicycle, which he still rode although he was in his eighties.

Each of us priests took responsibility for special parish ministries and I took over responsibility for marriage preparation. It happened that an elderly Jesuit priest from Liverpool made himself available to hold marriage talks for couples already married – some for many years. I have never met anyone so experienced in giving marriage talks. He came for three successive years and many of our parishioners availed of these four-night courses. He opened up whole new areas for personal communication – one couple with serious difficulties even found the answers to their problems. Every year we had about forty to fifty engaged couples who wanted to get married. We were so fortunate to have a married couple take them in small groups for two hours one night a week for four weeks.

Only a small number of our couples were both Catholic. Some of the others were baptised, some not. When I told them about the pre-marriage talks, they were not very enthusiastic and often reluctant to attend. I insisted they come to the first night. After that I had no problem. The couple giving the talks were so good, that those attending realised they were getting the recipe for a good marriage. After they did a personality profile for the couples, they spent most of the time talking about communication in marriage: communicating feelings from one heart to another; the importance of listening – not with one ear, but our hearts; knowing that the only person I can change is myself. What was most important was they got the couples sharing their own life experiences – most couples were already living together. There were many laughs as they shared very openly. They spent much time on how they managed conflict and how they made up after rows. The last night, they concentrated on the words of the vows they would make to each other on their wedding day. We ended with a party of cheese and wine.

It never ceased to amaze me that they were reluctant to come to the talks, but when they attended we had difficulty getting them to leave on the last night. They just wanted to keep talking and sharing with each other and the couple giving the talks. They often said, 'We have spent so much time on the trappings of the wedding; these few nights have put into perspective that preparing to have a good marriage is the only important thing.' The couples got different handouts for reflection. I will give one example on listening:

When I ask you to listen …

When I ask you to listen to me and you start giving advice,
you have not done what I asked.
When I ask you to listen to me,
and you begin to tell me that I shouldn't feel that way,
you are trampling on my feelings.
When I ask you to listen to me,
and you feel that you have something to solve my problem,
then you have failed me, strange as that may seem.
Listen! All I ask is that you listen,
not talk, or do; just hear me.
Advice is cheap, and I can do things for myself. I'm not helpless.
You contribute to my fear and weakness.
But when you accept as a simple fact
that I do feel what I feel, no matter how irrational,
then I can stop trying to convince you,
and get on with the business of understanding what's behind my feelings.
Perhaps that's why prayer works, sometimes, for some people,
because God is quiet,
and He doesn't give advice or try to fix things.
He just listens and lets you work it out for yourself.
So please listen and just hear me.
And if you want to talk, wait a minute for your turn, and I'll listen to you.

And when we don't listen …

An apocryphal story, but a good example of what happens when you don't listen … British Navy off the coast of Kerry:

Irish: Please divert your course 15 degrees to the South, to avoid a collision.

British: Recommend you divert your course 15 degrees to the North, to avoid a collision.

Irish: Negative. You need to divert your course 15 degrees to the South to avoid a collision.

British: This is the Captain of a British Navy ship. I say again, divert *your* course.

Irish: Negative. I say again, you will have to divert your course.

British: This is the Aircraft Carrier HMS Britannia. The second largest ship in the British Atlantic Fleet. We are accompanied by three destroyers, three cruisers, and numerous support vessels. I demand that you change your course 15 degrees North, or counter-measures will be undertaken to ensure the safety of this ship.

Irish: We are a lighthouse. Your call.

My niece Mairead and fiancé Dario came to the talks. I married them later in Kilcrohane, West Cork. She sent me a thank-you letter saying that the talks were 'surprisingly helpful'.

Many of the engaged couples got married in many different parts of the world. I must have sent marriage papers to at least twenty different countries. Some got married in our church in St Albans. Over the years, my understanding of a marriage homily changed so much. I was always reminded of the young priest who, maybe foolishly, asked an old woman what she thought of his marriage homily. She said, 'Very good, Father, but I wish I knew as little about marriage as you do.'

The love of marriage is a giving love, or to use a big word, altruistic love. The love that Paul spoke about in his letter to the Corinthians. I challenge every couple to give 100% to each other – an ideal that they may never reach. I repeat what they heard during the pre-marriage talks about quality time for

170

communication, and especially listening to the feelings of their partner. I tell them as they light the one candle, it will take them a long time to become one. But when it happens, it will be awesome. A few times, I have told them the story of my older brother Danny and his late wife Nellie. When she had to go into a home for two years before she died, every day, seven days a week, Danny drove through the road at the back of Curragh Racecourse to the home, some 8 miles away. He spent all afternoon in a large room with the residents, many of whom were quite senile. He went back to make his evening meal. Later, one of his daughters had to drive him back to the home, where he stayed till Nellie went to bed. They were truly one and it was awesome.

Many women's magazines keep on telling couples how to have a wonderful marriage. However, without the giving love that Christ taught us, which often involves some sacrifice, they won't have much success. There are some cases in the animal kingdom where male and female will bond for life. It was sad to read of two giant tortoises in a zoo in Germany who had been together for 115 years. Bibi and Poldi had been living in harmony and begot quite a few offspring. After 115 years they had a furious row. As the zookeeper said, 'We have the feeling that they cannot stand the sight of each other any more.' Bibi had started to bite off bits of her partner's shell. So there was a quick divorce. Even the best marriages can turn turtle!

Some of the TV channels have taken advantage of some travellers' weddings and made programmes called *My Big Fat Gypsy Wedding*. There is an enormous amount of money spent on lavish trappings, especially on some of the outrageous dresses for the bride and bridesmaids. I have done many travellers' weddings and most of them have been heartache. Most English priests would not do a wedding for them unless they conformed to the usual rules of preparation. Lots of them are very well off financially and they vie with each other as to who will have the biggest dress and most lavish wedding. There is very little interest in the church side, and they use it for the photo session. I have waited for up to an hour for the bride to arrive. They have several stretch limousines. On one occasion, the first arrived and when the door opened one bridesmaid was pushed out (because of her massive dress), followed by eight more bridesmaids. Kids run riot up and down the aisle of the church and jump over seats. The men never enter the church, but remain outside smoking and answering mobiles. As I receive their vows, I have to ask the groom to take his hands out of his pockets. Once his mobile went off. For them the serious bit is the many photos afterwards. But I kept on helping them. I think Jesus would have done so. I did have a few very good couples, which helped.

It was very sad when some years later, a family I knew very well and for whom I did some weddings, were convicted of exploiting vulnerable men and compelling them to work as slaves. This family was very well off and were multimillionaires. Why such cruelty and greed? I have visited some travellers in jail for using and selling drugs.

Some priests live to a ripe old age. Others get sick and die much younger. Fr Sandy Murray, who had been on the staff of St Albans, had a stroke at the age of sixty-one. Sandy was Scottish Presbyterian before becoming Catholic as a young man. He later decided he had a vocation to the priesthood and joined the MSCs. At the age of fifty he was ordained. Now the difference of being a secular priest and a religious one was that we took the responsibility of looking after Sandy as an invalid. We were able to create his own flat with his sitting room, disabled toilet and bedroom. He was confined to a wheelchair all day. Carers came in every morning to shower him. He was able to go to the toilet himself and came into us for his meals. He loved TV. He was frustrated he could not properly use a laptop. He had a speech problem, and although his mind was perfect, he could not pick out the words he wanted. His memory was perfect and he could sometimes sing early in the morning. Some wonderful ladies came in to share parish news with him. He was happy as a member of our community.

Fr Pat Coakley left for ministry in Ireland and later in the USA. We were very fortunate to get Fr Danny Cleary, who was on parish mission work from Ireland. He brought great vitality to the parish in liturgy and youth work. We had big numbers for baptism and first communion, but numbers dwindled to half when they were due for confirmation at the age of fifteen. The fall-off in the practice of churchgoing was getting very noticeable. Young priests like Fr Danny had a better chance of communicating with them.

At this time, Fr Fitzgibbon, with the parish finance committee, decided to make our rooms en suite. This was a great comfort. There were new developments in the working and effectiveness of parish councils. Ours was radically renewed.

You might be surprised if I did not mention golf. I applied to join my old club, Mid-Herts, as a five-day member. Mike Ringham and I played on Mondays for the high stakes of £1. On Thursdays, I joined a competition where our names were picked out of a hat, so we had different partners each week. After a shower, there was a social gathering for drinks and much-awaited results. There was lots of fun, especially when the unfortunate booby prize was given for the worst score. This was a most enjoyable afternoon, to which I looked forward every week. I made some very good friends there.

Some were a little nervous of me at first, having never spoken to a Catholic priest, and weren't quite sure how to treat me. When they got to know me, they felt free to ask me questions about religion. They knew that priests heard confession and sometimes made little jokes about it. But deep down I think they were looking for information, which they never got.

The men who ran the competition kept a record of the winnings for the whole year. My big boast was that I won the 'order of merit' one year. Of course, I was accused of having 'outside help', being a priest.

At this time, the greatest scandal ever to happen in the Catholic Church was slowly but unceasingly coming to light. Three priests in our deanery have been sent to jail for the sexual abuse of teenagers. Later, Marie Keenan, in her meticulously researched book *Child Sexual Abuse and the Catholic Church*, would locate the problem not exclusively in individual pathology, but other factors, such as the very institution of priesthood itself. The Catholic take on sexuality, clerical culture, power relations, governance structures of the Catholic Church and especially the process of formation for the priesthood and religious life – all coalesce to create serious institutional risks for sexual abuse. The great temptation to try to cover up and avoid taking responsibility became obvious. The Second Vatican Council promised a church which would engage positively with the human condition in the modern world. It would contribute to the dialogue out of the wisdom of its lengthy tradition and also learn from contemporary insights. It was hoped it would develop a healthy and holistic theology of sexuality.

Alas, this is not happening. All this seems to be choked by the Vatican Curia. As Fr Kevin Hegarty said in his address to the Association of Catholic Priests:

> So bishops are chosen on the basis of being in favour of compulsory celibacy, adherence to clerical dress, docility to papal teaching and above all contraception and against the ordination of women. Loyalty is defined in old narrow terms. And it is fearful of the feminine. Misogyny is dressed up in theological abstraction.

When talking to engaged couples, I have often suggested that unless they can share how they really feel, there will be no meaningful communication. Priests rarely share how they feel. Henri Nouwen was the exception. This great spiritual writer shared his feelings when he said:

> Today the small rejections of life are too much for me – a sarcastic smile, a flippant remark, a bitter silence, a coldness from a colleague, an indifference from someone I love, the lack of a soul mate, a loneliness I cannot explain. I feel empty, alone, afraid, restless. I look around for invitations, letters, phone calls, for some warm gesture to heal my emptiness. And right now I don't particularly want God, faith or Church. I want simply to be held,

embraced, loved by someone special, made to feel unique, kissed by a soul mate.

There are times when I felt a bit like that. But I also know that as a priest, maturity – emotional and spiritual – demands that ultimately we choose God, not on a basis of feeling, but on the basis of values, truth and goodness. Sometimes we may feel the pain of a child who is being weaned from her mother and may cry him/herself to sleep; but God, like a good mother, knows that giving an emotional breast back to the child only delays the inevitable. Maturity can only come about through sacrifice and self-denial.

Back to the mundane: as we moved towards the end of the twentieth century, I had an operation for my first hip replacement. A friend in the golf club told me of a new procedure for hip operations. He had just had his done. A Mr Derek McMinn, with the help of another Irish surgeon, has pioneered this new operation, where the prosthesis is a metal ball without the big spike that is hammered into the femur. It goes under the name of 'Birmingham Hip', or 'Resurfacing'. I went for a consultation with Mr McMinn and fixed a date.

On the morning of the operation, like most people, I was very nervous. When I was wheeled into the theatre it was so cold. I will never forget the kindness of a nurse who put a heated blanket over me. The operation went well. But it was so difficult lying in bed with one leg refusing to move. This private hospital in Birmingham had mostly agency nurses, who were awful. I had to have a catheter for a few days. I wore underpants only. Mr McMinn told me I could have a shower. They never helped. But when I exited from the shower they came into my room. They found it most hilarious as they said 'the old man could not take off his knickers'.

By a strange coincidence, while I was there Mr McMinn said a very good surgeon came over from Waterford to learn this new procedure, a Tadgh O'Sullivan. His aunt, the late Martha Newman, was a friend and parishioner in St Albans. Tadgh did my second hip three years later. The little hospital in Kilkenny where he did his orthopaedic surgery was old and lacked some facilities, but the nurses were out of this world. What a difference it makes. Since then, I have never ceased to wonder at the miracle of new hips; without them I would be a cripple. Getting back on the golf course, it took some time to build up my confidence again.

I think it was Dickenson who said, 'The turn of a century is the prince's kiss of time' – what a century we have lived through. It truly was the best of times and the worst of times. The latter is represented by the mushroom cloud that hung over two cities in Japan: Hiroshima and Nagasaki. During the century, in all the wars, more humans have been killed or left to die of starvation than ever before. The Nazi Holocaust still leaves a terrible mark, and we invented a power of destruction which can cause more havoc than all the natural catastrophes, earthquakes, volcanoes or tsunami. On the other hand, women's rights have at last been recognised with full human rights in most constitutions. In general, there has been emancipation from male dominance and gender oppression except where it is enshrined in the holy texts of a few religions. There are the spectacular advances in discoveries that have made life more bearable and pleasurable for billions of people, eliminating many epidemics, taking vital organs from dead bodies and transplanting them in living bodies, planes 10,000 metres high buzzing like birds – the list goes on and on. The moral atmosphere has changed, which you know when you can buy the three Cs from one vending machine: cigarettes, chocolate and condoms.

The old Celtic tiger is in great health across the water – it will be many years before he will need even a flu injection. A massive balloon is being created and gradually being filled with Anglo-Irish economic hot air. Those on the bandwagon of the financial boom change their cars for 4 x 4 petrol guzzlers, and when shopping for designer clothes would think it unseemly to look at the price tag. Plastic money can get you a second home or a second annual holiday in far-off places. There is no need any more for gospel values. True, maybe one million Irish people never get even a lick from the tiger, but doesn't the one sentence of the gospel that they can recall say 'the poor you will have with you always'?

Our parish was in Hertfordshire, but we belonged to the archdiocese of Westminster. We must have been the most fortunate of dioceses to have had for many years Cardinal Hume as our spiritual leader. And also to have had Bishop James O'Brien as bishop with responsibility for Hertfordshire. Bishop James lived beside us in the gatehouse of the Pastoral Centre at London Colney. I would like to give you in full Cardinal Hume's vision of the church in 1980:

I speak in my own name, and in my own name alone. I have listened to many speeches intently and attentively; well, that is not quite true. I confess that I have from time to time fallen asleep. During one of these, I had a dream. I will speak of my dream.

I heard a voice speaking, and it spoke of the Church, and I saw in my dream a vision. It was a vision of the Church. I saw a *fortress*, strong and upstanding. Every stranger approaching seemed to those who defended it to be an enemy to be repelled; from that fortress, the voices of those outside could not be heard. The solders within showed unquestioning obedience – and that was much to be admired: 'Theirs not to reason why, theirs but to do and die.' It seemed thus in my dream. And then I remembered, upon awakening – and it was only just to do so – that dreams distort reality. They exaggerate.

Then I had another vision. It was of a *pilgrim*, a pilgrim through history and through life. That pilgrim was the Church. The pilgrim was hastening towards the vision, towards all Truth. But it had not yet reached it. It limped along the road. But meanwhile there were signposts to show the way; or rather they told you that this or that road was not the right one. The pilgrim is always in search, I reflected, and that can be painful. The leaders, too, of the pilgrimage are often themselves not always clear. They must sometimes co-agonise with the other pilgrims. Co-responsibility will always involve co-agonising.

The fortress was a temple, but the pilgrims lived in a tent. It is sometimes better to know the uncertainties of Abraham's tent than to sit secure in Solomon's temple.

There was a time when most Catholics went to confession, especially at Christmas time and during parish missions. From 1968, when Pope Paul VI gave us his famous encyclical *Humanae Vitae*, the priest as confessor was caught between a rock and a hard place. Priests became aware of the incredible burden this places on the conscience of so many excellent Catholics. I always found refuge by telling people that their conscience is the final norm, and if their conscience found it an intolerable strain on their marriage, to follow their conscience.

Vatican II approved major constitutional changes in church structures. It backed, by a huge majority, the doctrine of collegiality – that the church is governed by the college of bishops, under the pope. He and they exercise *shared responsibility* – they are not his delegates but the original pattern of the apostles grouped around the leader.

But powerful figures in the Curia never accepted collegiality as valid. Pope Paul VI faced fearsome opponents in his own household. What would collegiality mean in actual practice? Having overseen and guided the collegiality doctrine into the printed council text, Paul VI would act in a spectacularly non-collegial way. The big issue on the agenda for Paul VI in the post-Council years was contraception. The commission he set up to examine the issue had concluded that the natural law arguments against contraception were not persuasive. He was in agony: 'How easy it is to study and study, how hard to decide.' He decided alone, with no reference to the principal of collegiality which had been so emphatically decided at the Vatican Council. Cardinal Leo Joseph Suenens of Belgium said how much greater the encyclical's authority would have been if it had been a collegial production.

It seems to me as a priest that forty years after *Humanae Vitae*, it has ceased to be an issue for the vast majority of Catholics. Most no longer go to confession, and the few that do go are in the latter quarter of their lives. I don't believe it has done papal authority any favours. Some will say quite openly that the church should keep out of the bedroom. It is probably time to say that most of the moral problems that occupy the minds of church leaders are to do, one way or the other, with sex and gender, divorce, contraception, gay unions, married priests and women priests. It has taken a hard line and resolutely refused to budge on the issue of contraception, even the use of condoms to prevent AIDS.

And it has made its views known to other Christian churches in dialogue with it that it would prefer it if they would also comply with Catholic practice in respect to women priests – i.e. have nothing to do with them. Some priests have spoken of how ill-prepared they were; living a sheltered life and knowing nothing about the real stresses and strains of marriage, trying to advise a young woman on the most intimate area of her relationship in a dark confession box. The reality was that once people were no longer uneducated and decided that church teaching on the use of artificial birth control within marriage did not make sense, they gradually lost faith in the church's capacity to have anything significant to say on human sexuality.

As the years went by, I realised as a confessor how much damage was done to the conscience of ordinary men and women due to the unnecessary amount of guilt they carried, some for years and years. Fr Daniel O'Leary, who is one of my favourite spiritual writers, says, 'In my travels, I have listened to a great number of bruised Catholics who find it difficult to understand the hard line that so many priests take, especially as regards total reception of the sacraments.' I remember attending a meeting for episcopal vicars in London. Someone suggested a wider use of general absolution and a more generous attitude towards many of those no longer allowed to receive holy communion. 'Good God!' one of those present exclaimed. 'If you go down that road, our church will be crammed with sinners every Sunday morning!'

But what the more experienced priests will now freely admit – especially those who are in their sixties and over and who are risking the inner spiritual journey into souls – is that they have stopped taking the hard line when that line is less than compassionate. They regret when they have placed restrictions on the unconditional love of God. God's extravagant compassion and mercy reaches well beyond the boundaries and categories of our prescribed certainties.

Fr Tony Flannery in one of his articles for *Reality* magazine, has this story:

I was chatting with an old man, sitting on a seat in a church in a west of Ireland town. He looked over at one of the confessionals, which were still the same as 60 years ago when he was in his late teens. He was going with a girl at the time. He explained that 'going with a girl' in the early 1940s meant going for walks to the next village a mile down the coast. He assured me that he hadn't got as far as kissing her. But when the parish missionaries came and he went to confession, all his training told him that he should feel guilty even about something as innocent as he was engaged in. So he confessed that he was 'company keeping'. He was roundly abused by the confessor and warned that unless he promised to stop seeing the girl, he would not be given absolution. Since the particular style of the confession box tended to amplify rather than subdue the voice, he said that one of the hardest things he ever had to do in his life was to face walking out of that box, knowing that the large queue outside had heard every word of the raised voice of the missioner.

No wonder so many of our good Catholics carry in their subconscious a fearful God. A God of endless demands and infinite reprisals. It is so difficult to tell them not to believe in such a God; he is an imposter and makes neurotics of so many.

A punishing God will become an unbearable God and is so far from the Christ of the gospel. Sinners did not flee from Christ. They sat at his feet, dined at his table, hung on his loving words. This God had a human face and it was lit with love. There was no raised voice, only forgiveness.

What we need to recover most of all is the tenderness of Jesus. We would do well to reflect on how patiently a mother entices out the humanity and personality of her baby.

Hans Urs von Balthasar wrote: 'After a mother has smiled for a long time at her child, the child will begin to smile back. She has awakened love in its heart, and in this awakening love, she awakens also recognition.' All this reminds me of a home where there are many children, and where when I visit the mum is often apologetic for the mess. I have come to realise that a 'holy home' does not mean everything in its place, no dust, tidiness. God can be very absent from the super-respectable, the gleaming surfaces. One super mum later reflected: 'I am reminded of God's presence by the stains in the carpet, where we had tea around the fire, and the children spilled some on the carpet. In the grime on the paintwork where small dirty hands have touched. In the rather uncomfortable sofa which has held so many tired bodies. In the chipped plates which remind me of the many happy meals we had together. Thinking of these things and so much more, I thank God for his presence in my family. God is in our reality, not in our dreams. He is in the now, not in the "might be" or "might have been". He delights in the mess, he rejoices in the successes, but is still present in our failures. He is the one constant factor.' All this is a beautiful image of our loving Father.

Life in the parish went on. My very good friend, Fr Pat Courtney, was the new parish priest. Fr Danny Cleary went to do further studies and was replaced by a young priest, Manus Ferry.

In his vision of the Pilgrim Church, Cardinal Hume spoke of how co-responsibility will always involve co-agonising. We were encouraged by our MSC leadership to exercise collaboration in all of our ministries. In our efforts to do so at parish level, there is the eternal problem of apathy. For so long, people let the priest do everything. We have to persuade people that the church is their responsibility and as priests get scarcer, they must 'step up to the plate'. It is an uphill battle, but perseverance pays off. Many parishioners have goodwill but lack confidence. Once you persuade them to take the plunge, they learn by doing and there are many resources and training courses available. Once they get involved, they get great fulfilment from it.

Preparation for the sacraments of confession and holy communion were taken out of the school and run by the parish. It involved getting very many catechists. Parents were encouraged to journey with their children in the preparation, and a special Sunday liturgy was held every month for children and parents.

Our beloved Cardinal Hume visited the parish for the school anniversary. His health was failing fast, yet he could still find time for people. He died a few months later. It is very obvious how frustrated he was with the lack of implementation of the Vatican II document of collegiality. It was said on the grapevine that on one of his visits to Rome, he was heard shouting at the head of one of the Curia congregations. Over and over again he asked permission to allow general absolution, and was always refused. Like his friend Cardinal Martini, he left letters to be published after his death telling of his sadness that the church was growing more and more out of touch with a changing world.

Pope John Paul II was also growing old and feeble from ill health. He started with such energy, showing himself to be a man of character, deeply rooted in the Polish Christian faith, a champion of peace, human rights and social justice. With his personal charisma, he became a media superstar and, for many, a living cult figure.

In this first encyclical *Redemptor Hominis*, John Paul made it clear that the emphasis was to be on him as the captain. It was the job of all bishops to follow his lead. They had to sing from the same hymn sheet and to his tune. When he went on his many journeys, the local bishop risked being reduced to a master of ceremonies. I have read so many times about bishops who went on their five-yearly visit to Rome. They came back feeling they were only messenger boys. Priests were leaving the ministry, very often to get married. There were a dwindling number of vocations to priesthood. Convents were becoming empty. Sunday congregations were rapidly getting smaller. None of these problems were being addressed. It seemed to me that there were now two different worlds. One was the world of Pope John Paul and the Vatican Curia. It revolved on it axis as it had for centuries. There is no need for new wineskins. There is no need for the householder to bring out new treasures. Reading the signs of the times is not necessary. Everything is set in marble. The kingdom of God is already here; it is not something that we are working towards. The mustard plant is fully grown.

But there is another world. Some may call it the real world, which is spinning at an ever-quickening pace, driven on by the evolutionary imperative. Things are forever changing, and fast. Jesus promised us He would be with us always and that the Spirit would lead us eventually into all truth. This is the only world that the kingdom of God can grow in. So much truthful and honest dialogue is needed. We must not block the Spirit and say this is not open for debate.

St John of the Cross wrote: 'One of the greatest favours bestowed on the soul in this life is to enable it to see so distinctly and to feel so profoundly that it cannot comprehend God at all.' And St Thomas Aquinas: 'What God actually is always remains hidden from us.' There is no such thing as the final word about God or religion.

One of the great shocks about family bereavement was hearing that my niece's husband, Flor, had died tragically while on holiday in Portugal. I later found out it was suicide. Flor was the most popular vet in west Cork – perhaps a workaholic. The family were on their annual holiday. The day before they were due to come home, which happened to be their wedding anniversary, he committed suicide. He rarely drank, but on that day imbibed a good lot. There was some small disagreement, after which he killed himself.

I have written already about suicide. One of the many books I have read tells us that suicide is not an act of despair. We are emerging from that mindset which said it was culpable and unforgivable. What is now understood is that it is an illness, pure and simple. We are made up of body and soul; either can snap. We can die of cancer or heart attacks, which are physical sicknesses. But we can suffer these too in the soul. We are told that in most cases suicide, like any terminal illness, takes a person out of life against their will. The death is not freely chosen, but is a desperate attempt to end unendurable pain, like a woman who throws herself from a window because her clothing has caught fire. That's a tragedy, not an act of despair. Our wounded loved ones who fall victim to suicide are safe in God's hands.

Another writer claims that there is always an aberrant biochemical cause or some chemical imbalance. The writer felt that he was one of the lucky ones. With his suicide already planned, he drew on some last gleam of sanity and realised he could not commit this desecration on himself and his loved ones. He woke his sleeping wife, who drove him to hospital. Through chemical adjustment he healed.

While writing this I read in a newspaper that since 1998, 3,288 people have died through suicide in Northern Ireland, almost the same number who died all through the Troubles. It is becoming a major issue among young adults. I have a personal feeling that another cause is the problem of not being able to communicate our feelings. The culture that says that big boys don't cry, or worse, tigers don't cry. Feelings get bottled up.

A few years later, my niece Marcella, who had suffered from postnatal depression after her children were born and who never quite recovered, also committed suicide after her husband died, as she could not cope. She was one of the most loveable and saintly persons. Both of their funerals were incredibly sad. Thankfully, both families have recovered from the trauma; with God's help, life goes on. The human heart is exquisitely fragile. God redeems everything and, in the end, all manner of being will be well.

After the death of Cardinal Hume, we waited for a few months before his successor was appointed. We were pleased to hear that Cormac Murphy-O'Connor was to be the new Archbishop of Westminster. Later that year, he received the Red Hat.

After meetings with all the priests of the dioceses, it was decided to have the Renew Programme in the diocese. It required lots of planning and meetings. It mostly consisted of having BCCs (Basic Christian Communities) in all the parishes. There was quite a lot of resource material for discussion in these small groups – sharing the word of God and how to minister to each other in pastoral, social and spiritual needs. The programme went well and we still have many active groups who meet on a weekly or monthly basis. Some have developed into scripture-sharing and prayer groups. The cardinal was also involved in moving the celebration of holy days of obligation to Sundays. On the few outings of clergy golfing days, he joined us. As we were both senior citizens, we shared a buggy. He may have been more impressed with my golf than vice versa!

All religious congregations were now realising that because of so few vocations, they were unable to meet the demands of the various ministries. They would have to withdraw personnel from some of them. The Missionaries of the Sacred Heart decided to start with withdrawing priests from some of the parishes. Perhaps because of limited and flawed consultation, it was decided to withdraw the priests from St Albans. There was shock and even anger among the parishioners, who had had recourse to over a hundred years of pastoral care from the MSCs. A vast petition was started. Older priests in the province were also very unhappy with this decision. As it happened, St Albans was set up as a Canonical Religious House and permission was needed from the Superior General in Rome to close it down. This permission was not sought and if it had been, would not have been granted. The decision to close St Albans was overturned. We all breathed a sigh of relief. Later, three other parishes were returned to the diocesan clergy. One of them was my beloved Tamworth.

Shortly after this, Fr Pat Courtney was elected the new Provincial. For six months, Fr Manus and I kept the parish going until the new parish priest, Fr Charlie Sweeney, came to St Albans. Fr Charles, as he was now called in St Albans, had the best pastoral and parish experience. He wisely reduced the number of Masses and rearranged the times of some of the rest. The whole idea of collaboration took on a new meaning, and after much parish deliberation with the laity, many took on new responsibilities. There was special outreach to the elderly, especially those living alone. Many and varied initiatives were introduced to bring them together in the parish hall. A number of volunteers offered to bring them in their cars.

After two years, he started training for volunteers to run a programme called 'Life's Healing Journey'. This was an incredible success. Now you had lay people empowered to bring healing and help to the bereaved and the separated and others suffering from different hurts. Those volunteers now felt that they were ministers of healing, empowered by the spirit of the living God. They spent hours with each person who needed healing.

The cardinal asked for vocations to the Permanent Diaconate. The ceiling age would be fifty-seven years. Steve Pickard, who had been Eucharistic Minister since the 1970s, volunteered, but he was over sixty. When the parishioners heard that he had not been accepted due to age, they started a petition, which I sent to the cardinal. He phoned me asking if I had initiated the petition and when I told him no, he graciously said, 'I made the rules and I can break them.' Steve was accepted and after three years of training, was ordained deacon. He could now preach, and assist, at marriage and funeral services. Also, he was now better trained to run the RCIA course for those wishing to join the Catholic Church.

Fr Manus was transferred to Liverpool and we were fortunate to get a replacement. Fr Tom Hewitt, who is one of our few English priests, came to join our team. He had been in St Albans in the eighties and was welcomed back with great joy by the parishioners. Cricket became a new subject of conversation at our meals, mostly to console Tom when the English lost yet another Test. But they were lucky once and won the Ashes. We had a special celebratory meal. This was a 'once in a blue moon' occasion! Tom was also known to shout boisterously when his rugby team scored a try. But most of all, Tom was able to share his deep spirituality with the people of God.

For security reasons, most city churches in England are locked after morning Mass. We were fortunate to have a very large prayer room at the back of the presbytery to which about sixty people had a key. They came at all times, day and night, to pray for a short while or for long periods. Some came as a group to say vocal prayers. In the early church, there was a praying ministry; people who had the gift of prayer. This should be encouraged in our hectic world. During Lent, we had very early Mass for people on their way to work.

It was a few years since we had had an ordination. Alan Neville, who had completed his studies, came for a year's pastoral experience before being ordained from deacon to priest. He got stuck into ministry to the youth, from tiny tots to over-twenties. There was a special Liturgy of the Word for children during 9.30 Mass. They all marched back in, some with a parent, for the offertory. The noise level increased dramatically, but it was family Mass. It was great to see mums with their prams there. I often spoke of my admiration for their efforts to get their children fed and ready at such an early hour. Alan remained with us for two more years when we appointed him as special youth officer full-time.

A young man in his twenties, Michael O'Rourke, felt he might have a vocation to the MSCs. We invited him to 'come and see'. He had done a degree in theology and he went daily to Heythrop College to further his studies. He went to the novitiate, but after discernment he felt he could not go on. It was a great experience for him though and we wish him well.

It wasn't all work and no play. Fr Charlie was an Arsenal supporter rather late in life, having followed the better team, Man United, for many years. We went to the Emirates Stadium quite a few times. The new stadium had a special cabinet built for silverware. So far it is rather empty. I suggested they sell it to United, as theirs is overflowing! But it is one of the best-built stadiums I have ever been to. Perhaps Arsenal might get into building stadia full time.

Every September there was a national golf tournament for the Catholic clergy of England, Scotland and Wales. Our Westminster team won it one year and we decided to celebrate our win. Rather foolishly, we chose to go over to France via the tunnel, play golf and, after a celebration dinner, return on the same day. We had three cars. All went well till we came back to the tunnel, which was closed for some reason. We had to take the ferry back. When I got back to Potters Bar with Tim O'Connor it was 3 a.m. I took my passport from the glove compartment. Some five months later, on a Saturday morning after Christmas, I was having a sleep-in when the phone rang. It was Tim O'Connor, asking me to look at my passport. He was with some other priests on his way to Heathrow and Spain for a golfing break. I had Tim's passport and he had mine. I told him I would do my best to get it to the airport. Luckily, the M25 was half-empty of traffic. I got there in forty minutes. I phoned his mobile and said I forgot to wish him Happy New Year. He used a very unclerical expletive and asked where I was. When I told him I was outside the main entrance, he came rushing out and threw me my passport and grabbed his. He just had a few minutes to spare. He did phone later to apologise.

* * *

And so to my golden jubilee celebration. I had often looked forward to celebrating fifty years of priesthood. I sometimes wondered if I would live that long. I know some of our priests have in recent years seen their platinum jubilee – seventy years a priest. But the golden jubilee was the big one for me, and I wanted to celebrate it in style. I had said to parishioners that I would appreciate very much if they would join me in a special celebration Mass of thanksgiving for fifty years as a priest. With some of my relations in England joining the congregation, it was quite an emotional occasion for me. The MSCs put on a very good buffet in the parish hall, with music and a very generous presentation from the parishioners. I often wondered why some parishioners go out of their way to say thank you – the little note after a wedding or funeral service, or the occasional thank you for a service they enjoyed. Or again, the ones who made the effort to join me in my thanksgiving Mass for fifty years as a priest. I sometimes think of Jesus having cured ten lepers – one made the effort to say thank you.

I also had a celebration in Cork with fellow MSCs celebrating different jubilees. I was able to invite some of my family to this. The last celebration was in the village of Kilcrohane; Our Lady Star of the Sea Church was where I received my early sacraments and where I said my first Mass.

I took the opportunity to go to New York to visit three nieces (all siblings) and to San Francisco to visit three nephews (all siblings). San Francisco is one of the most beautiful cities in the world. I played golf with my nephews in Napa Valley among the vineyards. I helped myself to some grapes that were overhanging one of the tees.

* * *

I have always tried to keep in touch with new developments in theology and how relevant they are to the changing world we live in. I would like to offer the following from John F.X. Harriott's *The Empire of the Heart*, which has given me great food for thought:

> The church is not a clear, well-lit place where everything runs smoothly. It is, in the word of the Gospel, a field of cockle and wheat growing up together and beyond human power to separate. The enthusiast will always be running up against a narrowness of vision, stoniness of heart. No great development in the Church has ever received a fair word from the start. The lover of good order, of uniformity of spirit and discipline, will always be confounded by a

spirit that blows where it will, by the sheer complexity of the human situation and individuals, by prophets and visionaries, and even non-conformists, who will not be regulated like an alarm clock. Whoever asks for a Church where everyone sings the same tune, will ask in vain. It will always have a dark side as well as a bright side. It is, after all, the people of God. And people are imperfect and contradictory. To know it, we have only to look at ourselves.

During the last twenty years, many Anglican priests have asked to join the Catholic Church as priests. In our diocese, at most there have been over a hundred. These eventually got parishes. So you had married priests working side by side with celibate priests. Parishioners had no problems with this. What they could not accept was when a Catholic priest left because he had felt that he had two vocations – one the priesthood, and one to married life – and was replaced by a married (Anglican) priest. Tony Caster was one of these. This is a short version of his story:

In September 1970, after agonising over the decision for six years and constant prayer, seeking God's will, I decided that the only honest and sincere thing to do was to withdraw from active ministry. I was convinced that I had a vocation to the Catholic priesthood, but I was equally convinced that I had a vocation to marriage. After seven years as a priest, the last thing I wanted to do was to bring shame on that ministry. During those years, I had not been 'involved' with anyone – I was a celibate up to my wedding day. But knowing human nature, I knew something would happen which would damage the good name of the priesthood. The decision to leave was made two years before I left and long before I met my future wife. We have been married for thirty-five years and have experienced the usual joys and sorrows of married life with four children. We are very involved with the local church. People have said to me, 'If it is alright for Frs Tom and Michael (Anglicans) to be married with families, why can't you be our priest?'

In 1997, I wrote to Cardinal Hume and addressed the question to him. He invited me for tea in the Archbishop's House, and after making the tea himself, asked me to tell him my story. He was a wonderful and humble listener. At the end of an hour together, he said, 'I can see no reason why you should not be back in active ministry. I have no problem with married priests and believe that it is wrong for the evident work of the Holy Spirit at this time to be blocked by the Church.' He went on to say that he was going to Rome in a few weeks and he would be very happy to present a petition from me to Cardinal Ratzinger. I submitted my petition. The cardinal said as I left, 'I'll do all that I can, but don't get your hopes too high. You know what Rome is like.' Four months later, I had a phone call from Bishop Thomas, telling me that the Cardinal had phoned with the news that Rome said 'no'.

Later, Tony Caster went on to say,

> I have no doubt that I am a better person for being married. I was unaware, while in active ministry, of my 'superiority complex' – I was 'Father' and I had all the answers. I was also very self-centred – I could plan my day, go or not go where I liked. I did not have to take another person into account (I didn't have to go shopping for hours). Changing nappies and getting up at night to attend to sick children is very formative. I had to learn that married love is more about patience than sex. I have learnt to be more generous and considerate.

It is possible to be very successful as a priest, to be super-efficient and competent, and do all manner of things well; as one priest said, it is a mental rather than a real faith that underpins all this priestly activity.

Fr Michael Golden, a Kiltegan missionary home from Africa and on holiday, was sitting in a convent chapel in Westport having doubts about his priestly vocation. He became suddenly aware of God's presence: 'And that awareness has never left me. I was simply carried past the way of mental faith into the realm of realisation. And I still have it. My merely notional faith was gone and my prayer became real. From that day on, whenever I took the bread in my hands, I knew I had Jesus in my hands, in my arms, in my soul. It was all so simple. One day, I believed in a notional way, the next I believed in a real way. Something had happened to me.'

I believe all of us priests need some sort of conversion or experience like that. I have had at least one such experience. These things are hard to describe. It is a raised level of consciousness, which comes to us as a gift.

The calling of the priest, like it was for Jesus before him, and like it is for the church and her sacraments now, is not to introduce something new to God's creation, but to reveal, purify and intensify what is already there. It is not easy to obey St Paul when he tells us that 'our unveiled faces reflect like mirrors the brightness of the Lord, growing brighter and brighter as we are turned into the image that we reflect'.

Parishioners are at their most vulnerable when told that they have cancer. Some have years of remission after surgery. Others are told that medicine can't help. This is a time when they need a priest most of all. Not just to give them the sacraments, but to journey with them in their pain, fear and isolation. It may mean just sitting and listening to them. In some situations, words can be meaningless. If I may tell you the story of one such parishioner: she had cancer in most of her vital organs and she was told that she had a couple of months to live. She survived eighteen months and baffled all the consultants. She had gallons of fluid drained regularly from her abdomen – a most painful procedure. Most of the time, she was at home. Her husband had died some years previously of cancer. They had no children. She was a midwife.

Twice a week, she went to the day hospice in St Albans.

Because of her amazing fortitude, all the others in the day room were drawn to her. She had some way of putting new heart into them, not through any outward show of religion, but just by being a sort of beacon of light and hope to them. She became a friend to all of them, mostly by being a good listener.

The eucharistic minister brought her holy communion on Sundays but I used to go every Friday to bring her holy communion and spend some time with her. I also did some house Masses when she invited special friends. Strangely, these were joyous occasions, with some laughter and fun.

I want to repeat one of her stories, as I have often mentioned it in homilies. Mary was a midwife, and this occasion was one of her difficult deliveries. For many hours while the mother was in labour, Mary stayed with her, often saying little prayers to God to help them. Eventually, the baby was safely born. The next day, the mother asked Mary to do her a special favour by being godparent to her baby. Mary said, 'Since you are not Catholic, I may not be allowed.' Shortly afterwards, she decided she would be godparent. She kept in contact with the family, who decided that they all wanted to become Catholics and became very active in their parish. Mary never preached to them, but her actions and devotion to help made a deep impression. People like Mary live gospel values every moment of their lives. They truly become salt and light to other people. Only God alone knows the cumulative good that people like Mary do. May she enjoy the company of the Risen Christ forever.

* * *

For the last fifty years, abortion has become the most contro-versial moral issue. Ever since abortion became available on demand in the UK, society has been divided into two camps – pro and anti. I have gone with many of our parishioners to rallies in London where we walked in silent protest and were heckled by all sorts of people. But parishioners felt that we should do something positive as well. Professor Jack Scarisbrick was invited to the town hall to debate the issue of abortion. As you might expect, there was some heated debate. I will never forget the ignorance of one GP who said that the Fifth Commandment, 'Thou shalt not kill', was Old Testament only. Through the help of Jack Scarisbrick and his wife, Nuala, a branch of the LIFE group was started. Kyra Audley Charles was the first president, with great support from the CWL and many parishioners. They started fundraising for accommodation for pregnant women who wanted to keep their babies. A hostel/house was officially opened by Bishop O'Brien in 1978. They also went into schools to give talks on the sanctity of all life. This LIFE group is still active and giving educational talks. I will always remember an article in a paper where a woman said she was pregnant but also had a dog. She could not afford a baby and a dog, so she was going to have an abortion.

In passing, I would like to mention that some great theologians in the past, among them Thomas Aquinas, said that at conception there was a negative soul which became an animal soul before becoming a human soul. But the church would ask us to treat all embryos as sacred.

I have already told you about one of our priests who was an alcoholic. Countless people across the world acknowledge the effectiveness and power of AA. We were fortunate that we had a parish room, which we rented to AA most lunchtimes during the week. There are twelve steps on the road to recovery with AA. The fifth one says: 'Admitted to God, to ourselves and to another human being the exact nature of the wrongs done while under the influence of drink.' Occasionally, a man would knock at the presbytery door and would ask me to listen to his story of wrongdoing. This was a most healing experience for them. I never asked what religion, if any, they had, but I offered them God's absolution, which they were always most grateful for. I have never ceased to wonder at the incalculable force for good the AA is. Only God could bring this about.

Being the second youngest of many siblings, it is a sad fact of life that I would assist at their funerals. Frank, who lived in Essex and had much tragedy in his life, was nursed at home by his daughter Angela. Shortly after having the joy of seeing his granddaughter, he died. He was one of the best human beings I have known. His simple faith will lead him into the company of the saints forever.

The second funeral was of my sister Martina. This was a sudden death. Although over eighty, she had got an air ticket and new clothes to go to New York for her granddaughter's first communion. It was a great shock to me, as I spent my summer holiday in Ireland with her. She loved company and had so many friends around Bantry. She took enormous pride in her seven children and many grandchildren. It was difficult doing the funeral, which was on Holy Thursday. I will remember her most of all for not being judgemental – she never seemed to say anything bad about anyone. She said she would like to live longer than me but she also wanted me to do her funeral; she got one of her wishes. May she rest in peace.

I have touched on parish funerals elsewhere. The bereaved are so sensitive in their loss of a loved one. Many have no experience of organising a funeral. A large number would not be churchgoing. They have to be guided gently to what is appropriate music for a church service. When they wanted the deceased's favourite music or song, I always suggested that the best time to play it was as the coffin was being taken out. So many of the Irish wanted 'Danny Boy' or 'The Rose of Tralee', or the more discerning, 'The Banks Of My Own Lovely Lee.'

Recently, a bishop in Ireland has banned all eulogies. I believe this to be a mistake. The time has gone for issuing these decrees. Funerals call for great understanding and sympathy. We priests know what a pain eulogies sometimes are; many of the congregation will feel the same. But we must try to manage them rather than rule them out. And if we sometimes fail, it is a better alternative to blanket condemnation.

In St Albans, we were especially blessed in having a professional singer to lead the congregation, which she did in a most powerful manner. Julia White is a gift. Her husband Jeremy, an operatic singer at Covent Garden and elsewhere, plays the organ.

I used to try to vary the funeral homily to the circumstances of the deceased. However, I always came back to the great mystery of the resurrection. Maybe sometimes it went over their heads – who knows? Resurrection is as earthy, local and intimate as our sweat and blood, our dreams and nightmares, our drives and passions. It is as real as whatever or whoever drives and draws us. Resurrection, in fact, is the deepest meaning of everything that brings a smile to our faces, a tear to our eyes, a vitality to our bodies, a tenderness to our touch. Every hope you carry inside you can come true because with the resurrected Christ you can do all things. You can mend a broken world because now all things are possible. But there is one condition: you must dare to believe it.

During my last year at St Albans, we got a new translation of the missal. There was *no* consultation. The archbishop wrote a letter to be read out in church extolling the virtues of the new translation. Having read this on Sunday, I boldly told the congregation that I did not believe any of these reasons to be true – least of all that it was more prayerful. I may have shocked some people.

Fr Michael Maginn, writing in *The Furrow* some time later, gave his views: 'Some of the ponderous, heavily Latinised translations are truly dreadful in their syntax and choice of vocabulary. No amount of positive good will can change this unavoidable conclusion.' For example, the word 'suffering' is never mentioned; it is always replaced with 'passion'. Now the common meaning of passion as found in the *Oxford Dictionary* is: 'strong emotion; outburst of anger, sexual love'. The prayers that the priest must now read from the missal are gold medal-winners for their sheer linguistic density and lengthy unreadability. As Fr Michael says, 'these words will never trip lightly from our increasingly tangled tongues'. I have a personal problem with the substitution of the word 'many' instead of 'all'. Christ died for all mankind. I will continue to use the words 'for all'.

For over a hundred years, the Missionaries of the Sacred Heart have been running this parish. Many of the priests who worked here have also spent time on the missions. We have always tried to emphasise that the church is missionary. Over the past few years, there has been an active group, led by Barbara, collecting funds for an AIDS hospital in South Africa called Tshwaranang. They have managed to raise over £10,000 every year for this most necessary cause. Recently, there has been much publicity in Ireland about the obscene salaries given to senior staff who run the many charities. So much of the money given to good causes never finds its way to that cause. In our parish, every single penny raised for Tshwaranang finds its way to that hospice.

The clock has been ticking away for fifteen years in St Albans. I will soon be celebrating my eightieth birthday. I have decided that I will retire. Before I go, there are a few things I would like to mention. All of us priests know that in any parish, you will get many unsung heroes who do so much voluntary work in the parish. I want to mention the handyman who will come at a moment's notice to solve some problem, and if it is too much for him he will get someone to do it. The lady who spends six mornings a week doing an infinite variety of chores in the church and presbytery, including the garden. The ladies who cooked and did our laundry. The lady who keeps all the altar linen spotless and never expects any thank you. The six people who come every Monday morning to count the collection and bank it. The retired accountant, who is not a Catholic but comes to church every Sunday with his wife, who spends countless hours paying bills and keeping check on all the finances, reporting to the finance committee every month. The ladies who come to answer the door and phone so that the secretary can get on with her work. The CWL and St Vincent de Paul keep going with a few older members. Your reward will be out of this world – in the next.

Mobile phones can be a problem when they go off in public places. You may not believe this story. Once a man came into confession, and as he knelt down his mobile went off. He took it out and had a conversation before saying, 'Sorry about that, Father.' If he only saw me! I was laughing. I have lived to see everything. When teenagers clutch their phones in their hands,

I call them 'life support necessities' – without them, they couldn't cope.

I forgot to mention a health crisis I had. One Sunday morning I had to get Fr Charles to take me to the A&E at Watford Hospital. I had difficulty trying to explain my problem. The junior doctors worked so hard in the A&E. I was transferred to the Acute Assessment Unit and wired up to a heart monitor. During the night, I was shaken awake by a lady who said, 'I am the doctor on duty – your pulse is very low.' I thought, 'What can I do about it?' I went to sleep again to be awoken by a nurse, who said, 'I am the nurse – your pulse is very low.' I decided I had better stay awake. I heard the staff talking in the morning, saying that I was getting a pacemaker. Late that afternoon, a cardiac consultant with no notes came to visit me. He put his fingers on the pulse in my throat and said, 'Some people have a low pulse; you can go home.' I said that a doctor and nurse woke me during the night saying I had a very low pulse. He said, 'How low was it?' I asked him how was I to know. I was discharged. Fr Charles was worried and we made a private appointment with Mr John Baylis, a cardiologist. I wore a monitor for twenty-four hours. He called me in immediately and said I needed a pacemaker very badly – my heart was stopping for nine or ten seconds during the night.

Unfortunately, I had booked to take my car on holiday to Ireland a few days later and I foolishly told him I would have it done when I returned. I got the problem again in Ireland and had to have a pacemaker put inserted in University Hospital, Cork. Everything was so professional and I was very proud of my hometown hospital.

The pacemaker has made an incredible difference to my life, although I have had to endure little jokes about 'Jerry and the pacemakers'. Apparently, I will need a new battery in seven years' time, if I am still alive!

I had a low-key celebration for my eightieth birthday in Sea View Manor Hotel in Bantry, with a few of my family. Two days later, in the worst summer in Ireland, I went for a game of golf on Bantry Golf Course on my own. What happened was sensational. On the ninth hole, with the most beautiful panoramic view of beautiful Bantry Bay, I had my first hole-in-one. For forty years I had been trying and now it happens two days after my eightieth birthday, with no one to witness it. The ball went directly into the hole. I wasn't sure what had happened to it, so as I approached the green I was wondering where the ball was. I walked slowly up to the hole and there it was, resting quite happily at the bottom of the hole. I started to laugh and laugh. Will it ever happen again – who knows?

I told the parishioners I had decided to retire. I gave them a few months' notice – I would retire in October after fifty-five years active in the ministry. Fr Jimmy Stubbs had come to replace me, so I had plenty of time to hand over everything to him.

There is one little story that has touched my heart. I always find children so fascinating in their beautiful innocence. There was this little girl called Caroline, who was about three or four years old and brought to church by her dad. It is impossible to explain what happens in the mind of a child, but she always insisted that her dad would take her to me as they left the church. She would jump up and down as children do when excited and smile at me. One day, when I had done the Mass and was busy opening the doors to let people out, I looked up and there she was with tears coming to her eyes. I asked the dad what the matter was and he said, 'She thinks you are ignoring her.' I almost wanted to cry myself. When I left St Albans, I was certain that I would be 'out of sight, out of mind' and she would have forgotten me. Not a bit of it. A few months later, at Easter, she was in playschool making little Easter cards and she insisted on making one for Fr Jerry, which her mum sent me. I sent her a lovely storybook, which told of all the stories of the unconditional love of mum and dad. The mother told me she was sick and tired of reading the same stories every night! I have been to see her once while in St Albans. She never says anything, but just looks at me with a lovely smile on her face.

So while I am at it, I want to tell you a story of the innocence of a child that can sometimes cause a little embarrassment. A mother was telling her husband about a visitor they had for the evening meal. When he came, he had a drink or two before the meal and during the meal was enjoying several glasses of red wine. Eventually he said to the four-year-old girl, 'Why are you staring at me?' She replied, 'Well, I heard Mummy tell Daddy that you drink like a fish.' What could poor Mummy say? Little kids have such big ears.

I was quite surprised that so many parishioners came to my farewell Mass. It was sad for me to say goodbye after so many years. But I also felt happy that it was the right time to go. It was a celebration of everything that the Lord did through me over these years. I could not refrain from telling them about a priest who, at his farewell Mass, said very piously, 'Jesus has brought me to this parish and Jesus is taking me away.' Soon afterwards, the organist began to play 'What a Friend We Have in Jesus'. The dean told an apocryphal story about me. He said that one day as we were walking back to his presbytery, there were some men working on a building using some very profane language, but when one of them spotted that we were wearing the dog collar, he apologised and said, 'Sorry, vicars.' A few minutes later, the dean said to me, 'Did you mind their language?', to which I responded, 'Oh no, but I did object to being called vicars.' The parish put on wonderful refreshments and gave me a very generous farewell gift.

Part VI

The next day I packed everything into my car and left for Ireland. I stayed at my nephew's house in Dublin. The following morning, as the mother was driving her teenage daughter to school, she asked, 'Has Fr Jeremiah got all his belongings in that car?' When told yes, she said, '*All* his belongings?' When told again yes, there was a long silence. As I said before, I believe in travelling lightly.

The Missionaries of the Sacred Heart were proactive in building some retirement homes for an ever-increasing number of older members. This one in Cork City was opened in 1999. This was the final bus stop. My room number was 13 – lucky for some! There are ten priests and one Brother living here, but only about six are retired. All our needs are wonderfully catered for. There were lots of small formalities to be seen to: re-registering my car, applying for my non-contributory pension and even a PPS number, which I had never had. Having done all these, I felt that I would like to be involved in parish ministry in some small way. Fortunately, there was great need in a vast parish nearby. Fr George O'Mahony, the parish priest of Ballincollig, invited me to do the 10 a.m. Mass every Sunday in the old church, and also two weekday Masses. I have found all of this very fulfilling. Maybe I have some inner need to be before a congregation. I think they are happy with me. I do try to keep my homily short but to the point.

The next formality may sound morbid, but it is very practical for the Provincial to know where a member wishes to be buried. It used to be in a community grave nearby. Now, priests may decide otherwise. I told him I want to be buried in the family grave in Kilcrohane. I suggested an epitaph, which I am sure they will ignore: 'This priest died computer-illiterate.'

But I have no thoughts of dying just yet. My first problem was to find a golf course. I went to the first well-known one; having met the manager and enquired if there was a joining fee, he mentioned a sum. I said, 'I am getting deaf. Did you say 14,000 euros?' He said 'yes'. The chances of making some concession to an octogenarian priest were slim. Then I went to Cork Golf Club in Little Island. The very friendly Matt Sands told me that because I was clergy I could join without paying the large joining fee. Moreover, they would reduce the annual subscription by quite a bit. They are the only golf club in Ireland that makes such a concession. There are actually very few priest members. My next stroke of luck was that I met Jim McKenna and Pat O'Hara, who have become my golfing buddies. We very often get someone to make up a four-ball.

* * *

Very shortly, the Irish state will celebrate the 1916 uprising in Dublin. They will be celebrating one hundred years of nationhood – some of it very troubled. During this century, the role of the church in Irish life has changed dramatically. I wonder how much thought will be given to thanking the nuns and Brothers for their incalculable input to education and health in Ireland. Nearly every big town in Ireland had a Mercy convent school, primary and secondary. In some they also had a small hospital for primary health care. They got very little funding from the State until the second half of the century. It is impossible to know the countless number of Irish girls who owe their education to the Mercy and other orders of nuns. Recently, in the town of Kerry, I noticed that at the back of some of the churches were large plaques thanking the Christian Brothers who had departed their towns for the priceless work of education in their town. How many of these young men, who were able to advance to university because of the Brothers and later took over responsible positions in government, ever publicly thanked the Brothers?

The contribution of the Brothers and Sisters was no less important in our Irish cities. Will the Minister for Education, whoever he might be, have a word of gratitude for all those Brothers and Sisters, instead of hounding them for money? During the celebrations, will there be anyone to raise their voice in praise of Catherine McAuley, who established the Mercy congregation and whose Sisters went out in their thousands to the English-speaking world? To give one small example: Sr Vincent Whitty set off for Australia in 1860 – months before the Mater Hospital opened in Dublin. Even though she was pivotal in this project, she set off for Queensland, where she founded twenty convents. When she died in 1892, there were 222 Mercy Sisters there. This was repeated over and over again in the English-speaking countries of the world.

They were equally involved in healthcare in some of the largest hospitals in these countries. In England, where I worked for many years, the contribution by the Irish Sisters, especially the Mercy Sisters, could not be overestimated.

Some Sisters have suffered some bad press recently. Very near our retirement home is the convent of the Good Shepherd Sisters. They once ran what are now called the Magdalene Laundries. When we were students in Sacred Heart College, they did our laundry. I met one of the Sisters recently and we spoke about all the publicity they have received. She told me that one night they got a telephone call from the UK. The lady said she was very angry that the nuns had done nothing to give another side of the story – the words she used were that 'they have not defended themselves'. The lady went on to say that she spent one year in their laundries. She was put there because she was rebellious and difficult. Her family put her in there but took her back after a year. She went to the UK, became a nurse and married a doctor. She went on to say, 'That year in the laundries was the making of me – I owe you so much.' The Magdalene story never mentions the unjust society that put those girls in the convent. Very often they were made pregnant by those for whom they worked. The girls took all the blame and were very often not the guilty partner. The father took no responsibility in supporting the child for which he was responsible.

The church and society acted like the people in the gospel who brought the woman who had committed adultery before Jesus. The Sister told of one case when a girl made pregnant by the next-door neighbour was put into a convent. After a year they took her back. When the parish priest, some months later, saw her talking to the same man, he went to her family and he himself drove her to a convent and had her put in there for the rest of her life. Does the church or society take any of the blame? Do the men who made those girls pregnant take any of the blame?

Twenty years ago, Fr Tony Flannery wrote his first book, called *The Death of Religious Life?* Its main thesis was that the style of religious life, known as 'apostolic', which was lived by most congregations of men and women in Ireland and elsewhere, was in terminal decline. As a general rule, whistle-blowers or prophets are rarely listened to. It was dismissed as defeatist. But the reality of the book's message is slowly being accepted. For nuns especially, the sad reality is that there are no vocations for years and years. Convents are closing at an alarming rate; many of their younger nuns have gone back to a lay state, some to get married. My heartfelt message to them is to rejoice like Mary at the wonderful things that the Lord has achieved through all your apostolates. You have achieved what the Holy Spirit inspired you to do. Have no regrets. The Spirit moves where it wills. There will be new apostolates involving lay people. New founders will be born; God's work will go on in a new way.

* * *

As a priest returning to Ireland after fifty-five years and still doing a little bit of parish ministry, the first shock was the lost generation who have stopped coming to church regularly, but also the almost complete change in the practice of going to confession. There were the usual penitential services of Christmas and Easter, but 95% of those who attend were in the latter part of their lives. Private confession was dead in the water. The Second Vatican Council declared in two key documents that confession, or the sacrament of penance, was a reconciliation that took place not only between God and the individual soul, but also between the fellowship of the people of God and each individual Christian as a member of the congregation. They wanted to bring back the long-neglected social nature of the sacrament and of sin. The Second Vatican Council sought to rectify this emphasis by recovering the idea of communal reconciliation practised in the early church. This is why the rite of general confession and absolution was so popular in the 1970s, and why it brought so many people back to the faith who had been lapsed for years.

In Rome, however, the new pope, John Paul II, elected in 1978, and his new doctrinal enforcer, Cardinal Joseph Ratzinger, were unhappy. The time had come, they thought, for another overhaul of the theology of the sacrament of penance. In 1983, John Paul convened a synod of bishops in Rome to discuss 'Reconciliation and Penance'. In the verbal and written submissions made by the bishops from all over the world, the issue of general absolution was raised repeatedly. Bishops from missionary countries, especially from Africa and South America, spoke of the advantage of administering the rite to large congregations. The issue was again raised by the Cardinal Archbishop of Milan, Carlo Mario Martini, who was charged with collating the 200 verbal and written views expressed on the matter by the synod of bishops. A year after the synod, John Paul issued an 'apostolic exhortation' ignoring the concerns raised by most of the bishops. As with Paul VI's encyclical *Humanae Vitae*, it was the pontiff taking upon himself the ultimate teaching role, ignoring the collegial authority of his bishops. In its final section, individual as opposed to general absolution was advocated as the only means of healing the soul in mortal sin. The ritual of general absolution was banned.

So, you may all ask the question, does a sinner require the absolution of a priest to return to God? The view of many theologians and the practice of so many Catholics is that a penitent is reconciled to God before going to confession, not as a result of it. The late Fr Herbert McCabe, a Dominican theologian, gave a homily on confession not long before he died: 'You are not forgiven because you confess your sin, you confess your sin and recognise yourself for what you are, because you are forgiven.' The theologian Karl Rahner, citing St Augustine, made the same point. Cardinal Martini, talking of discussion within the church said: 'We are in the 1990s, but some Catholics are mentally in the 1960s, and some in the 1940s, and even some in the last century. It is inevitable there will be clashes of mentalities.'

Listening to a discussion among very serious Catholics about how they felt forgiven, one said: 'I have a spiritual director, a lovely Carmelite Sister, who gives me direction in my prayer life. The deepening of my relationship with God occurs through contemplative prayer.' In this fast-moving and noisy world, the return to the old practice of private prayer and praying the scriptures would seem a most healthy way forward to gaining reconciliation with God. Catholic life is no longer compliant with the catalogue of precepts governing every detail of our behaviour. They spoke about John O'Donohue's idea of the Celtic 'Soul Friend' (*Anam Cara*). The good younger generation of Catholics will find in Christianity a duty to combat social, economic and political injustice. Their moral concerns focus not on the exquisite state of their souls, but on the alleviation of poverty, homelessness, hunger and disease; care for the environment; and peace building. They seek to combat the sins of racism, sexism, child abuse and the oppression of minorities.

As I come to the end of this book, I would like to reflect on the sad fact that Ireland's traditionally strong missionary record is in danger of ending. The facts are so clear. Where there were once 8,000 Irish Catholic missionaries in the field, there are now only 1,500, stretching across eighty-three countries, and the recent records show the number is falling by 100 a year.

In 2008, there were nearly 2,000 priests, Brothers and Sisters in the missions – last year there were only 1,500, almost all over the age of fifty. In fifteen years' time, it will be down to 150. Now Europe itself is becoming missionary territory. Dr Daniel Murphy has written a wonderful resource book on *The History of Irish Emigration and Missionary Education*. What a wonderful opportunity we have in celebrating our first century of national freedom to also celebrate 1,500 years of Irish missionary sacrifice in bringing the message of the gospels and in uplifting people through education and healthcare.

During the past century, great missionary giants like Bishop Shanahan and Bishop Galvin left their homeland with countless numbers of Columban Holy Ghost Fathers, African missionaries, St Patrick's missionaries and from every order and congregation in Ireland, not to mention the missionary Sisters and Brothers. The Medical Missionaries of Mary brought a new dimension to healthcare in Africa. All of these missionaries have fostered indigenous vocations and most countries do not need foreign missionaries any more. We Irish have carried out Christ's command to 'Go out to the whole world'. We have tried to help in mind, body and soul.

About the missionary's role in uplifting people – Robert Calderisi, former director of the World Bank (he was Country Director for Central Africa), in a lecture in London in 2014 said: 'The Catholic Church has probably lifted more people out of poverty in more countries than any other organisation in human history.' He also went on to say: 'Since the 1990s, however, there has been a rapid reappraisal of the role that faiths can play in development. Many now believe them to be some of the most effective means for delivering aid.'

An encouraging new trend has been slowly taking place: young men and women feel a calling to help in the Third World. If I may give an example, Aisling Foley gave up her job in a leading law firm to go to South Africa to help the underprivileged: 'I thought people would think I was absolutely crazy or having a mid-life crisis, but when I go home, people say "We really admire what you have done."' Aisling works with the Home of Hope charity in Cape Town, a unique school, community home and foster care support service for children born with foetal alcohol syndrome disorder. 'They are not all from poor families, but among the poorest the problem is exacerbated by malnutrition and physical and sexual abuse. It is financial suicide for me, but what I am doing is so important to me and to them.' Maybe more will follow the example of Aisling and become missionaries of hope to the poorest of the poor.

Some two years ago, Fr Joe McDonald from Dublin, at the end of an article on the lost constituencies of the church, asked the question 'Where are we going?' He goes on to say that there is one very important group that is almost non-existent in the fabric of the leadership of the Irish church today, and that is the prophets. He genuinely believes that if we are looking from them for some prophetic witness – by which he means a courageous, self-effacing voice that disturbs, challenges and inspires us – we will for the most part be disappointed. He thinks there may be one or two exceptions.

When Joe speaks of prophets, I am sure he has in mind someone like Hélder Câmara. Câmara spent his first twenty-eight years as a priest in a diocese of Rio. In 1952, he became the auxiliary bishop. He was among six of Brazil's bishops appointed to the preparatory commission for the Second Vatican Council. Frustrated, like so many others, at the control by the Curia, he was one of the most energetic organisers, with Cardinal Suenens, of the revolt of the Council Fathers, who broke this stranglehold: 'Very often I dance with rage as I listened to some of the speeches during the Council.' His statement on episcopal authority attracted the most attention: 'Let us end once and for all the authority which insists in practice on making itself more feared than loved, on being served rather than serving.' He also urged the bishops to abandon titles like 'Your Lordship' and 'Your Eminence', and much of the ornate garb: 'Let us put an end to the impression of a prince-bishop living in a palace, isolated from priests and people.' He was appointed Bishop of Recife during the Council.

The day before he arrived in Brazil, an army coup set up a conservative military dictatorship. The new archbishop became enemy number one. His secretary, a young priest, was murdered; but agents sent to kill the archbishop, disguised as beggars, could not bring themselves to do so and asked his pardon. He abandoned his palace and lived with one of his sisters in a flat, where he was accessible to the poor. He used public transport, like Pope Francis did. 'When I queue for a bus,' he said, 'my people see I am one of them.'

He gave church land to provide settlements for the landless poor, started a credit union, brought priests and laity into the running of the diocese, took his clerical students out of the seminary and sent them to small communities in parishes, and set up a theological institute where those future priests would study with lay people and receive some lectures from women. He struggled to make people aware of the abominable lack of any social justice that kept 85% as economic slaves. The church was on the side of the rich.

As can be expected, his fellow Brazilian bishops did not agree with his attitude to social problems; a few called him a communist. At seventy-five years of age, he resigned and was succeeded by a canon lawyer, who at once began to dismantle all that he had done. Hélder Câmara was treated as a non-person by the church. He often said, 'If I give money to the poor, I am a saint. If I ask why the poor are poor, I am a communist.'

Hélder Câmara took his seminarians out of the seminary to live with communities and attend a simple theological institute with lay people, even having some women lecturers. To me, one of the greatest disasters in the church is having one model of seminary for the whole world. And this model is many hundreds of years old. The vast cultural, economic and social differences in this enormous church are not taken into account. Take Africa as an example. Think of taking future seminarians from poor rural areas and moving them into Western-type seminaries where they are taught philosophy for two years – not modern philosophy, but old scholastic philosophy – then theology for four years. All of this in a male-oriented institution where any contact with women is out. The whole lifestyle of the seminary is in strong contrast to the rural village where they come from. Very little time is given to discussing the problems they will face when they return to a rural setting. Celibacy will not be a choice for them. But for me, the greatest indictment against our seminary training was written by an elderly Irish priest. He wrote a few beautiful articles in the magazine *Intercom* in the 1990s, under the pseudonym 'Pastor Ignotus'.

This is part of the final article he wrote in May 2006:

Back in the corridors of Maynooth in the early Fifties: memories abound of the rigid formation we experienced and how little space or time there seemed to be for a human life.

Fifty-plus years on, the religious certainties on which so much was based seem like sand running through our fingers. The unthinking acceptance of a credulous authority and the submission of the will that attended it through a life of blind obedience seemed at the time laudable, heroic, even at times lyrical. Now it seems redundant, infantile, redolent of a forgotten world, a world of Catholic fatwahs and clerical imams.

In Maynooth there was a distrust of art and literature. Even a paring down of ritual so that the aesthetic was drained out of it. Theology was an exact science when it should have been like literature, a way of exploring truth that accepted as a first principle the impossibility of expressing the inexpressible. Like literature and music and art, theology should have developed a healthy respect for its limitations. Eliot, I think it was who described poetry as a 'raid on the inarticulate'. Real theology, or rather for theology to be real, it has to be free. If you find yourself pretending that the Song of Songs is not a celebration of human love or that apologetics – a way of insisting that your own tradition is infallibly correct – become theology, you not only lack intellectual credibility in today's world but worse still you stunt the kind of exploration that opens a window on transcendence.

Priests, of course, don't talk about faith or hope of love. Football, yes. Politics, too. Sex, occasionally, in a distracted and disembodied way. But theology, never. Been there, done that, half a century ago. A huge theological grid was constructed where logic rules and all the bits fitted neatly together. A system was constructed like a vast Lego set, which held together provided you accepted a list of basic propositions. Transformation took place when the personal and the human were subsumed into the system – rather than the other way around.

I now tend to live in the present moment, savouring the unpredictable beauty of every day. Seeing life as a gift. Reading my favourite psalms, Isaiah, the Gospel of John the Evangelist, the writings of John McGahern, listening to the pure music of Beethoven. Searching for whatever enhances my life.

Trying to undo the damage of my Maynooth days and most of my priesthood when the practice of religion diminished me, stunted me, dehumanised me, demanding assent to a series of improbable mysteries rather than encouraging me to see my life as exploration and pilgrimage.

Religion for me now is not discovering this truth or finding that meaning. It is about living as fully as possible in the present moment, and finding echoes of a longing for the sacred in the ordinariness of things: the beauty of a rose, the laughter of a child, the variegated pattern of a sun shower on the glass of the bay window on an August day. Above all, it is a gathering sense of God's presence in my life, not because I've managed to find my way through the maze of a snakes-and-ladders morality where sin and virtue demand pre-packaged responses, but because I have come to a place where I sense that, extraordinarily and disconcertingly, God actually loves me. There is now no other place that I want to be ... Adieu.

I have already mentioned the scholarly study of child sexual abuse by priests by Marie Keenan. She says:

Absent from the priest's education was an approach to morality, conscience and ethics in which moral judgement could be based on reasoned debate, personal reflection and a relational principle that would encourage the capacity to put oneself in the shoes of the other (the abused). They had learned a morality that relied solely on moral absolutes and were not ignorant of these moral absolutes. The problem was that the norms were impossible to live by and they lacked the emotional and relational intelligence to enable them to make right judgements. The seminary, with its lack of emphasis on personal awareness, personal reflection and human engagement, was not a context in which the men in my research could develop emotionally and relationally. (This is not to say that they are not responsible for the abuse that happened.)

In spite of all these insights, seminaries, with the few students they have, will not change.

Victoria White, who is not a Catholic, writing in a national newspaper, says, 'Tarring all the Catholic religion with the sex abuse brush is a horrible injustice.' She goes on to say:

Catholic priests are no more likely to abuse minors than men of any other profession. They are no more likely to abuse minors than ministers of any other denomination. They are less likely to abuse minors than teachers. That is what the international research says. I am not a Catholic. The only reason I am writing this article is because I cannot stand seeing such injustice done to any group in society as is being done to the Catholic religion. The vast majority of the Catholic religion is wrongly accused in the public mind of hideous crimes and their entire life's work is being rubbished.

I would like to add to this the fact that over 90% of child abuse takes place in homes, involving family or extended family. The clergy can be a smokescreen behind which the shocking abuse of children continues unknown and unchecked.

Recently, on Easter Sunday, the thought that came uppermost in my homilies was the role of women during those days in Jerusalem. I find it hard to believe that Mary the mother of Jesus, who on Good Friday was there at the foot of the cross, was not present at the celebration of the Passover in the upper room with all of Jesus' disciples. On Good Friday, there was one brave woman, Veronica, who extended a towel to wipe his sacred face. Mary and a few women stood by the cross with one apostle, John. They would have administered to the dead body of Jesus taken down from the cross. Early on Easter Sunday, women were on their way to the tomb for the final burial rites. Jesus appeared personally to Mary of Magdala and she became the first preacher of the Easter story, the good news for all mankind. They would have been present at the ascension and were back in the upper room with the apostles for the coming of the Holy Spirit. In spite of all that, some fifty years later they seem to be airbrushed out of the early church. St Jerome's negative views on marriage and sexuality, as well as the pessimistic theology of St Augustine, and his inability to include sexuality in any positive way within his commitment to Christianity, led to the sidelining of women in the church. But this pales into insignificance compared with what St Epifanio wrote: 'A woman is the creature of the devil from her head to her feet. A man, on his part, is only God by half, from the waist upwards he is a creature of God. So the union in marriage between a man and a woman is therefore the work of the devil.' They say some of the saints were mad – St Epifanio was totally batty.

Pope John Paul I, in his extremely brief time as pope, said that 'God was as truly Mother as God was Father'. That statement was erased by his mysteriously early death. Many women are now starting to explore their own theological and spiritual resources, rooted in their bodily identity as women, and pursue their God and their story from that perspective. This new movement is called Christian feminism. They believe very strongly that, apart from the first twenty-five years of Christianity, women have not been accepted as Christians on an equal footing with men. During the worst years of the Inquisition, it was mostly women who were burnt as heretics and witches.

One of these Christian feminists, Mary T. Malone, has written a book, *The Elephant in the Church*. I found this book fascinating and would like to quote from her final chapter:

And what of the women down the centuries? How were they 'there'? As we have seen, they were there among the first and most faithful disciples, as house-church leaders, apostles, teachers, prophets, and presiders at the agape meal, the initial form of Eucharist. They were there, to men's great surprise, as martyrs and virgins, not having been deemed capable of either role in male theology. They were there as abbesses and founders, writers and preachers, mystics and scholars, reformers and mission-aries, not only at home on the continent of Europe, but in far distant lands, again demonstrating virtues of courage and ingenuity that they were not supposed to have. And in our own time women have been there as theological scholars and biblical exegetes, parish leaders and pastoral guides, chaplains in a huge variety of settings, and ministers of the gospel at bedsides and graves, birthing rooms and schools, publishing houses and universities. And all of this has been done entirely on their own initiative, without any official calling from the Church because the Catholic Church does not consider itself capable of calling women.

It took centuries before the church could reconcile sanctity and matrimonial sexuality. There is one interesting line in the first letter of St Paul to the Corinthians (1 Cor 9:5): 'Have we not any right to eat and drink? And the right to take a Christian woman round with us, like all the other apostles and the brother of the Lord and Cephas?' Paul has no problem with marriage and leadership in the church. He even said a bishop should have only one wife.

I would like to speak of four priests who have made very valuable contributions to the changing church in Ireland. The first is Fr Sean Fagan, an elderly, erudite moral theologian of the Marist order. For many years he has raised his voice that a radical re-examination of human sexuality should take place in the light of modern psychological and anthropological insights and the lived experience of lay people. He has been censored by the Congregation for the Doctrine of the Faith (CDF). He is silenced. He has taken it all with saintly resignation. Now, for the first time, a bishop in the UK (Middlesbrough, Terence Drainey) has called for the upcoming synod in Rome to re-examine the whole question of human sexuality. That could lead to a development in church teaching in areas such as contraception, homosexuality, divorce and remarriage, cohabitation, and the role of women in the church.

Fr Brian D'Arcy is one of the best-known priests in Ireland and the UK. Every week, through his newspaper columns and radio broadcasts, he has fearlessly spread the message of the good news to people eager to hear it. Like any priest who dares put his head over the parapet, he has encountered difficulties with the institutional church. But he has soldiered on, giving hope and insight to thousands of readers and listeners. His recent book *Food for the Soul* is well worth getting for your bedside reading. Each contribution is a gem – for many, a great contrast to what you might hear on a Sunday morning.

Fr Tony Flannery has been a Redemptorist priest for over forty years. He is well known the length and breadth of Ireland as a preacher of parish mission. But most of all he is known for the great crowds that come to his novena services. His homilies and services have been inspirational. He has published a number of books including *From the Inside* and *The Death of*

Religious Life? The latter caused quite a sensation, but it has proved to be a prophetic message. He also wrote many articles for the Redemptorist magazine *Reality*. One of these has got him into trouble with Big Brother, the CDF. In talking about the history of the priesthood, Tony will admit that his words could have been misunderstood by lay people.

Tony has written a book called *A Question of Conscience*, which gives full details of the long-drawn-out confrontation and secret meeting with representatives from the CDF. Strange that Veritas, the official bookshop for the Catholic Church, was not allowed to sell this book. With the coming of Pope Francis, they seem to have laid off him, but no reconciliation has yet come about. Fr Tony is off the ministry. Mary McAleese writes in the foreword, 'But I ask myself, what mother treats a son like Tony Flannery has been treated?'

The last of the four priests is Fr Brendan Hoban of the diocese of Killala. I remember reading his book, published in 1995, *Change or Decay: Irish Catholicism in Crisis*. There is lots of discussion about whistle-blowers in the Irish Garda and the controversy that it has caused. Brendan Hoban was the first clerical whistle-blower. Most often, whistle-blowers are not recognised or appreciated. Most clergy and laity feel that things will never change, so we don't have to worry about the future. Let tomorrow take care of itself. Twenty years later, everything that he said in the book is being realised.

Fr Brendan has written another book, *Who Will Break Bread for Us?* In it he talks about the disenchantment and isolation that many priests feel:

> The field of dreams that opened out before us on ordination day is now for many a thicket we try to break through to preserve the vestiges of an ordinary life. In the small hours and the quiet moment, questions surface about the wisdom of the whole enterprise and our role in it. What is left of me when so much is subsumed into priesthood? What can I do to live a human life in whatever time God gives me?

The stats he gives are alarming. In eighteen years' time there will be only four to twelve elderly and very elderly priests in his rural diocese of Killala. The vocation for priesthood and religious life has dropped from 750 in 1920 to just fifty in 2006. In the last eight years, it has got worse. From the million Catholics in the archdiocese of Dublin, there was only one vocation last year.

Fr Brendan discusses some possible solutions. He speaks eloquently on the reason for abolishing compulsory celibacy. He suggests that there is no reason not to accept priests who have left to get married and come back to active ministry. There is the possibility of men who are able to take early retirement and feel they have a vocation; these, whether single or married, would be some help. The question of women priests will not go away: 'There is a huge disconnect between the attitude of Catholics in the pew and the present teaching of the Catholic Church. In the ACP survey in 2011, 77% of Irish Catholics believe women should be ordained.' I believe that all these solutions, good as they are, are only temporary solutions.

Before I give my dream for the future of the priesthood as now exercised and having such a bleak future I would like to quote Cardinal Newman, who said: 'I have not a shadow of misgiving that the Catholic Church and its doctrine are directly from God. And I believe great changes before now have taken place in the direction of the Church's course, and that new aspects of her aboriginal doctrine have suddenly come forth.' This is my dream: that some more aspects of her aboriginal doctrine are due to come forth. Because of incredible evidence of the scarcity of future priests, one of these aspects will be about a new understanding of priesthood.

The New Testament writers avoided calling the apostles or any other individual disciple of Jesus a priest. In Acts 18:2–6, we find a husband-and-wife team cooperating in giving further instruction to Paul. In Paul's own letters, there are so many whom he regards as 'apostles', who perform various functions in the service of the community. They are teachers or leaders, both male and female, evangelists, prophets and deacons. Never are they called priests, and the hierarchical governing body is a later historical development.

Jesus instituted a new kind of authority, an authority of pure service. People may be surprised to hear noted scripture scholar Raymond Brown say, 'speculating on who did preside at the Eucharist, I confess ignorance ...' Schillebeeckx says, 'In the house churches of Corinth, it was the hosts who presided at the Eucharistic meal, but these were at the same time leaders of the house churches.' These were often referred to as elders.

Joe McDonald wrote in an article entitled 'Who or What are Priests?':

It is by their sharing in the one, unique priesthood of Christ that the Christian faithful collectively constitute a priesthood in the same way as, by their baptism, they constitute the Church. What this comes to is that the distinction made by many in the Church today between priest and people in respect of sacrifice or ritual is false. There is certainly a legitimate difference of function within the Christian Church; the offices of presbyter, bishop and deacon were not introduced for nothing. The Church is an ordered and orderly community and ordination is correctly referred to as a sacrament of holy orders.' The Mass is celebrated by all the faithful attending by virtue of the priesthood of Christ which they share through baptism. As *Lumen Gentium* puts it, 'Taking part in the Eucharistic sacrifice, which is the source and crown of the whole Christian life, they (the People of God) offer the divine victim to God, and offer themselves with it.'

There is a retired bishop in South Africa, Bishop Fritz Lobinger, who for many years worked in the Lumku Institute training catechists and helping new missionaries with African languages and inculturation. In his latest book, he proposes the ordination of community elders to work with full-time priests who are getting scarcer and scarcer. He has travelled widely in Southern Africa and is touched by the few times many Catholic communities can celebrate the eucharist. He laments that for centuries we have become used to the pattern that religious leadership is not entrusted to local people, is not combined with secular life, but is reserved for special people who are set apart for religious work (priests). He goes on to say:

> We see the great value of a professional clergy that surrounds the bishop and is anchored in the diocesan centre. But besides that professional clergy that is anchored in the diocese, we need a second, different type of ordained ministry that is anchored in the local community. We do not want them to be called 'clergy' and we do not want them to act as 'clergy'. We want them to be Elders who remain part of their community.

To me, that is the way forward for the universal church.

One of the recent spiritual writers who I find most helpful is Fr Daniel O'Leary. One of his books is *Treasured and Transformed*, which consists mostly of articles he had already written for *The Tablet*. I would like to give a lengthy quotation from this book, which says exactly what I want to say, but infinitely better:

> We need to remember that Revelation is the amazing love story of God's desire to be intimately among us in human form. Full of intense compassion, God wished to create out of pure love, and then, in time, to become that creation. That becoming happened in Jesus Christ. In him it was revealed that God's heart beats in all our hearts, that all our bodies are temples of the Holy Spirit, that every creature is a divine work of art. How different that is to the awful picture painted for some of us of the angry God in search of vengeance!
>
> Revelation is now seen to be about the beauty of being human since humanity is the 'raw material', so to speak, of God's presence in the world. Revelation is about the graced possibilities of humanity, graced at its centre from the very beginning. It is about God's desire to be known

and loved in the humanity of Jesus Christ. It is about God's delight in being visible and tangible in human form. This is how it became possible for God to be close to us, to share completely in the experiences of creatures, the fruit of God's own womb. We can say with saints and theologians from the time of Christ, that the Incarnation happened not because creation went wrong at some early stage, but because in God's plan to share God's own divine joy with others, creation was first necessary so that Incarnation could take place. I hope this does not sound complicated.

When God was creating Adam, Tertullian reminds us, as do both Vatican Councils, it was the human form of the Son, the ever-present Word, that was motivating God. Adam was the long-term preparation for Jesus – a sort of prototype of the lovely redeeming Human One who was to come later. All of this we have tumbled to in the Revelation that is Jesus. Now we know that all humanity is heading toward divinity. You and I are growing into God, as the mystics put it. In fact all of creation is already sacred, and reveals something of the glory and splendour of God. That is why we say that the event of Incarnation has ended all dualism. Heaven and earth are forever mysteriously intertwined since the Word became flesh. And deep in our own inner being the kingdom of God forms an intrinsic part of our true nature …

I never cease to be amazed at such glimpses into the meaning of Revelation. And whenever we share it with others, the reaction is similar. After talks, workshops and presentations about such an understanding of the mystery of Incarnation, invariably there will be those who say something like, 'What you have said is not new. We have always known it in our hearts. We have never doubted the sacredness of our lives, of our childbearing and our daily work, of our struggles to survive and grow, of our efforts to forgive and start again. Our hearts have always told us that these are holy tasks. All that's new is that now we have heard it said.' What a deep transformation it would trigger off around the Christian world were this good news to be proclaimed wherever the people are gathered around the table of the Lord.

But as a dream of what the Holy Spirit may bring about in the not-too-distant future: it would be the tsunami change of talking about God's kingdom rather than the church. Jesus continually referred to the kingdom of God in parables and stories. He even asked us to pray to His Father that this kingdom would come about. If we hope for the unity of Catholic and Orthodox, as well as the many Christian churches, the term 'God's kingdom' would appeal to them. The keys of the kingdom would be with the pope, working with his bishops or senior church leaders. Through the Holy Spirit, it would finally become an eternal or universal kingdom, a kingdom of truth and life, a kingdom of justice, love and peace. In this kingdom, gender would not be an issue; the communities would choose suitable candidates to be empowered by the bishops to preside at the eucharist.

Hopefully, stories like this would not be uncommon in God's kingdom:

I was in a big foreign city many years ago, coming to the last hours of the several days I had spent there. I was almost entirely out of money, completely exhausted, and was suffering the pain that shakes the animal in the rational animal that we are: the pain of loss brought by death, the several deaths of those who were of the same flesh as mine. I do not believe that I represented any social category. The clothes I was wearing had nothing particular about them.

I had been walking through the streets for several hours while I waited for my train. And why not say it? I was crying. But I didn't care any more, and I waited for it to pass. A foreigner. A stranger. A sorrow that all people know, one that brings tears just as certain forms of work bring sweat.

It started to rain; I was hungry. The few coins remaining to me determined what I was permitted to eat. I went into a tiny café that served food and ordered what I could afford: some raw vegetables. I ate them slowly, so that they would be more nourishing and also to give the rain a chance to stop. Every once in a while my eyes filled up with tears. Then, all of a sudden, a warm and comforting arm took me by the shoulders. A voice said to me: 'You, coffee. Me, give.' It was absolutely clear. I don't remember exactly what happened afterward, which is lucky for me because I don't much care for melodramatic scenes.

I have often spoken about this woman, thought about her, and prayed for her with an inexhaustible gratitude. When I look today for an example of goodness in flesh and bones, she is the one who comes to mind.

What makes this woman a Christian sign, a distant but faithful image of the goodness of God, is that she was good because goodness dwelled within her, and not because I was 'one of her own', familially, socially, politically, nationally, or religiously. I was a 'stranger' without any identifying marks. I was in need of goodness, and even that goodness that goes by the name of mercy. It was given me by that woman. Today she represents an absolute example of goodness because I was just 'anybody'; it didn't matter what or who I was, and because what she did for me she did simply because there was goodness in her. In her simple gesture, I discovered everything that goodness has to be in order to be goodness.

The wonderful retired Bishop Willie Walsh puts his dream more modestly:

I believe we have to try to move to a model of church which begins to take ownership of the local church. Moving towards a model of church in which baptised people play their rightful part is not a journey which will be accomplished overnight. It requires real change of mindset in both clergy and laity. We can set out on that journey in a spirit of dialogue, openness and collaboration. The journey is an endless one. We will never arrive at the perfect model. But then sometimes the journey is more important than the arrival.

* * *

Back to my retirement home by the banks of my own lovely Lee. Shakespeare wrote an epitaph on the final stage of age: 'sans teeth, sans eyes, sans taste, sans everything.' Not an accurate or positive observation. Each one has still their own personality, and personality, unlike muscle or memory, need not wither like a leaf or fade like a flower. Some might say that the elderly can be quirky and cantankerous, given to unreasonable demands and seeing everything through condemning eyes. 'Yet the old can be so different, mellow wine, red Burgundy, imparting a kind of glory to their presence.' Most of our elderly priests would have suffered in different ways, but they can still sing and celebrate. They have known the storm; it has been their strength. They may have had to sail against a headwind and discovered their capacity.

One of the younger priests is a keen gardener, and in summer there is a wonderful display of colour outside the dining room and in front of the house. In short morning visits he seems to communicate with every single flower. The young Fr John, parish priest and Superior, rides his lawnmower while listening to Radio Kerry. He says it provides some stories for his down-to-earth homilies. Another elderly member is a rose enthusiast and tends the many rose beds around the church. He is very active in spring and autumn, but during summer days he is observed standing quite still in the middle of the rose bed. Some may think it is standing meditation, but others know better. He is casting a cold eye on each rosebud, and woe betide the greenfly that may perch on one of them. Hidden in the palm of his hand is a deadly pistol that squirts a fluid on the fly – dead meat.

One of the priests spent years teaching art and later spent time in parish work – he still does the odd inspirational painting. He has an incredible memory for stories. In one of them, an elderly couple had celebrated their golden wedding anniversary. They are sitting one summer evening on a veranda overlooking Dingle Bay as the sun is setting. They have had more than one glass of wine. After a long silence, she says, 'I don't know how I could have lived without you.' He says, 'Is that you or the wine speaking?' She says, 'No, it is me speaking to the wine.'

Some have drawn the short straw in terms of health – one is most restricted in movement. Occasionally at breakfast, for a little excitement, he offers a wager of fifty cents as to which of the two pigeons perched on the wall will fly away first.

I wrote to Fr Brendan Hoban asking to join the Association of Catholic Priests, which now has almost eight hundred members. As they have often said, they are not against church teaching – they cherish and value it. They are not damaging unity, they are working for it. They have the right and duty to openly discuss the problems facing the church.

Who are the spiritual heroes that I have looked up to during my long life as a priest? The first is Pope John XXIII, who was responsible for Vatican II and whom I saw in audience in 1961. Then there was Archbishop Denis Hurley, who for over fifty years never gave up the fight against apartheid. I have already mentioned Hélder Câmara. There was Cardinal Basil Hume and, lastly, there is Oscar Romero. His appointment as Archbishop of El Salvador in 1977 was met with some surprise, as it was feared that his conservative reputation would negatively affect commitment to the poor. However, an event would take place three weeks after his election that would transform the ascetic and timid Romero. One of his priests was ambushed and shot down along with two parishioners because of his defence of a peasant's rights to organise a farm cooperative. That night, as Romero drove out to see the dead body of his priest, as well as the old parishioner and seven-year-old who were murdered, marked his change. The sad eyes of the mourning peasants asked the question, will you stand with us as this dead priest

THE LIFE OF A PRIEST

did? Romero's 'yes' was in his deeds; as he said later, 'God needs His people to save the world – the world of the poor teaches us that liberation will arrive only when the poor are not only on the receiving end of handouts but when they themselves are masters of their struggle for liberation and justice.' Three years later, Romero was shot in his cathedral as he lifted the consecrated chalice, spilling his blood with the blood of Christ on the altar. You would have expected that the course for his canonisation as a modern martyr of the church would have gone forward. It appears that it was withheld by the Congregation for the Doctrine of the Faith until Pope Francis asked them to release it.

Part of a long reflection which he used daily was: 'We cannot do everything and there is a sense of liberation in realising that. This enables us do to something, and do it very well. We may never see the end results, but that is the difference between the master builder and the worker. We are workers, not master builders; ministers, not messiahs. We are prophets of a future not our own.'

My last reflection is about falling in love again with the beautiful sea and landscapes around the coast of Ireland. One of my new favourites is the coastline around Ballyferriter and Slea Head on the Dingle Peninsula. What a contrast to the Costa del Sol, with its hundreds of square miles of concrete jungle – yes, they have the sun, but what a price to pay for it! For many years the islanders survived and eked out an existence from rocky little fields and the fruit of the sea, even harvesting the sea birds and their eggs. There is an old Irish proverb that 'nature breaks through the eyes of the cat'. From this small community of islanders have emerged many poets and writers. The most famous of these was Peig Sayers, who was illiterate. She may be unlettered, but not unlearned and was the inheritor of a considerable art: the art of storytelling. Peig became the queen of Gaelic storytelling.

As we celebrate the first century of independence, we realise how often nature has broken through the eyes of the cat. Our deep Celtic roots have produced so many famous writers and poets – Shaw, Yeats, Joyce, Beckett and Heaney, to name but a few. So, as a nation we remember the road we have travelled from the great flourishing of learning and culture nurtured by the great monastic movement of early Christian Ireland, which produced the *Book of Kells*. Then the wave after wave of invasions, the looting and plundering of the monasteries, the hundreds of years of barbarous oppression from the ethnic cleansing of Cromwell to the Great Famine.

We now accept and appreciate the hand of friendship and respect from the queen of the United Kingdom and its prime minister. It seems so different from the Disraeli declaration of 1836: 'The Irish hate our order, our civilisation, our pure religion. This wild, reckless, indolent, uncertain and superstitious race has no sympathy with the English character. Their ideal of human felicity is an altercation of clannish broils and coarse idolatry (Catholicism).' And during the Famine, another English prime minister, Robert Peel, used to stand on a chair with a glass of port and propose the Orange Toast: 'To the glorious, pious and immortal memory of the good and great King William, who delivered us from popery, slavery, brass money and wooden shoes, and here is a fart to the Bishop of Cork.'

So my final dream is that the Irish nation, which has the most educated younger generation (to give one example, of twelve siblings in one family in Mayo, all became GPs and some went on to become consultants – apparently this has gone into the *Guinness Book of Records*), will in the second century of independence scale new heights, not only in literature and the arts, but in every discipline of human endeavour; that they will be at the forefront in stretching the limits of human technology; that they have learnt the valuable lesson that the greed and naked materialism that brought about the birth and demise of the Celtic tiger should never be repeated. In all of this dream, I would hope that Celtic spirituality and the gospel values of the kingdom would be the inspiration for this new generation. Is all this an impossible dream? Well, we can try. Hitch our nation to a star. For some, that spirituality of the heart of Christ may inspire them to work for the poor and starving of the Third World.

In this, my life as a priest, I have become an endangered species. I will finish by saying that what counts are not the special and unique accomplishments in life that make me different from others, but the basic experiences of sadness and joy, pain and healing, which make me part of humanity. Mourning and joy can now both deepen my quiet desire for the day when I realise that the many kindnesses and embraces I received were simple incarnations of the eternal embrace of the Lord himself.

This book is about the truth, nothing but the truth – but maybe not the whole truth.

Afterword

One of the reasons for writing this book was a small effort to make people aware of the massive contribution that missionaries have made to advance the kingdom of God. So the last word is from a recipient of the work of the Missionaries of the Sacred Heart in Papua New Guinea. Before the advent of the MSCs in the late nineteenth century from France and Germany, followed later from Ireland and Australia, Papua New Guinea was a mountainous country with each valley having its own tribe and language. There was constant warfare and cannibalism was part of the culture.

Fr Rochus Tatamai MSC, in an address to the MSC Assembly in 2004, had this to say:

As Missionaries of the Sacred Heart, you helped us to respect ourselves and to love each other, especially to love our traditional enemies. You gave us the teaching of Jesus Christ, the Good News. You baptised us into the Body of Christ.

As linguists, you learned and you spoke our languages. You wrote our dictionaries and you taught us our own grammar.

As diplomats, you negotiated with civil authorities for us. You taught us about our own human rights and about religious freedom.

As mediators, you reconciled tribes that were at war. You promoted other cultural values such as the mutual exchange of gifts in order to reach reconciliation. You courageously opposed the traditional law of vengeance (pay back). You won the trust and respect of our people.

As builders, you built our churches, our schools, our clinics, our roads and our bridges.

As teachers, you taught us to read and write.

As anthropologists, you studied our social structures and you entered into our Melanesian vision of the world. You used our chants and dances to express our faith in the liturgy and in the celebration of the sacraments.

As mystics, you studied our religious beliefs and our initiation rites. You explored our sacred space and time. We recognise you as spiritual men, men of prayer, men of God.

As experts in agriculture, you taught us new ways to cultivate the earth and to produce crops.

As doctors, you healed us with your 'miracles' when you gave us your medicine and your knowledge.

And as Missionaries of the Sacred Heart, you gave us a God of love who fills us with hope.